". . . A LEGEND, A CERTIFIABLE HOUSEHOLD WORD . . . THERE'S NO ONE LIKE MARGARET. . . ."*

Now, in *Blackberry Winter,* Dr. Margaret Mead reveals the intimate personal story behind her remarkable experiences and their effects on her as a woman—her childhood, her school days, her three marriages, and her early field trips.

"More than an account of her professional beginnings, this book—presumably the first half of Dr. Mead's autobiography—is a hymn to her own family in particular and the idea of families in general."   —*Jane Howard,
                              The New York Times Book Review*

"Everything that has been so appealing about Miss Mead's previous writing is on hand here. . . . The fact that she is writing about herself instead of about others adds greatly to the book's interest, allowing Miss Mead's fans to learn how this remarkable woman happened. . . . There are plums galore. . . ."   —*The New Yorker*

Margaret Mead at sixteen

MARGARET MEAD

BLACKBERRY WINTER

My Earlier Years

WASHINGTON SQUARE PRESS
PUBLISHED BY POCKET BOOKS NEW YORK

Grateful acknowledgment is made to Norma Millay Ellis for permission to quote from "Second Fig," by Edna St. Vincent Millay, from *Collected Poems* (Harper & Row), copyright 1922, 1950 by Edna St. Vincent Millay; and from "Blue Flag in the Bog," by Edna St. Vincent Millay, from *Collected Poems* (Harper & Row), copyright 1921, 1948 by Edna St. Vincent Millay; and to Mrs. George Bambridge, Methuen & Co. Ltd., and Doubleday & Company, Inc., for permission to quote from Rudyard Kipling's "When Earth's Last Picture is Painted," from *The Seven Seas* (Methuen) and *The Collected Verse of Rudyard Kipling Definitive Edition* (Doubleday.)

WSP

A Washington Square Press Publication of
POCKET BOOKS, a Simon & Schuster division of
GULF & WESTERN CORPORATION
1230 Avenue of the Americas, New York, N.Y. 10020

Published by arrangement with William Morrow and Company, Inc.
Library of Congress Catalog Card Number: 72-7187

ISBN: 0-671-43299-0

First Pocket Books printing January, 1975

12   11   10   9   8   7   6

WASHINGTON SQUARE PRESS, WSP and colophon are
trademarks of Simon & Schuster.

Printed in the U.S.A.

ACKNOWLEDGMENTS

This is not a book about the South Sea peoples I have studied through the years. I have written about them in many books and the interested reader can find there what is taken for granted in this narrative of my own life. Although the focus of this book is not on them, they are nonetheless present and I thank them.

It would be impossible for me to thank all the people who have welcomed me, tolerated me, and cared for me wherever I have come in almost fifty years of travel. It would be equally impossible to thank all those who have had a part in shaping the life I record here.

I can only thank, specifically for their criticism and help with this manuscript, Marie E. Eichelberger, Geoffrey Gorer, Leah Josephson Hanna, Caroline Kelly, Rhoda Métraux, and Elizabeth Steig, and for their able assistance, in its preparation, Florette Henri, Mary Beth O'Connell, and Eleanor Pelham Stapelfeldt.

New York, May 1972

To the eight peoples who have admitted me to their lives I dedicate this book in which I try to give of my own life as they have given of theirs.

Contents

Blackberry winter, the time when the hoarfrost lies on the blackberry blossoms; without this frost the berries will not set.
It is the forerunner of a rich harvest.

BLACKBERRY WINTER
My Earlier Years

1 Prologue: For Whom and Why

When I was sixteen years old, I read a text set like a flowered valentine on the office wall of an old country doctor: "All things work together for good to them that love God." I interpreted this to mean that if you set a course and bend your sails to every wind to further the journey, always trusting that the course is right, it will, in fact, be right even though the ship itself may go down at any time during the voyage.

I have spent most of my life studying the lives of other peoples, faraway peoples, so that Americans might better understand themselves. Living primitive peoples, having neither script nor any records but their own spoken words, have only themselves to embody what they are. In much the same way, I bring my own life to throw what light it may on how children can be brought up so that parents and children, together, can weather the roughest seas. Already young people are asking, "Will we be as alienated from our children as we have been from our parents?" I do not think so. I brought to this life the awareness my parents and grandmother gave me of the culture in which we were living. It has been sharpened by many years of work among South Sea peoples. But I think we can build this kind of awareness into our own lives.

The South Sea peoples I have described—Samoans, Manus, Arapesh, Mundugumor, Tchambuli, Balinese, and Iatmul—gave generously when I explained that an account of their lives was needed. Sometimes it was difficult to explain to a people still living in the Stone Age

why I had come to live among them and what I was
doing. But I always tried. At first I had to let them work
out their own fantasies about what I was doing, and in
those days I often felt that although I might come to
understand them, they did not understand me. But when
I went back again in the years after the war—to Manus,
to Bali, to Iatmul—I discovered with great delight that
there were men and women there who were themselves
concerned about the fate of their people in the midst of
rushing change and who could now understand why I had
come—and come again—and what they were contributing
to the rest of the world.

In the past, in our own country, when people, especially young people, used to ask me how it was that I
seemed to understand what they were trying to do and
say, I used to answer, "Because I am an anthropologist."
But now this does not seem to me a sufficient answer.
And, in any case, how much use is it as an answer? After
all, very few people are trained as anthropologists or can
take the time to share for months and years in the lives
of another people and come home with newly opened
eyes. Moreover, it now seems to me that this answer
omitted two things that were vitally important in my
life. One was brought home to me when one of my oldest
friends said, "In my house I was a child. In your family's
house I was a person." The other, which I have come to
realize with fresh appreciation in the last ten years, is
that in many ways I was brought up within my own
culture two generations ahead of my time.

As I have worked on this book—and writing it has been
rather like editing a film for which the photography has
been done so generously that there is a great abundance
of material from which to choose to make any point—I
have rediscovered how it happened that I grew up ahead
of my time. In part it came about because during my
whole childhood I shared my grandmother's lively relationship to the past and the present. But it was also
because I was the child of social scientists who were
deeply—and differently—concerned with the state of the
world. For me, being brought up to become a woman

who could live responsibly in the contemporary world and learning to become an anthropologist, conscious of the culture in which I lived, were almost the same thing.

When I ran with the other children across the fields in the Buckingham Valley to watch a fire or to test the ice on the winter ponds, I knew how the lives of the people around us differed from the lives of their ancestors. And I was aware how our lives were changing before our eyes. When my grandmother decided to learn how to make butter, it was not the same thing as making butter at home in the days before mechanically made butter could be bought in a store. When a zeppelin floated lazily in the sky above our meadows, I related it both to the first flights in balloons and to ideas about air travel as yet unrealized. And when our neighbors in the many places we lived during my childhood behaved in ways that were different from ours and from one another, I learned that this was because of their life experience and the life experiences of their ancestors and mine—not because of differences in the color of our skin or the shape of our heads.

One does not need to go to Samoa or New Guinea to learn these things. This way of seeing the world and thinking about it is something children can—and today often do—learn at home. It is true, of course, that if earlier anthropologists had not gone to far-off places and recorded what they found, my mother would not have had the same things to teach me. And if the question, "Who then is neighbor unto him?" had not been part of my grandmother's religious experience, it is possible that neither my mother's nor my grandmother's concern for the human race would have made sense to me. And certainly I would not have interpreted in the particular way I did my father's conviction that the most important thing any person could do was to add to the world's store of knowledge.

In this book I have tried to describe the kinds of experiences that have made me what I am, myself, and to sort out the kinds of experiences that might become part of a way of bringing up children and of seeing the world that includes the past and the future as aspects of the present—the present of any generation. At the same time, as I have evoked the earlier experiences of my personal life, they have become newly woven into the tapestry of my relations to others who have long been close to me. For I have written this book in many different places around the world, but always close to someone who was part of what I was writing about—in Cincinnati, where members of my grandmother's family live; in Australia, where Caroline Tennant Kelly has been part of my life in the South Pacific during all the years I have come and gone through Sydney; in Cambridge, where my sister Elizabeth and my daughter Catherine could read what I was writing about our family; in Hungary, at an international seminar on housing, which I was attending with Geoffrey Gorer, whom I did not meet until 1935 but who has shared with me an understanding of the growth of anthropological theory and the adventure in making sense of the modern world; and, finally, in New York, where I shared with Rhoda Métraux, who had just returned from field work on the Sepik River, this overview of my own field work that now extends back almost fifty years.

Halfway through the book I returned to the South Pacific to retrace those of my own journeys to the field which began in 1925—in Samoa—and ended in 1938—in New Guinea. It was then, while we were traveling from Bali to the Iatmul, that we heard on a radio on a little Chinese trading boat on the Sepik River the ominous news of Chamberlain's visit to Hitler that was to avert war "in our time." Not many months later, as we were leaving for home just before the tragedy of Czechoslovakia, we realized that war would not be averted. We were leaving the field to face the war that had seemed so certain that all my work in the preceding nine years had been paced against its coming.

Past and present were juxtaposed as I made that summer journey, carrying the unfinished manuscript with me. And I realized that just as the events of the war divided the peoples of the world in two—not as enemies, but as the members of two generations, born and reared before the war or after the events that changed the human condition—so also this present account of my life would have to end with the war. In 1939, when we came home, the situation within which this unique generation break occurred was already taking shape. My contemporaries were already deeply concerned about young people. In their eyes young men and women appeared to be alienated, apathetic, and lacking in moral fiber—the very words they used are still familiar phrases today. At the same time there were those who said that young people must learn to live without high ambition, for which there was only a limited scope in the contemporary world. My own response was foreshadowed in an article about the younger generation, some of whose members it seemed to me were thinking through our traditional themes in a new way as they asked, "Ought one to have a conscience?"

This week, searching through old photographs among the archives that Marie Eichelberger keeps safe for me—the photographs taken through the years by so many of the people with whom I have worked closely—Karsten Stapelfeldt, Gregory Bateson, Jane Belo, Paul Byers, Ken Heyman, and Robert Levin—I found no sharp break with the past. Setting side by side pictures of my daughter and my granddaughter, of my grandmother as a young woman and as I last knew her, of my father with my young sister and, many years later, with my mother, of myself, as a child, with my brother, and of my brother and sisters growing up, I found that all these pictures echoed each other. Each was a picture of a person at a particular moment, but spread out before me I saw them as the pattern my family made for me.

The course that my life has taken was set long ago. But since the 1940's I have moved in new directions. This book is about the present, but the present as I first understood it in a world that has changed out of measure.

Today young people, young enough to be my own great-grandchildren, often say, "You belong to us." The temptation is great to agree. It would be an extraordinary thing to belong to this generation, just coming into its own. But, in truth, I have to answer, "No, I belong to my own generation. Because we are now seeking many of the same things, this does not mean I belong to your generation. I cannot ever belong to your generation, as you cannot ever belong to mine. But I can try to explain, I can try to lay my life on the line, as you speak of laying your bodies on the line."

This is what this book is about and why I have written it.

PART ONE

2 Home and Travel

For many people moving is one kind of thing and travel is something very different. Travel means going away from home and staying away from home; it is an antidote to the humdrum activities of everyday life, a prelude to a holiday one is entitled to enjoy after months of dullness. Moving means breaking up a home, sadly or joyfully breaking with the past; a happy venture or a hardship, something to be endured with good or ill grace.

For me, moving and staying at home, traveling and arriving, are all of a piece. The world is full of homes in which I have lived for a day, a month, a year, or much longer. How much I care about a home is not measured by the length of time I have lived there. One night in a room with a leaping fire may mean more to me than many months in a room without a fireplace, a room in which my life has been paced less excitingly.

From the time I can first remember, I knew that we had not always lived where we were living then—in Hammonton, New Jersey, where we had moved so that Mother could work on her doctoral thesis. I knew that I had spent my first summer at a resort called Lavallette, a place I did not visit again until I was seventeen, there to have the only authentic attack of homesickness I have ever had, brought on by the sound of the pounding surf. I knew also that we had lived on St. Marks Square, Philadelphia, because the next winter we lived near St. Marks Square and still knew people who lived there.

Every winter we went to live in or near Philadelphia so that Father would not have to travel too far or stay in the city on the nights that he lectured at the University. From the time I was seven years old, we went somewhere for the summer, too. So we moved four times a year, because for the fall and spring we returned to the house in Hammonton.

All the other houses were strange—houses that had to be made our own as quickly as possible so that they no longer would be strange. This did not mean that they were frightening, but only that we had to learn about every nook and corner, for otherwise it was hard to play hide-and-go-seek. As soon as we arrived, I ran ahead to find a room for myself as far away as possible from everyone else, preferably at the top of the house when I would always be warned by footsteps that someone was coming. After that, until we were settled in, I was busy exploring, making my own the new domain. Later, when I was about fourteen, I was in charge of unpacking, getting beds made, food in the icebox, and the lamps filled and lit before nightfall.

The next step was to explore the neighborhood. I had to find out what other children lived nearby and whether there were woods, wild flowers, tangles, or jungles—any hidden spot that could be turned into a miniature forest where life could be quickly shaped to an imaginary world.

In Hammonton we had five whole acres, a good part of which was second-grade bush, studded with blueberries, which the little Italian children who were our neighbors picked and sold back to us. In Lansdowne and Swarthmore there were bits of woodlot. But in Philadelphia there was nothing, only stone walls of different heights on which to walk. Nothing, except for the winter when we lived at the edge of the park near the zoo.

However far away we moved and however often, we always came home again to Hammonton and the familiar and loved things that were too fragile to take with us— although Mother was very permissive about allowing us to carry along all the objects each of us wanted. In Hammonton there was the same blueberry thicket in which to wander along old paths and make new ones, the same surrey, which we hired from the livery stable, and the same door which was never opened—a second door on the front porch which was used only on one occasion, on the night the neighbors pounded on it to tell us that our chimney had caught fire.

There was the great tree from which a hornets' nest blew down in a storm. I had been dancing in the wind when it blew down and, still dancing, plunged my hands into it. I can still remember the wind but not the stings with which I was said to have been covered. There were the tall evergreen arborvitae that divided the lawn into little squares, where Grandma played games with us until one day she put her hand to her heart and then she did not play running games anymore. And outside the mock-orange hedge we once found faeces, and Mother said, in a tone of disgust close to horror, that they were human faeces.

There was the well with a pump that we used to prime with hot water, until one day my five-year-old brother and a desperado friend a year younger threw everything detachable down the well, and then it was never used again. There was an old dinghy in which we grew flowers until the boys tore it up. And once, when the barn had been reshingled and the old shingles had been piled in the barn for the winter, the two little boys threw all of them out. Grandma said it just showed how two children, each one quite good by himself, could get into mischief. You never could tell, when you put two children together, what the outcome would be. This enlarged my picture of what boys were like.

It was contrapuntal to an engraving in a homemade copper frame that stood on the mantelpiece. This showed a pair of children, a little girl diligently sewing a fine seam and a boy, beautiful and remote, simply sitting and looking out at the world. Long years later, the same picture provided the central image in a bitter little verse of feminine protest that I wrote when Edward Sapir told me I would do better to stay at home and have children than to go off to the South Seas to study adolescent girls:

Measure your thread and cut it
To suit your little seam,
Stitch the garment tightly, tightly,
And leave no room for dream.

. . .

Head down, be not caught looking
Where the restless wild geese fly.

There were treasures on Mother's dressing table, too—
a Wedgwood pin dish, a little porcelain Mary and her
lamb, the pale green, flowered top of a rose bowl that
had broken, and Mother's silver-backed comb and brush
and mirror. All these things held meaning for me. Each
was—and still is—capable of evoking a rush of memories.

Taken altogether, the things that mattered a great
deal to me when I was a child are very few when I
compare them to the overloaded tables and overcrowded
shelves through which children today have to thread
their way. Only if they are very fortunate will they be
able to weave together into memories the ill-assorted
mass of gadgets, toys, and easily forgotten objects, objects
without a past or a future, and piles of snapshots that
will be replaced by new, brightly colored snapshots next
year.

The difficulty, it seems to me, is not—as so many older
people claim—that in the past life was simpler and there
were fewer things, and so people were somehow better,
as well as more frugal. It is, rather, that today's children
have to find new ways of anchoring the changing moments of their lives, and they have to try to do this with
very little help from their elders, who grew up in an
extraordinarily different world. How many of the young
people who are rebelling against the tyranny of things,
who want to strip their lives down to the contents of a
rucksack, can remember and name the things that lay
on their mother's dressing table or can describe every
toy and book they had as a child?

It has been found that when desperate, unhappy
youngsters are preparing to break away from a dis-
ordered, drug-ridden commune in which they have been

living for months, they first gather together in one spot their few possessions and introduce a semblance of order among them. The need to define who you are by the place in which you live remains intact, even when that place is defined by a single object, like the small blue vase that used to mean home to one of my friends, the daughter of a widowed trained nurse who continually moved from one place to another. The Bushmen of the Kalahari Desert often build no walls when they camp in the desert. They simply hollow out a small space in the sand. But then they bend a slender sapling into an arch to make a doorway, an entrance to a dwelling as sacrosanct from invasion as the walled estates of the wealthy are or as Makati, in Manila, is, where watchmen guard the rich against the poor.

I realized how few things are needed to make a "home" when I took my seven-year-old daughter on her first sea voyage. The ship—the *Marine Jumper,* an unrenovated troopship with iron decks—was crowded with over a thousand students. They were bunked below where the troops had slept, while Cathy and I shared one cabin with six other members of the staff. Cathy climbed into her upper berth, opened the little packages that had been given to her as going-away presents, and arranged them in a circle around her. Then she leaned over the side of the berth and said, "Now I am ready to see the ship."

Home, I learned, can be anywhere you make it. Home is also the place to which you come back again and again. The really poignant parting is the parting that may be forever. It is this sense that every sailing may be a point of no return that haunts the peoples of the Pacific islands. On the very day I arrived in Samoa, people began to ask, "When will you leave?" When I replied, "In a year," they sighed, "Alas, *talofai*"—our love to you— with the sadness of a thousand partings in their voices. Their islands were peopled by voyagers who set off on a short known journey and whose canoes were blown hundreds of miles off course. But even when a fishing canoe goes out there is a chance that it will upset on the dangerous reef and that someone will be drowned. The smallest journey may be forever.

I have seen something similar on the seacoast of Portugal, where every year for four hundred years fishermen set out in their frail boats for the fishing banks across the treacherous Atlantic and no one could tell when—or whether—they would return. Portugal is still a widow's walk. The old women, dressed in black, still seem to be looking out to sea for the men who disappeared into the distance and an unknown fate.

In all my years of field work, each place where I have lived has become home. Each small object I have brought with me, each arrangement on a shelf of tin cans holding beads or salt for trade or crayons for the children to draw with becomes the mark of home. When it is dismantled on the last morning—a morning that is marked by the greed of those who have little and hope for a share of whatever is left behind, as well as by the grief of feeling that someone is leaving forever—on that morning, I weep. I, too, know that this departure, unlike my forays from home as a child, is likely to be forever.

In Manus, in 1928, the men beat the death drums as our canoe pulled out of the village. In 1953, when I made my first return visit to Manus and was leaving again, old Pokanau bade me a formal farewell: "Now, like an old turtle, you are going out into the sea to die and we will never see you again." Then Kilipak, a much younger man, remarked insightfully, "He is really talking about himself!"

Going away, knowing I shall return to the same place and the same people—this is the way my life has always been. When I set off for Samoa, for my first field trip in 1925, we had a last dinner in the dining room of the farm, the farm in Holicong, Bucks County, to which we moved when I was ten, after we had sold the house in Hammonton. Father and Mother and Grandma were there, and my brother and sisters, Richard, Elizabeth and Priscilla, and my student husband, Luther Cressman. Father and Richard sang, partly to tease me and partly to cover their own feelings, alternating "The smoke goes up the chimney just the same"—a song that had become a family joke when we moved to the farm and all the chimneys smoked—and "We shall meet but we shall miss her."

After dinner we drove to Philadelphia to the old Baltimore and Ohio station, which I had never seen before. I kissed them all good-bye and walked through the gate. Afterward my father said, "She never looked back!" This was a next step in life. I was going to the field and Luther had a fellowship to travel in Europe, the thing he wanted very much to do. No one was permanently bereft. I would be coming back to the farm when the hollyhocks were in bloom again.

I have never been without a home to return to. First there was Hammonton and then the farm, which was not sold until 1928. Then, in 1926, after my return from Samoa, I came to the American Museum of Natural History in New York City, where I was given as my office an attic room under the eaves up in the west tower of the old Seventy-seventh Street building. It was just like the room I had at the farm and the kind of room I had always chosen in each rented house we lived in. Among other advantages, there were two stairways leading up to the tower, just as there had been in all the better houses we had rented; this meant that one could creep down one stairway while someone whom one did not want to meet—in my childhood, my mother or the person who was It in a game, or later, a too solicitous elderly curator—was coming up the other.

Perhaps it was because I was given that little attic room with a view out over the city roofs that I decided within a few months that I was going to stay at the Museum all my life. I saw the elderly men, retired curators—one of whom was even named Mead—puttering among their books and specimens. Far from being repelled, I felt secure. Evidently the Museum did not evict its curators as universities evicted their professors when they were too old to rearrange their papers in some other place so that they could find them again. I would manage to stay there, always.

Only a few years before I came to the Museum, that office had been the bedroom of the building superintendent's apartment in which he had lived with his family. He used to stand in the doorway and tell me how all his children had been born in that room. There was also a bathroom large enough for a massive sink in which to wash specimens and, in the room across the little hall, a tiled fireplace that later held a gas jet. For those of us who worked in the tower, there was no endless hall lined with storage cases to walk along and no limits like those set by the large handsome offices downstairs, each one reserved for a curator and anyone he happened to have to help him.

After the superintendent and his family moved out, my attic had become a cataloguing room presided over by Mr. Sabine, formerly the Museum president's butler, who had become an assistant in the Department. He had a fine eye for detail and spotted at once in my Manus collection the anomalous javelin that was hurled by a twisted cord in the same manner as a Roman javelin. When I arrived, Mr. Sabine was moved out in order to give me a place to work, at least temporarily, until one of the big offices downstairs would be free.

At first my office seemed large and bare. The only furnishings were a few half-size metal cabinets, a bookcase, and an old rolltop golden oak desk that had been banished from some office down below. I hung tapa-patterned cotton curtains at the window, spread Samoan mats on the floor, and on the wall hung a map of the world on which the archeologist Erich Schmidt and I used to plot our future field trips.

Slowly through the year, after I had been offered a proper office and had refused it, I increased my attic domain. First I acquired the inside room of the old apartment, which, during Mr. Sabine's regime, had been labeled "Unidentified Specimens" and had a secret cabinet in which the Peruvian gold was stored. This is where my staff worked, for I have kept as my own the outer office. In one sense, this has been my most permanent home for many years.

Since the late 1920's, I have had no permanent house to go back to, only a series of rented apartments between field trips or part of the brownstone houses belonging to friends, in which I have lived, which I have cherished, but without a householder's responsibilities. After my parents sold the old farm in the Buckingham Valley, they bought another one which burned down soon after. So the office in the Museum became the successor to the rooms in which I had grown up.

When the farm was gone, my parents also lived in rented houses, at first a very large one which my brother and younger sisters left to get married, and then, after Father retired, a tiny house, about which Mother complained that the rooms were too small for committee meetings. Now my brother owns a house, but it is far away in California. My daughter also has a house in New Hampshire, but no country house today is safe from rodents, vandals, and arson.

The office at the top of the Museum is where all my valuable things—notes, manuscripts, photographs, and films—are stored and where, over time, I have had to find additional space for the notes and manuscripts and films of my collaborators—in the room across the hall, which was once the superintendent's kitchen, and in the window alcoves of the tower next to high racks of stored specimens.

"The Museum is a very safe place," the Department chairman, Dr. Wissler, used to say. "Once when we were going away for the summer, I brought all our silver down and we didn't find it again for eleven years. Mrs. Wissler wasn't very pleased. But we did find it."

That sense of total safety has diminished over the past thirty years. During World War II, when I used to practice imagining the Empire State Building bend and crash under bombs, we packed away some of our most valuable specimens and notes. So thoroughly were they put away that the carbon copies of our Balinese notes have not turned up yet. There have been occasional robberies, too. One thief, an ingenious and interested student of native materials, altered ethnological specimens to suit his fancy, which made it much harder to locate them in the city's pawnshops. There was also a well-publicized robbery of the Star of India from the Museum's gem collection. And there have been bomb scares and telephoned false alarms, one of them during the period when the man known as the Mad Bomber was still at large in New York.

As in wartime, now in this troubled peacetime no place is wholly safe. Still, up in the tower, with two flights of stairs between me and the milling crowds below, I feel as safe from intrusion and loss as once I did at home in my third-floor room where the night wind whistled through the closed shutters and the sparrows racketed in the ivy outside my windows every dawn. For all my years of traveling, I have always had somewhere to return to, somewhere where everything is just where I put it away twenty, thirty, or forty years ago.

It was a little hard, a few years ago, to find on my desk, accompanied by a rather curt letter of obviously unwilling apology, a skit written by a member of another department, which he labeled something like "The Department of Unimportant Information." In the skit the writer reported that although he constantly encountered me in print and on the radio and on television, he had not seen me in the Museum for many years. Finally, he penetrated the west tower to find my office deep in dust. (My hard-working, harried young student assistants particularly resented this bit.) Eventually he made his way into the big corner tower room. There he did find live files. These revealed that I had been dead for years, but that ample funds were still being provided by a series of impersonators, each of whom was murdered when she asked for a larger share of the take, and was replaced by another.

It was a cruel little piece. But I must admit there was a germ of truth in it. I always did—and still do—come into the Museum at very odd hours, so that I seldom have a chance to greet my colleagues in the elevator, and I have underwritten most of the expense of my own research with my own earnings.

As my activities have grown and as I have found room under the eaves and in the alcoves for my associates, the style of decoration of my office has changed with the interests of the young people who work with me. For a long time two reproductions of *le Douanier* Rousseau hung on the wall of the inner office. Then for a time Japanese lanterns hung from the ceiling lights, and the wastebaskets and stepladders were painted bright nursery colors. Later the students put up a picture of Martin Luther King. At present a huge beautiful portrait of an American Indian covers most of the slanting ceiling of of the inner office.

My personal possessions can all be contained in part of the colleagues' apartment, which we share. But the accumulation of research materials continues to grow as the years go by. We still need attics for those pieces of the past we find it hard to discard altogether, for someday, finding them, grandchildren may puzzle over them like old buried treasure.

3 The Original Punk

I was a first child, wanted and loved.

When I was fifteen, I asked my mother whether she had planned her children. She answered, "Goodness, no! There are some things that are best left to the Lord!" In fact, "the Lord" was only a figure of speech. She did not believe in a personal God, but she had an abiding trust in a generally benevolent providence.

Before my birth, my mother kept a little notebook in which she jotted down, among other things, quotations from William James about developing all of a child's senses, as well as the titles of articles on which she was working for various encyclopedias, and here she wrote, "When I knew baby was coming I was anxious to do the best for it."

Pictures of me as a baby show me in the arms of my mother or grandmother, with their hair down and wearing wrappers, dressed in a way I have no memory of seeing either of them. Only now, after so many years, I realize that it was for her children's sake that my mother pinned up her hair so carefully every morning as soon as she got up. Earlier, when I was too young to notice, she let it fall softly around her face—but later, never. In turn, the first thing I do in the morning is to comb my hair, and when my daughter was young I put on something pretty—as I still do when I am staying in a house where there are children.

Another picture shows me, a three-month-old baby, prone and head up, in a Morris chair. Years later we still had the Morris chair, and by the time I could think about it, I knew both that the chair represented some kind of revolution in furniture design and that it was somehow a good thing to have slept in a Morris chair instead of a crib, like other babies.

I was the first baby born in a new hospital, so Mother had the attention of the entire staff. She made a modern choice, but when I began to read school poetry—including "I remember, I remember the house where I was born" and "Over the river and through the woods,/To grandfather's house we'll go"—I felt somewhat aggrieved that I had no house where I was born and no grandfather's house to go on Thanksgiving Day, because both my grandfathers were dead and my paternal grandmother lived with us in our house.

These two views of my childhood, our houses, and my unusual upbringing persisted all through my early years. I took pride in being unlike other children and in living in a household that was itself unique. But at the same time I longed to share in every culturally normal experience. I wished that I had been born in a house. I wanted to have a locket, like other little girls, and to wear a hat with ribbons and fluffy petticoats instead of

The original punk, 1902

the sensible bloomers that very advanced mothers put on their little daughters so they could climb trees. The prevailing cultural style, as it was expressed in stories, poems, aphorisms, and the behavior of our neighbors, fascinated me in every smallest detail. I longed to live out every bit of it. But I also wanted to be very sure that I would always be recognized as myself.

My father called me, very affectionately, "Punk." Then, when my brother was born two years later, I was called "the original punk" and Dick was known as "the boy-punk," a reversal of the usual pattern, according to which the girl is only a female version of the true human being, the boy.

Before Dick was born, my parents made the common mistake of promising me a playmate in the new baby. As a result I found his newborn ineptitude very exasperating. I have been told that I once got him, as a toddler, behind a door and furiously demanded, "Can't you say anything but 'da da da' all the time?"

I was a sturdy child and had no ailments. But my brother was fragile, always—it seemed to me—ill and a worry to my parents. I early learned to expect that any disasters that occurred would happen to Dick and I even conveniently displaced onto him frightening memories, like being locked up in a dark cupboard by a German governess, who lasted no more than a week in our household. When I told the story later, I believed that it had happened not to me but to my brother, as I also recalled, mistakenly, that it was he, not I, who had been bitten by a rabbit in the zoo. Even today I have some difficulty in keeping in mind unpleasant things that have happened to me. So I learned long ago to check my memories very carefully and to write down what I found out, but I still tend to erase small misfortunes from my mind. Later other people have to recall them to me.

My father was six feet tall, which was very tall in 1901. He called my mother, who was just five feet tall, "Tiny Wife," and that was. what I called her, too, when I first learned to talk. She was slight and had very blue eyes and golden hair, and I delighted in her gentle beauty. However, she seldom allowed herself to enjoy pretty clothes or elaborately dressed hair. Life was real, life was earnest—it was too serious for trivial things. She had babies to care for and a house to manage. She also felt it was important to continue her own intellectual life and to be a responsible citizen in a world in which there were many wrongs—wrongs to the poor and the downtrodden, to foreigners, to Negroes, to women—that had to be set right. Long afterward, near the end of her life, when she was recovering from a stroke and allowed herself to take pleasure in pretty bed jackets, she confided in her son-in-law, Leo Rosten, "Margaret wanted a little rosebud mother." When she died, we dressed her in pale blue with a spray of sweetheart roses. Then, for those last hours, my father felt that his young wife had been given back to him.

Gotthard Booth, who is very much interested in inheritance in family lines, gave the Rorschach test to both my parents when they were in their seventies. I spent one of the pleasantest hours of my life discussing with him my mother's Rorschach, in which she discerned, disentangled from the chiaroscuro shadows, rare and tiny images, tinkling brooks and kissing children. Out of my own earliest memories I could bring back the poetry that evoked these images:

> Hast thou seen, with flash incessant,
> Bubbles gliding under ice,
> Bodied forth and evanescent,
> No one knows by what device?

and

> When all at once I saw a crowd,
> A host, of golden daffodils;
> Beside the lake, beneath the trees,
> Fluttering and dancing in the breeze;
> . . .
> And then my heart with pleasure fills
> and dances with the daffodils.

My mother grew up on the shores of Lake Michigan. Her Chicago childhood was so real to her that I, too, thought of the past as "before the Fire"—in 1871—from which my grandfather's house on the North Side just escaped destruction, or "before the Fair"—the Chicago World's Fair in 1893. One of my treasures, as a child, was a miniature can of Van Houten's cocoa that came from the Fair. For years I kept it carefully on my prayer desk— the prie-dieu my mother had bought at a sale, not realizing what it was. "Someday," I thought, "someday I will open that little can and actually taste the essence of the World's Fair contained in it." Meanwhile, since this could be done only once, I kept the can standing next to a miniature jar made from the clay of the Holy Land. For all her slightness and delicate beauty, my mother

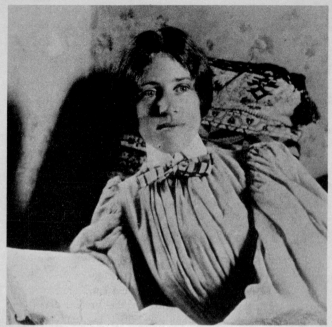

My mother as a student

had been a determined and impetuous young girl. She
told us stories of how she had led the whole high school
out on the streets to celebrate the election of Grover
Cleveland and how she had refused to kiss a boy, who
was later lost on an expedition to the interior of China,
because, instead of kissing her, he had said, "Emily, I am
going to kiss you!"—and so, of course, she had said he
couldn't. Father countered with the story of how he saw
Mother sitting in the front row of a class at the University
of Chicago and sat down beside her, announcing (probably only to himself, but we never knew for sure), "I am
going to marry you." Fifty years later, an elderly lady,
the mother of a colleague, came up to me after a lecture
and announced in a menacing voice, "I am responsible
for your existence. I introduced your father to your
mother."

Mother wore a wedding ring, but she never had another ring until, thirty years after their marriage, Father gave her a turquoise ring. Turquoise is my birthstone, and as a small child I learned to say, "December's child shall live to bless the turquoise that ensures success." But I didn't find out about being a Sagittarian—someone who goes as far as anyone else and shoots a little farther—until I was sixteen, when we learned about astrology from the physicist husband of one of my mother's college friends.

It was always difficult to give Mother a present. She felt that the money would be better spent on a good cause. Once Father, in a fit of remorse, I suspect, about some fancied infidelity and remembering how Mother had often said she would like a string of blue beads, went to Tiffany in New York, where he bought her a lapis lazuli necklace for ninety dollars. Mother reacted to this flamboyant gesture with horror and insisted that the necklace be taken back. The credit was given to me to use when I got married. And so, ten years later three undergraduate friends and I rode down from Barnard on the top deck of a Fifth Avenue bus to pick out Tiffany teaspoons and coffee spoons and an unappreciated gravy spoon that was not shaped like a ladle.

Whenever a question arose about how money was to be spent—should we buy a new rug or give the money to the fellowship fund of the American Association of University Women?—my mother always tried to capture the money for the more worthy purpose. Between the quotations of sheer delight, from Wordsworth and Browning, that came so readily to her lips, there were also the stern phrases of her American forebears and the impassioned declarations of early feminists, for example, about freeing women from the ignominy of being classified, along with criminals and imbeciles, as incapable of voting.

Mother's vehemence was reserved for the causes she supported and her fury was directed at impersonal institutions, such as political machines—the Vares of Philadelphia or Tammany Hall—the Telephone Company,

Standard Oil, or the Chicago Stockyards. As a matter of principle, she never wore furs; and feathers, except for ostrich plumes, were forbidden. Long before I had an idea what they were, I learned that aigrettes represented a murder of the innocents. There were types of people, too, for whom she had no use—anti-suffragettes (women who probably kept poodles) or "the kind of woman who comes down at ten in the morning wearing a boudoir cap and who takes headache powders." But these were never people whom she knew.

For actual, living people she had only gentleness and generosity and a radiant smile that lives on in the memory of those who knew her and of everyone who turned to her for help. Her vehemence was wholly disinterested, and so she could argue with an intensity that upset my grandmother, who had been used to quieter family meals.

The lack of any contradiction between my mother's ardent support of good principles and her fury at injustice, on the one hand, and her deep personal gentleness, on the other, came out clearly in her response to the advice given mothers in a baby book that was published just about the time I was born. The author, L. E. Holt, was an advocate of the kind of regimen, such as schedules for bottle-fed babies, that ever since has bedeviled our child-rearing practices. She read the book, but she nursed her babies. She accepted the admonition about never picking up a crying child unless it was in pain. But she said her babies were good babies who would cry only if something was wrong, and so she picked them up. Believing that she was living by the principles of the most modern child-rearing practices, she quite contentedly adapted what she was told about children in the abstract to the living reality of her own children.

All her life she kept a kind of innocence that we all too readily interpreted as an inability to appreciate humor. Once, on Groundhog Day, she reported that she had seen in Doylestown a barrel with a sign on it that read, "Ground hog, just caught." When she looked inside the barrel, she found that it contained sausage. "Why

My mother and I, 1905

sausage?" she asked, very puzzled. Or quite seriously, she would make some intellectual conversion, as when she transformed "pep" into a lament. "This horse has no pepper!" By putting the promptings of the senses and of the unconscious at a distance, she also distantiated humor.

In fact, she had no gift for play and very little for pleasure or comfort. She saw to it that we had wholesome food, but it was always very plain. It was only toward the end of her life that I began to suspect that both the plainness of our food and, in some measure, her own fastidiousness were due to a sensory deficiency of smell and taste.

She herself conscientiously filled the eighteen lamps we needed in our house in Bucks County, but she let me arrange the flowers. Indeed, she gave far less attention to the flower garden than to the vegetable garden. Changes in style—giving up tablecloths for doilies—were made not for the sake of fashion, but to save work for servants. Her two younger sisters were far more pleasure-loving and often criticized my mother for her austerity. But she easily accorded to her sister Fanny McMaster a sense of beauty and style which she felt she herself lacked. Yet any room in which she lived, filled with books and papers, had lamps that were good for the eyes and an air of welcome. It never gave one the sense that here were things among which children had to walk warily. The few precious things we had—the Wedgwood coffee service and the Meissen "onion pattern" china, which everyone in my mother's family was given by Great-aunt Fanny Howe—were always used and only briefly regretted when a piece was broken or lost in one of our many moves from one house to another. My mother did, however, reserve a little impersonal rage for the unfair way long-dead ancestors had distributed the family silver.

As she had no real gift for play, she also could neither tell nor make up stories, and there was always a touch of duty in the parties and games she planned for us. By the time I was eight, I had taken over the preparations for festivities. I made the table decorations and the place cards, filled the stockings, and trimmed the Christmas tree, while Mother sat up half the night finishing a tie for Father's Christmas present. She could neither cook nor sew, although intermittently she did a little cross-stitch embroidery or some enjoined knitting. What household skills she had were primarily managerial—providing a safe and comfortable home in which children were fed nutritionally, book salesmen and nuns collecting for charity were invited to lunch, other people's children were welcomed and treated as people, and in which there were rooms large enough for committees to meet.

In many ways she shared the intellectual snobbishness of the tradition that was so characteristic of families of New England origin, Unitarian or once Unitarian, college-bred, readers of serious novels and deeply imbued with the attitudes and imagery of the nineteenth-century essayists and poets, especially Robert Browning. The world, as she saw it, was divided into "people with some background"—a charitable phrase which accorded neither credit nor blame, but somehow divested them of privilege—"ordinary people," and a special group of "fine people"—a term that was most often applied to "fine women."

Ordinary people let their children chew gum, read girls' and boys' books, drink ice cream sodas, and go to Coney Island or Willow Grove, where they mingled with "the common herd"—a phrase we never let Mother forget she had used. They also read cheap paperback novels and were riddled by prejudice—prejudice against Labor, against foreigners, against Negroes, against Catholics and Jews.

In contrast, fine people were highly literate and had taste and sophistication. Even more important, they engaged actively in efforts to make this a better world. They fought for causes and organized community efforts. Mother believed strongly in the community, in knowing her neighbors and in treating servants as individuals with dignity and rights. In fact, by insisting on their rights, she often alienated servants who might well have responded more easily to expressions of warm but capricious affection.

Her involvement in causes carried with it a fixed belief in the value of walking. She gave walking as her main avocation in her listing in *American Women*. For years she was famous in Bucks County because, during the summer we moved there, she walked to Plumsteadville to attend a sale and back home again, a journey of some fifteen miles, and also because she herself painted the kitchen ceiling—two strange and, in local terms, unfeminine activities. It was a kind of criticism she did not mind.

All these things were part of my consciousness of my mother, but for me she had two outstanding characteristics. One was her unfailing and ungrudging generosity. In my life I realized every one of her unrealized ambitions, and she was unambivalently delighted. The other was that she was absolutely trustworthy. I know that if I had ever written to her to say, "Please go and wait for me on the corner of Thirteenth and Chestnut Streets," she would have stayed there until I came or she dropped from sheer fatigue.

But I, as the eldest—the original punk, the child who was always told, "There's no one like Margaret"—had the clearest sense of what she was. When my youngest sister Priscilla was twenty-two, she prepared an autobiographical account for one of my social science projects. In it she wrote, "Dick was Dadda's favorite, Elizabeth was Grandma's favorite, Margaret was everybody's favorite. I was Mother's favorite, but Mother didn't count for much in our house."

Priscilla wrote this in the days when she, the last child, was leaving home and Mother was struggling, unhappily, to pick up the threads of graduate work she had dropped twenty-five years earlier. And Priscilla was one of the children born after the death of my nine-month-old sister Katherine, my parents' third child. It was a death that drove a wedge between my father and my mother and made my father vow never again to give his heart so wholly to a child.

4 My Father and Academia

When my father entered the house, my mother's and my grandmother's absorption with the children was likely to be interrupted by his immediate demands. "Emmy-Tiny," he would shout, "where is my . . ."—whatever he was looking for at the moment. Mother never was able to anticipate what he would ask for; it might be anything—a book he hadn't read for years, an issue of one of the Western magazines that were his favorite light reading, a telephone number or a name he had forgotten. His voice was loud and direct and the imperative mode was very congenial to him. When he felt particularly executive and considered that his orders were being obeyed too slowly, he would catch the tip of his tongue tightly between his teeth. I do this myself—with a small ache in my left cheek—on occasions when I feel frustrated by stupidity or recalcitrance. Father used the telephone constantly, so we all learned a great deal about his current interests and also how to answer the telephone and how to take messages correctly. He had no time at all for inaccuracy or blundering or for people who didn't use their head. His secretaries adored him and tirelessly carried out his most inordinate demands, while he apostrophized them, "What is that you have on top of your neck, anyway?"

Fairly early I had a pretty good idea of how life was organized. Father was a professor at the University of Pennsylvania—known at home simply as "the University"—and he had an office there which overlooked the entrance to the morgue of the medical school. When Mother

My father as a young professor

asked him to take charge of one of us, as small children, he would take us to the office and hand us over to a secretary. She would try to keep us from staring at the morgue and, instead, might take us to the Museum to wonder at some fact such as that, although Mother disapproved of rouge, the Egyptians had painted their fingernails.

When I was a young child, in the years when we lived in Philadelphia in the wintertime, faculty members and students came to Sunday morning breakfast to talk and eat Spanish mackerel. Among my toys I had a string of strange animals that had been put together as a joke about Professor Simon N. Patten's lectures on evolution and were then given to me as the first child in the faculty of the newly organized Evening School.

Father's position in the Wharton School of Finance and Commerce meant that his attention was early concentrated on practical matters, and he soon became one of the editors of *Railway World*. I learned to draw on the back of proof sheets, the shiny, glazed surface of which was unresponsive to anything but the hardest pencil. Today I use a soft pencil and almost shudder when I get a hard one by mistake.

As I grew up within an academic environment, I heard constant talk about university politics and financing, about the stratagems and ruses adopted by ambitious men, and about those who made their reputations by quoting, or almost quoting, without acknowledgment from the work of others. Living in the midst of university politics and academic disputes, I very early got a sense of what academic life was like. I also came to recognize my father's deep conviction as to the necessity for trust between men and loyalty to the "organization."

He was unrelenting in his disapproval of anyone who failed to stand by his colleagues. A dean who had let down the men who had trusted him was the subject of unending reprobation. In 1915, when Scott Nearing was dismissed from the University, my father helped to organize the group of men who guaranteed his salary for the next year. Former students, too, always had a claim on his time, and he expected the same kind of loyalty from them. He used to say, "I can go into any bank on the East Coast and find a former student behind a front desk." Much later, when he retired from the University, which had in fact treated him rather shabbily, he was offered a new position to build up the School of Business Administration at Temple University, a private institution that was ambitious but still was playing very second fiddle to the University of Pennsylvania. The offer attracted my father, but he felt that to accept it would be treason to his own institution, so he refused. Loyalty was one of his strongest sentiments—unconditional loyalty through thick and thin.

At the same time his enormous respect for facts made his standards of academic work rigorous but totally lacking in ambiguity. You either had the facts or you did not, and the facts—not any abstract theory—dictated the conclusions. He taught by the case method and each of his students had to make an original study of a business or an industry. As most of them were sons who expected to inherit some family enterprise, they usually made the easy choice of studying their own family business. Partly in this way Father built up an enormous store of teaching materials which he valued so highly that once, when Logan Hall caught fire, he stood in the doorway of his office to prevent the firemen from entering it. How could he teach without his files? Luckily they were not destroyed. Yet when he retired, he made no effort to save these masses of material. They were part of the equipment of a teacher and writer of contemporary textbooks and commentries.

For a man who spent so much of his life in the academic world, he was extraordinarily uninterested in the work that was being done by other members of his discipline. Even the word "discipline" sounds odd as applied to him, for he never used it. After a few years of membership, he stopped attending meetings of the American Economic Association. Instead, he devoted himself to building up the Wharton School and the Evening School, on the one hand, and on the other, to understanding the contemporary realities of the American economic system. One of the few comments he ever made about fame or reputation was a remark that the amount of space accorded someone in the obituaries in *The New York Times* was proportionate to the amount of good a man had attempted to do, not to the amount of money he had made.

However, although teaching was at the center of his life, he had a large number of other interests, few of which Mother appreciated. When she met and married him, he was a theoretical economist concerned with such problems as the quantity theory of money. But working on the quantity theory of money led him to look at gold itself, instead of treating it as a mere abstraction with special concrete properties. So he became interested in gold mining and even wrote a little book on the whole sequence of processes connected with it, *The Story of Gold*.

Father always had a close male confederate in whatever extracurricular activity engaged his interest. Whether this confederate was a faculty member, an itinerant inventor, or a businessman—once his student and now struggling with a failing family business, who had come to him for help—or the current farmer on our farm, Mother treated him—and all others like him—as on the whole basically undesirable. She would have liked my father to be a prominent and admired member of the wider community.

But he preferred to spend his spare time finding out about the concrete processes of economic life. He had, for example, a life-long interest in the possibilities of using the waste products from coal mining. Even on the first Christmas after they were married, my mother told me, Father left her alone to trim the Christmas tree while he was "somewhere watching an experiment on briquettes"—molded blocks of compacted coal dust. At one time an attempt was made to use molasses as the binding agent. World War I ended that experiment. Then pitch was used, and one winter our whole house was filled with the smoke of great unbound hunks of coal dust. Then there was the "creek" where the barely economically profitable fine coal was pumped out. Of course, the machinery continually broke down, and this gave Father excuses for taking trips upstate to Shamokin, where he sat and gossiped with the rough engineers who ran the cranky enterprise. There was also "the plant," a brick factory in Trenton, that was supposed to consume the coal that came out of the creek. Finally, after I was ten, there was the farm, as well, as another project that absorbed my father's attention. When it rained too much for the benefit of the farm in Bucks County, it was good for the creek, further upstate. Besides these activities, there were also the Extension Schools in Harrisburg, Wilkes-Barre, and Scranton, which my father helped to organize and in which he faithfully lectured two nights a week for many years.

Father was interested in money, very interested in it as a subject of thought and manipulation, but he felt it would have been unbecoming for him to have made a great deal of money. Although he made more than his academic salary, we always had to borrow for the summer. His motto was: If you need more money, make it; don't skimp and save. Sometimes he made some money through the experiments in which he was involved, but more often he lost some.

Usually he tried to conceal from Mother the fact that he was short of money. But it was lack of funds, in 1919, that lay back of his unwillingness to send me to college. The reason he gave was that, since I was going to get married, I would not need a college education—he having married a wife who was working for her doctorate when I was born! And besides, he commented, I would have the same old-maid teachers at Wellesley who had been there when my mother was a student.

He had a way of putting things that offended my mother's sense of the proprieties, a streak of vulgarity combined with a tendency to see things in rather crude—and, I suspect, lurid—colors. Certainly there were occasionally very different women in his life. One of them had red hair, and one almost persuaded him to marry her. This was at the time when he bought the farm. Mother used to grit her teeth and say that she knew—and hadn't forgotten—why the farm had been bought. But he told me later, a woman who would try to persuade a man with four children to leave them wasn't any good. And anyway, after Mother had established how much money she would need to bring us up properly, there wouldn't have been anything left.

This was in 1912. From then on, his infidelities were expressed in the interest he maintained in inventions and manufacturing processes of various sorts and, finally, in the new possibilities of commercial agriculture. His last important book was *The Ebb and Flow of Investment Values,* in which he related activity in the stock market to the question of whether a particular type of stock came from a declining or an expanding industry.

During all these years my father spent a great deal of time watching and listening to the people who actually did the things about which he taught and wrote. My first experience of field work was through my mother's work among the Italians living in Hammonton, New Jersey, where we had moved in 1902 so that she could study them. But Father's vivid accounts of how a street railway in Massachusetts had failed and of the fate of a pretzel factory also gave me a sense of the way theory and practice must be related. And it was his knowledge both of the concrete sequences of activities necessary to carry out any process and of the men involved—the workmen, for example, who alternately cursed and made the sign of the cross over the recalcitrant machinery used to dredge the "creek"—that gave me a sense of how important it was to link together the concrete and the abstract.

In spite of his lifelong interest in how things got done, my father himself had virtually no bodily skills. He was awkward in his handling of his children, and his determined touch hurt. I have many memories of this—of having my shoes put on the wrong feet the morning my brother was born, of being held too tightly, of once having my hair brushed far too vigorously.

He did not trust his own body, although he had worked on his uncle's farm every summer during his boyhood, and he had an enormous amount of physical anxiety. He was afraid for us to ride bicycles and he forbade horseback riding after a minor mishap when my brother and I fell off a led horse. I resented furiously what I regarded as his entirely arbitrary intrusions into our lives represented by such dicta and by his very occasional acts of discipline. His own intensity, when he would send me away from the table because my neck didn't look clean, roused such a corresponding fury in me that I would bang every door—and there were six—between the dining room and my third-floor refuge. In general, however, he left the supervision of his daughters to my mother and concentrated, instead, on worrying about and overprotecting his son.

Looking back, it seems to me that his physical anxieties must have arisen out of early fears connected with his father's death—from pneumonia—for which, in the typical struggle of a small boy over managing his own aggression, he must somehow have blamed himself, for he had seen his father die. A much later episode with a gun, in which one fellow student had almost killed another, also made an indelible impression on him, and he was terrified of any kind of physical violence.

Yet the superficiality of this repression showed up in his endless enjoyment of Westerns, stories which he read over and over again with exactly the same absorption. He did not like other types of novels and did not enjoy any book of any sort that Mother—and later his children —recommended to him. His university club had a first-class library and all the current periodicals, and he spent a great deal of time there. At home he either read the endless Westerns or reread certain great favorites, such as John L. Motley's *Rise of the Dutch Republic* and *The Writings and Speeches of Edmund Burke*. At other times he figured and figured on the back of used envelopes, making long columns of neat numbers, or added some bit to his diary in which throughout his life he wrote down accounts of every interesting conversation. Whenever people came to the house, brought by Mother or the children, he tried to find out whether they knew anything special; if they did, he questioned them sharply and listened carefully.

I think I respected most of all my father's capacity to listen, his powers of concentration, and the aptness of his criticism. And I knew that he respected me. When I made Phi Beta Kappa at Barnard, he grasped the key that was hanging on a chain around my neck, and said, "That cost me ten thousand dollars, and it's worth it!" In later life, especially after my mother died in 1950, I used to accept speaking engagements in and near Philadelphia, and he would come to listen and criticize. "You should never speak from behind a podium," he would tell me. "Too much between you and the audience." Or he would advise me not to lose weight, saying, "You are too small anyway. You need a little weight to give you presence."

From the time I was a small child and had to recite in public, he started to train me to look him in the eye, when he sat in the audience, and to avoid what he called "the lawn sprinkler method," in which a speaker scatters his words over an audience without ever meeting a pair of eyes. But as often as not, on such occasions, he would promise to come and then, in the end, would beg off. I learned to count on this and on the dollar he offered me instead. My mother and Dick never ceased to be disappointed. But as I saw it, money is not like love, which is irreplaceable. If Father thought his attendance at some affair could be negotiated, then I would treat it as negotiable.

In this way, very early, I came to terms with his ethics. So I could not be bought in situations in which I myself did not set the conditions in advance and was not willing to accept the consequences. Initially, when Father decided that I was not to go to college, it was Mother who fought for me and invented the appealing idea of sending me to DePauw, which was his college, instead of to Wellesley. Two years later, when I developed a severe neuritis in my right arm, there seemed to be a good medical reason for keeping me home—which again fitted the state of Father's finances—and I did not rebel. I admitted his right to spend his money as he wished. But I considered running away and taking a job as a cook. The endless stream of runaway wives and daughters who had staffed our kitchen through the years provided me with a model and, anyway, cooking was my only fully developed skill. But it turned out not to be a necessary move.

Without Mother as the anchor for his life, his financial uncertainties and worries undoubtedly would have made him interfere in our lives much more than he did. In 1928, my mother took my sister Elizabeth to Italy and I left for the field in New Guinea, both of us reassured that my youngest sister's college plans had all been safely settled. Almost immediately, Father reversed everything

My father with Elizabeth, 1911

on the grounds that Priscilla had a tendency to hypothyroidism and that the college to which she planned
to go was in the goiter belt. Ruth Benedict, struggling
with the problem of what to do with an eighteen-year-old
girl who had been allowed to come to New York for the
summer but was not allowed to go to the University of
Wisconsin, wrote to me, after a lunch with Father, "My
congratulations, Margaret, I don't see how you ever grew
up!"

But in a sense I had always been a match for Father.
One of the stories he loved to tell was about taking me
for a walk in a square in Philadelphia when I was about

three. The pavement was covered with wet, fallen leaves which I insisted on kicking. He threatened to abandon me unless I stopped, and finally he did walk off. Thereupon I sat down on the wet pavement and wailed, "Bad Dada to go off and leave his poor little baby girl!" Of course, he had to come back, facing the condemnatory glances of other Sunday strollers, and pick me up and comfort me.

I greatly respected the way my father thought, but not his ethic or the tone of his thinking. While I granted his right to set the conditions when he paid, I was prepared to combat to the finish his conservative, money-bound judgments. What I found most difficult was his frequent recourse to sarcasm and bitter parody. When I was eleven, I elected to be baptized. My father did drive me to church, but when we approached the tollgate, where churchgoers did not have to pay toll, he galloped the horses through and shouted, "Going to be baptized, Lou!" Then, for a year or more afterward, he would threaten to have me unbaptized whenever I did something he did not like. I did not really believe he could do this, but I wrote in my diary, "I think it is wrong to jest about such subjects," and I confided my troubles to one of the nurses who lived with us during the summer to take care of my brother, who had a broken leg.

I accepted my father's ethic that he w ɔ pays the piper calls the tune. I simply was very careful not to put myself in a position in which he, who called the tune, had too much power over me. When I graduated from college, Father offered me a trip around the world and a very liberal allowance if I would give up my plan to get married. He was moved to do this by my grandmother's conviction that I was getting married because, in my mind, this was the expected thing for a girl to do after college. She was right in this judgment. In addition, he did not like my choice of a husband. Unquestionably, he sensed how much I valued in Luther exactly those abilities in which I felt my father was lacking—his precise physical skills and his sensitivity to other human beings. Of course, I promptly refused my father's offer.

Two years later the situation was different. I had a chance to do field work in Samoa, where I wanted to go, instead of working with an American Indian tribe, which was what my professor, Franz Boas, wanted me to do. Then, partly out of sheer countersuggestibility to the proposal made by Boas, but out of his genuine capacity to share in another person's ambitions, my father again offered to pay my fare around the world. This time I accepted.

It is hard for me to differentiate what my father contributed to me as a person and what he contributed to me as a girl learning to know what a woman is and what a man is. He certainly gave me a great deal of affection. He loved to hold my hands and comment on their shape and how they felt, and all my life I have enjoyed using my hands for activity and for communication. He taught me the importance of thinking clearly and of keeping one's premises clear. I learned to value male skills as something he did not have and was somehow diminished by not having. From the beginning I certainly repudiated his fearfulness and determinedly allowed my adventurous, but properly cautious, young daughter to climb the tallest pine.

In many ways I felt that my father had been cut down to size, to the pattern of academic and social virtues in which my mother believed, and that he wasted a great part of his birthright in small acts of rebellion against this. I used to wonder why it was necessary for him to do these things—wait to wash his hands until the dinner bell had rung, crumble bread on the dinner plate that later would be exchanged for another, refuse to carve, or make wicked jokes about Mother's stylish and serious friends. He once bought a couple of heifers from a friend of Mother's and named them after this rather pompous woman and her secretary; later he delighted in pointing out their names and milk yield on the chart in the dairy shed. Or he would go to a sale, bid for a cow, and then change his mind; afterward he would make out a check from, to, and endorsed by himself which, naturally, the perplexed auctioneer would refuse to accept. And once, when Mother insisted that we join the Farmers Club and become part of the community, we were asked to bring cheese to a community dinner; Father brought Lieder-kranz or Limburger cheese, which only one old Pennsylvania Dutch farmer and he himself would eat.

I have the feeling that in many ways my father lost out in life—that all the adventures with coal and bricks and farming and, at the very end of his life, with methods of recycling water were substitutes for something he missed that was important to him. But the failures he recognized—losing the chairmanship of his department before he retired and not being made an emeritus professor—these he regretted mainly for my mother's sake. He was sorry about them because they were things that mattered to her, and he knew she would mind.

It seems to me that in some way he thought of purely intellectual endeavor as feminine. He had barely known his father and he had the same kind of mind as his mother. Characteristically, he was very proud of my mother's achievements and honors—the award she received as a "useful citizen" from the alumnae of the University of Chicago and, when she died, the long obituary in *The New York Times.* Although her publications were few in number, since most of her life was devoted to caring for her children and various good works, he spoke of them with a pride that never dimmed. It was proper for women to be committed to pure goodness and purely intellectual activities and for their male relatives to take pride in their achievements.

Although he regretted it when my mother fretted because he did not receive the academic recognition she would have valued for him or when she raged because other men claimed his ideas, it mattered less to him. He always had other arenas in which the battles were fiercer than they were in the academic world and the stakes much higher. Year after year he played what were substantially intellectual games with industrial enterprises that could not be made to succeed but that could be made to fail less disastrously. But these games, too, were marred. Once he said to me, "It's a pity you aren't a boy, you'd have gone far." I think he only meant by this that I might have become a titan of industry—something from which he himself was debarred by the standards he had learned from his mother and had accepted in his wife. The fees connected with the different enterprises in which he was continually involved augmented his income—but only a little. Lack of success made the whole affair intellectually respectable and at the same time ministered to his respect for the real world and his underlying contempt for the men who only lectured about that world but never entered it.

However, the academic world was the real world to us, even though Father seemed to treat it as a mere shadow of the world about which he taught. Books, galley proofs and new editions, lectures, students, departmental changes, marriages of professors to their secretaries, bachelor professors who asked impertinent questions or kissed you when you didn't want to be kissed, awards and honors, and all the paraphernalia of academic life were very real to us in a way they never were to my father.

However, we responded to the reality of the academic world in very different ways. For my brother, at least in the beginning, it was a burdensome reality. I remember that when he was a young member of the Wharton School faculty, my father asked him whether a report on which he was working was to be published. Dick replied that it was going to be mimeographed, and when Father looked contemptuous, Dick flung angrily out of the room. That night he walked in his sleep and tried to make a printing press out of his wife's hanging plants.

A generation later it had a very different reality for my eight-year-old daughter. Realizing that she had not been fully appreciative of the book *A Club of Small Men,* which Colin McPhee had dedicated to her, she decided, "I will write him a review of it." She did so, and Colin sent it to *The Saturday Review.* When I explained to her that the review might not be published, she answered philosophically, "Well, anyway, I will have written something that might have been published when I was only eight." However, they did publish it and paid her half-

My parents, 1949

price because she was a child. As she held the check in her hand, she said, "I think writers don't make much money."

The way in which one's parents grow old matters a great deal. My mother had a severe stroke and had to learn to talk and walk and relate to the world again. It took her a year to do it, and once she had fully recovered so that she could find any book in the house and locate any name we wanted to know, she died. Her death left my father free because he would not have wanted her to make the long, weary recovery again.

Although he was now alone, he stayed on in the little house into which they had moved on his retirement and in which the rooms were too small for committee meetings. He was as forgetful and as careless of material things as he had always been, but as he did not smoke and the furnace had an automatic fire arrangement, the principal hazards were to himself and not to the neighbors in whose children he was deeply interested and for whose sake he had taken down the fence so that they would have more room to play. My youngest sister thought he ought to live in a home for the elderly. She feared that he might fall down the steep little staircase or be run over when he absentmindedly crossed a street against the light. But I stood out against this. I believed he had a right to run risks in his own way.

As my father grew old he became more eccentric. He became parsimonious, where once he had been open-handed, and complained about the bills run up by the students who sometimes lived with him. He often woke up at four in the morning and started to go out of the house. And he mislaid things, but he had never in his life had to find anything or file anything. He told the same stories, but he had always repeated stories, absorbed in the telling and unaware of the listener's expression of recognition or boredom. Now he had fewer stories to tell and told them oftener.

But the structure of his personality remained intact and his mind was as keen and fresh, as alert to anything new and interesting as it had ever been. The spring before he died I gave a seminar to a group who thought of themselves as avant-garde, but his were the most searching questions.

In the summer of 1956, after he had to move from the little house in which all the mementos of his life were in place, he was obviously failing. Although his grandchildren found a hotel in which he could live independently and still cause little trouble by leaving his door open or the bath running, because there was someone to watch out for such things, he felt close to the end. When summer school was over, his club, which he had founded and in which he ate lunch every day, closed. He was more alone, but the nephew of an old friend had breakfast with him to be sure that he had one good meal a day and he himself made a last effort to see those of his old friends who were still alive. He died in his sleep the night he knew I was crossing the Atlantic on my way home.

It was my father, even more than my mother, whose career was limited by the number of her children and her health, who defined for me my place in the world. Although I have acted on a wider stage than either my mother or my father, it is still the same stage—the same world, only with wider dimensions. I have been fortunate in being able to look up to my parents' minds well past my own middle years. And I watched my father grow— shed his earlier racial prejudices and come to respect new institutions of the federal government, such as Social Security and public ownership, which he had earlier disapproved of on the premise that the best government is the least government. Watching a parent grow is one of the most reassuring experiences anyone can have, a privilege that comes only to those whose parents live beyond their children's early adulthood.

5 On Being a Granddaughter

My paternal grandmother, who lived with us from the time my parents married until she died in 1927, while I was studying anthropological collections in German museums, was the most decisive influence in my life. She sat at the center of our household. Her room—and my mother always saw to it that she had the best room, spacious and sunny, with a fireplace if possible—was the place to which we immediately went when we came in from playing or home from school. There my father went when he arrived in the house. There we did our lessons on the cherry-wood table with which she had begun housekeeping and which, later, was my dining room table for twenty-five years. There, sitting by the fire, erect and intense, she listened to us and to all of Mother's friends and to our friends. In my early childhood she was also very active—cooking, preserving, growing flowers in the garden, and attentive to all the activities of the country and the farm, including the chickens that were always invading the lawn and that I was always being called from my book to shoo away.

My mother was trustworthy in all matters that concerned our care. Grandma was trustworthy in a quite different way. She meant exactly what she said, always. If you borrowed her scissors, you returned them. In like case, Mother would wail ineffectually, "Why does everyone borrow my scissors and never return them?" and Father would often utter idle threats. But Grandma never threatened. She never raised her voice. She simply commanded respect and obedience by her complete expectation that she would be obeyed. And she never gave silly orders. She became my model when, in later life, I tried to formulate a role for the modern parent who can no longer exact obedience merely by virtue of being a parent and yet must be able to get obedience when it is necessary. Grandma never said, "Do this because Grandma says so," or "because Grandma wants you to do it." She simply said, "Do it," and I knew from her tone of voice that it was necessary.

My grandmother grew up in the little town of Winchester, in Adams County, Ohio, which two of my great-great-grandfathers had founded. She was one of nine children who reached adulthood. Her father was a farmer, a small entrepreneur, a member of the state legislature, a justice of the peace, and the Methodist local preacher. His name was Richard Ramsay, and in our family there have been so many Richards that they have to be

My paternal grandparents

referred to as Uncle El's Richard, Grace Bradford's Richard, and so on.

My grandmother began school teaching quite young, at a time when it was still somewhat unusual for a girl to teach school. When my grandfather, who was also a teacher, came home from the Civil War, he married my grandmother and they went to college together. They also graduated together. She gave a graduation address in the morning and my grandfather, who gave one in the afternoon, was introduced as the husband of Mrs. Mead who spoke this morning.

My grandfather was a school superintendent who was such a vigorous innovator that exhausted school boards used to request him to leave after a one-year term—with the highest credentials—to undertake the reform of some other school. We have a few examples of my grandmother's letters to him while they were engaged, including admonitions not to go on picnics on the Sabbath. He died when my father was six. Two days later the principal took his place and my grandmother took the principal's place. From then on she taught, sometimes in high school, sometimes small children, until she came to live with us when my parents married. It was the small children in whom she was most interested, and I have the notes she took on the schools she observed during a visit to Philadelphia before my parents' marriage.

She understood many things that are barely recognized in the wider educational world even today. For example, she realized that arithmetic is injurious to young minds and so, after I had learned my tables, she taught me algebra. She also understood the advantages of learning both inductively and deductively. On some days she gave me a set of plants to analyze; on others, she gave me a description and sent me out to the woods and meadows to collect examples, say, of the "mint family." She thought that memorizing mere facts was not very important and that drill was stultifying. The result was that I was not well drilled in geography or spelling. But I learned to observe the world around me and to note what I saw—to observe flowers and children and baby chicks. She taught me to read for the sense of what I read and to enjoy learning.

With the exception of the two years I went to kindergarten, for Grandma believed in training the hands early, though not with too fine work, and the year I was eight, when I went to school for a half-day in the fourth grade in Swarthmore, she taught me until I went to high school and even then helped me with my lessons when my teachers were woefully inadequate, as they often were. I never expected any teacher to know as much as my parents or my grandmother did. Although my grandmother had no Greek, she had a good deal of Latin, and I remember that once, on the Fourth of July, she picked up one of my brother's Latin texts because she had never read Sallust.

She was conscious of the developmental differences between boys and girls and considered boys to be much more vulnerable and in need of patience from their teachers than were girls of the same age. This was part of the background of my learning the meaning of gender. And just as Grandma thought boys were more vulnerable, my father thought it was easier for girls to do well in school, and so he always required me to get two and a half points higher than my brother in order to win the same financial bonus.

Grandma had no sense at all of ever having been handicapped by being a woman. I think she played as strong a role among her brothers and sisters as her elder brother, who was a famous Methodist preacher. Between them they kept up an active relationship with their parents in Winchester and, returning often for visits, they supervised, stimulated, and advised the less adventurous members of the family. This has now become my role among some of the descendants of my grandmother's sisters, who still live in various small towns and large cities in Ohio.

Grandma was a wonderful storyteller, and she had a set of priceless, individually tailored anecdotes with which American grandparents of her day brought up children. There was the story of the little boys who had been taught absolute, quick obedience. One day when they were out on the prairie, their father shouted, "Fall down on your faces!" They did, and the terrible prairie fire swept over them *and they weren't hurt.* There was also the story of three boys at school, each of whom received a cake sent from home. One hoarded his, and the mice ate it; one ate all of his, and he got sick; and who do you think had the best time?—why, of course, the one who shared his cake with his friends. Then there was the little boy who ran away from home and stayed away all day. When he came home after supper, he found the

My grandmother with my father, 1878

family sitting around the fire and nobody said a word. Not a word. Finally, he couldn't stand it anymore and said, "Well, I see you have the same old cat!" And there was one about a man who was so lazy he would rather starve than work. Finally, his neighbors decided to bury him alive. On the way to the cemetery they met a man with a wagonload of unshelled corn. He asked where they were going. When they told him that they were going to bury that no-good man alive, the owner of the corn took pity on him and said, "I tell you what. I will give you this load of corn. All you will have to do is shell it." But the lazy man said, "Drive on, boys!"

Because Grandma did so many things with her hands, a little girl could always tag after her, talking and asking questions and listening. Side by side with Grandma, I learned to peel apples, to take the skin off tomatoes by plunging them into scalding water, to do simple embroidery stitches, and to knit. Later, during World War I, when I had to cook for the whole household, she taught me a lot about cooking, for example, just when to add a lump of butter, something that always had to be concealed from Mother, who thought that cooking with butter was extravagant.

While I followed her about as she carried out the endless little household tasks that she took on, supplementing the work of the maids or doing more in between maids—and we were often in between—she told me endless tales about Winchester. She told me about her school days and about the poor children who used to beg the cores of apples from the rich children who had whole apples for lunch. She told me about Em Eiler, who pushed Aunt Lou off a rail fence into a flooded pasture lot; about Great-aunt Louisian, who could read people's minds and tell them everything they had said about her and who had been a triplet and so small when she was born that she would fit into a quart cup; about Grace, who died from riding a trotting horse too hard, which wasn't good for girls; and about the time Lida cut off Anna Louise's curls and said, "Now they won't say 'pretty little girl' anymore." My great-grandfather used to say such a long grace, she told me, that one of her most vivid memories was of standing, holding a log she had started to put on the fire, for what seemed to be hours for fear of interrupting him. All this was as real to me as if I had lived it myself. I think that if anyone had tried to repeat the Bridie Murphy case, I could easily have impersonated, in trance, the child and girl my grandmother had been.

One of the stories I loved most was about the time the Confederate soldiers came through the village and shot down the flag. In the face of the danger, my grandmother's younger sister ran out and held the flag aloft. It was only another Barbara Frietchie episode and the story gained a great deal from the fact that we had learned to recite, " 'Shoot, if you must, this old gray head,/But spare your country's flag,' she said." But this particular Barbara Frietchie had been young and was my great-aunt. Later, I tried to immortalize her in a story called "A Strip of Old Glory," which was published in the Doylestown High School magazine, of which I was the editor.

I never saw Winchester until recently, when the town was holding its sesquicentennial celebration. I took my daughter with me, and as we walked through the streets, I looked at houses that were completely familiar. I saw the house in which my great-grandparents had lived and in which my father's cousin Cally had heard the sound of a ghostly coffin bumping on the stairs until her mother made her get down on her knees and promise never again to indulge in that strange, outlandish Aunt-Louisian kind of behavior. I saw the house in which the Bradfords had lived and where they had been such warm hosts to the next generation. And I recognized the sites of the fires. For part of the history of Winchester, a little town that never grew, is written in fire.

I was treated as an honored guest in a handsome house with peacocks on the lawn that had been bought by a successful man who had returned from a large city to buy the house where he had once been the stableboy. The husband of one of my cousins also was being honored for his success, and people told me how pleased

Grandma

Grandma in 1918

they were; as a boy he had been so poor, they explained, that he had had to ride a horse bareback to school. One of the peculiarities of the little town, which was never reflected in my grandmother's stories because she saw life ethically and not in class terms, was its incredible snobbishness. This came home to me as I watched how people with strange ticks and deformities seldom seen in a city entered the house humbly in order to shake the hands of the guests of a leading citizen who now owned the garage, as once her father had owned the livery stable.

My grandmother was indifferent to social class, but in her stories she told me about poor people, unfortunate people, people who were better off, and no-count people who drank or gambled or deserted their wives and children. Her own family, for all their pride and their handsome noses, had a fair number of charming, no-count men in each generation and, appropriately, a fair number of women who married the same kind of men. There were a number of stern, impressive women and an occasional impressive man, but a lot of weak ones, too—that is the family picture. My cousins suspect that our great-grandfather was not a very strong character, but that he was kept in hand by our great-grandmother.

This indifference to social class irritated my mother, who used to complain that Grandma could get interested in the most ordinary people. Sometimes she went on a holiday to the seaside. When she came home she told us endless narratives about the lives of the ordinary people with whom she sat on the steps of the seaside hotel. This used to make Mother mutter. Grandma and Mother looked a good deal alike. They were of the same height and weight, and had similar enough features so that people often mistook them for mother and daughter. This, too, did not please Mother.

Mother never ceased to resent the fact that Grandma lived with us, but she gave her her due. Grandma never "interfered"—never tried to teach the children anything religious that had not previously been introduced by my mother, and in disagreements between my mother and father she always took my mother's side. When my father threatened to leave my mother, Grandma told him firmly that she would stay with her and the children.

When Grandma was angry, she sat and held her tongue. I used to believe that this involved some very mysterious internal, anatomical trick. She was so still, so angry, and so determined not to speak, not to lose her temper. And she never did. But not losing her temper came out of her eyes like fire. Years later, when I was given a picture of her as a young woman, I felt that I had looked very like her at the same age. But when I actually compared pictures of me with the one of her, I looked milky mild. Not until the birth of her great-great-granddaughter, my daughter's daughter Sevanne Margaret, did that flashing glance reappear in the family. Looking at her black eyes, inherited from her Armenian father, I see again shining out of them the flash of Martha Ramsay's furiousness.

I think it was my grandmother who gave me my ease in being a woman. She was unquestionably feminine—small and dainty and pretty and wholly without masculine protest or feminist aggrievement. She had gone to college when this was a very unusual thing for a girl to do, she had a firm grasp of anything she paid attention to, she had married and had a child, and she had a career of her own. All this was true of my mother, as well. But my mother was filled with passionate resentment about the condition of women, as perhaps my grandmother might have been had my grandfather lived and had she borne five children and had little opportunity to use her special gifts and training. As it was, the two women I knew best were mothers and had professional training. So I had no reason to doubt that brains were suitable for a woman. And as I had my father's kind of mind—which was also his mother's—I learned that the mind is not sex-typed.

The content of my conscience came from my mother's concern for other people and the state of the world and from my father's insistence that the only thing worth doing is to add to the store of exactly known facts. But

Grandma with Elizabeth and Priscilla at the farm at
Holicong. *Watercolor by Elizabeth Mead Steig*

the strength of my conscience came from Grandma, who
meant what she said. Perhaps nothing is more valuable
for a child than living with an adult who is firm and
loving—and Grandma was loving. I loved the feel of her
soft skin, but she would never let me give her an extra
kiss when I said good night.

After I left home I used to write long letters to
Grandma, and later, when I went to Samoa, it was for
Grandma that I tried to make clear what I was doing.
She was not entirely happy with my choice of a career;

she thought that botany would have been better than savages. Even though she herself hardly ever went to church—she had decided that she had gone to church enough—she taught me to treat all people as the children of God. But she had no way to include in her conception of human beings the unknown peoples of distant South Sea islands. When I was a child and would come into her room with my hair flying, she would tell me that I looked like the wild man of Borneo. For her, that was only a figure of speech.

Throughout my childhood she talked a great deal about teachers, about their problems and conflicts, and about those teachers who could never close the school-house door behind them. The sense she gave me of what teachers are like, undistorted by my own particular experience with teachers, made me want to write my first book about adolescents in such a way that the teachers of adolescents would understand it. Grandma always wanted to understand things, and she was willing to listen or read until she did. There was only one subject, she decided rather fastidiously, that she did not wish to pursue. That was birth control. At eighty, she said, she did not need to know about it.

When I returned from Samoa, Grandma had already left for Fairhope, Alabama, where she had taken my two younger sisters to an experimental school. So I never had a chance to follow up the letters I wrote her from Samoa with long talks through which she would have understood more about what I was doing, and I would have learned more about how to say things useful to teachers.

In her later years she had devoted herself with almost single-minded passion to my sister Elizabeth, the one of us who was least like the rest. At the end of that year in Fairhope, Elizabeth graduated from high school. I have a vision of her standing in her white graduation dress in the garden where Grandma was sitting. I am sure Grandma felt that her hardest task—protecting and educating Elizabeth—was finished. She died on the way home, while she was visiting a favorite niece in Ohio.

The closest friends I have made all through life have been people who also grew up close to a loved and loving grandmother or grandfather.

6
The Pattern My Family Made for Me

From my earliest childhood I compared my own family with the kinds of families I heard about, learned about in songs, and read about in books. I thought seriously about the ways our family resembled other families, real and fictional, and sometimes sadly about the ways we did not fit into the expected pattern.

I felt sad that I did not have a house where I was born and that I had no grandfather's house because both my grandfathers were dead. Although my father's father had died when my father was a child, Grandma continued to wear black until at last I coaxed her into wearing lavender. I knew that it was my grandfather's big campaign bookcase that stood in our hall, and one of the few things that made him real to me was knowing that he had cared tremendously about the way people treated books. My mother's father, a handsome man who had, I was told, the same gentle blue eyes as my mother, had seen me as a baby, and I took some comfort from that. He had come to visit us at Lavallette, where we lived in a cottage next to Woodrow Wilson. Later, when Wilson became President, I liked to remember that he, too, had seen me as a baby. Somehow I got the feeling that my sense of having been seen by important persons lay back of my ease in public appearances and my enjoyment in being recognized as myself.

As a child I found having two grandmothers in some way an embarrassment. I thought of my father's mother as my real grandmother. She was Grandma, who lived with us, while my mother's mother was Grandma Fogg, who only came to visit. And when she did come, she mainly wanted to help Mother. She was a small, handsome woman with snapping black eyes, a sharp tongue, and a dutiful but lackluster relationship to children. Once she described me as a tiresome child who was always writing plays that no one wanted to listen to. I made what I could of Grandma Fogg's cleverness and superficial zest for life, her distaste for the elderly, and her search for people who made her feel young. When I was about sixteen I gave her a volume of stories by de Maupassant, which I inscribed, "To my wicked little grandmother." She died in her late nineties, after she had run away with her youngest son from the comfortable retirement home in which her children had placed her.

Grandma Fogg had a quality of inconsequential triviality that my mother and my youngest sister Priscilla shared with her. Typical of this was an incident, long after my childhood, that led me to think of her as Grandmother Gloves. When her favorite and most devoted son Lockwood died, she whispered to me as I arrived at the house for the funeral, "Margaret, I haven't any gloves. They put Lockwood into my room and I can't get at them."

My mother could fasten on some small detail in much the same way. While I was in college a group of us joined a picket line during a strike in midtown in New York City. Mother approved of strikes and disapproved of scabs, and so she was undisturbed by my stories of how the scabs had thrown empty spools out of the windows at us and by the idea that we had been in imminent danger of arrest. But her expression changed when I told her that we had been taught to say to the scabs, "Ain't you got no conscience, dearies? Don't you know every hour you work is an hour we lose?" Then she exclaimed, horrified, "Margaret! You didn't say *ain't!*"

Similarly, in 1928, when I was getting ready to go to the field, Priscilla came to New York to visit me, looking

Margaret and Richard, 1906

very grown up and smartly dressed. I asked her to go downtown and buy my round-the-world ticket, which meant carrying some $1,200 in cash with her. When she made a moue of distaste, I explained, "I'm sorry, dear, but I haven't anyone else to send. I know it's a lot of money to be responsible for." Priscilla still looked distressed. "I don't mind that," she said, "but I'll have to take my *white* handbag because it has a better snap!" And I thought to myself, "Just like Grandma Fogg."

Tracing old patterns was something I began to do very early, as I noted family resemblances—who in the next generation had the eyes or the nose or the curling hair or the sharp wit of some member of the generation before.

I was the eldest of five children. But I have very few memories of my early childhood in which my brother does not play a part. I remember my second birthday party and I remember spoiling my new red shoes by going out in the snow that winter. Then in the spring Richard was born, and very soon Margaret and Richard were expected to do everything together.

We used to have our supper together, wearing white nightclothes (with feet) and eating cereal or, on Sunday night, browis made of the dried remains of Saturday's Boston brown bread and baked beans soaked in hot milk. We were taught to sing the same songs together until it became obvious that while Richard's voice was true and clear, I had no voice at all. We even were dressed alike in blue coats with brass buttons and round stiff berets, and I passionately wanted a hat, but it was only when I was seven that I got permission to wear an old embroidered hat that a young aunt had left behind.

Richard was my little brother. He was valiant in my defense, standing in front of me and proclaiming, "You let my sister be!" But he was also frail, and his frequent illnesses reinforced my father's overprotectiveness toward his only son. I have a few memories of genuine battles—there was a doll he smashed and the broken latch to my door at the farm, which he battered with a hammer, and once I was spanked because I had hit him. But in general our life together was placid and unexciting. Most of the pranks we played were my inventions, and whenever he tried to conceal any of our misdeeds he would blush scarlet under his fair skin, for he was embarrassingly truthful.

I longed for an older brother and also for a brother who would be a ringleader in positive wickedness. This wish for a naughtier brother was temporarily gratified when I was thirteen by the arrival of my cousin Philip, who lived with us for two years while his home was broken up. He was as practiced in juvenile wickedness as my brother was in virtue, and we became firm allies. I also succeeded in getting Philip baptized and so became his juvenile godmother, but my father successfully blocked my efforts to bring Richard within the fold.

Two years younger and far less strong than I, Richard was not only prevented from doing boyish things that I, as a girl, was not permitted to do, but he was also kept from doing many of the rough-and-tumble things that I was allowed to do. Far from having any sense that I was being shut out of a male world, I felt that my little brother was always being kept indoors because he had a cold or an earache or a cough. My only feeling of deprivation was that I had to dress like a boy instead of as a frilly girl.

When I was four and Richard two, a baby sister was born whom I was allowed to name Katherine. She was a happy, responsive baby, and we delighted in her peals of laughter when she pulled off her socks. Once when she was about three months old I decided that we three children would secede from the household. I locked the doors to the nursery wing and made desperate plans to meet the need for hygiene and food. Food, I decided, we could obtain at night when everyone else was asleep, but the problem of the bathroom, which was outside the locked door, baffled me. Katherine slept on peacefully while Mother, speaking in a low voice that masked her desperation, pleaded with me to open the door. Finally, after an hour, I gave in.

Margaret and Richard in Nantucket, 1911

Christmas, when Katherine was six months old, was glowing and happy. The tree was hung with beautiful little Viennese ornaments and under the tree there was a doll dressed in white fur for the baby. Then in March she died. The house was hushed and filled with terror for two days and so, when Grandma told us that Katherine had gone to be with Grandfather, I knew what this meant.

Richard was not as clear about what had happened and for months he would wander disconsolately through the house looking for Katherine. I knew she had died, but my lost little sister lived on in my daydreams. At first I daydreamed about a lost twin sister. Later I dreamed of finding Katherine herself again. And finally, when I was in my twenties, I had a daydream of being stolen away to educate a child; when she was grown, my friends recognized that she must have been my pupil, for only I could have brought her up.

Katherine's death made a gap in the family. Instead of our being five stair-step children, we fell into two pairs. The younger girls, born two and four years later, were treated almost like a second family and for years they were called "the babies." With Katherine's death something also happened to my parents' relationship. Deeply grieved, Father withdrew, unwilling to give as much love again to a baby, and Elizabeth and Priscilla never had as much warmth and affection from him. Dr. Jarvis, who had been brought in during Katherine's illness, had been too late to save her, but we believed that somehow, had he been summoned in time, he would have kept her alive. He became a close friend of my father's and, at the same time, a hostile rival and sharp critic of my mother, whom he criticized as emotionally inadequate.

In this atmosphere of estrangement through grief and doubt my sister Elizabeth was conceived and born. She was a child my mother found it very difficult to carry. She was so ill through all that troubled pregnancy that it seemed again and again it might be necessary to take the baby. But at last Elizabeth, seven years younger than I, was born screaming, every hair on her head at odds with the world around her. Soon after her birth we went for the summer to a country cottage in the Poconos, and one day, when the baby almost choked to death, my distraught mother sent me tearing down the road in search of a physician. It was thought necessary to put metal mitts on Elizabeth's hands to keep her from scratching her face, and once when I was playing with a forbidden penknife and accidentally cut my nose I said that the baby had scratched me—a cardinal sin I have never forgotten. She was a frail baby, and in the autumn she was very ill again. I do not know whether it was our doubt that she would stay with us or whether it was her vividness and charm that so captivated me, but I felt that she had been sent to take the place of the baby who had died. This feeling had a decisive effect on my life as it gave me an abiding faith that what was lost would be found again.

Elizabeth became my delight. Mother became pregnant again very soon and my youngest sister Priscilla was born only eighteen months later. Grandma, who shared my concern and delight with Elizabeth, resented the birth of another baby who would absorb Mother's care, and she devoted herself especially to Elizabeth. So the new baby, quieter and very patient, came into a family all of whose members were in some sense already occupied.

Priscilla, named after my father's paternal grandmother, was born at home, and now, once again, there were two children who could be paired as Richard and I had been. After Priscilla's birth, Mother suffered from what today would be called a postpartum depression and she was sent away to live with an old family doctor in Bucks County. The rest of us lived in Swarthmore in a great cold rented house, a house so cold that at night the water used to freeze on the bedside tables. That winter we all had whooping cough, and at Christmas Mother came home at last to take care of the two very sick babies.

They were already beginning to show clear contrasts in temperament, which Grandma pointed out as she set

My brother Richard

me to work taking notes on their behavior—on the first
words Priscilla spoke and on the way one echoed the
other. She made me aware of how Priscilla mimicked the
epithets and shouts hurled up and down the back stairs
by the Swedish nurse and the Irish cook and of how
Elizabeth was already making poetry of life. Told that
her dress was ragged, she replied happily, "Yes, I's the
raggedy man." I learned to make these notes with love,
carrying on what Mother had begun. I knew that she
had filled thirteen notebooks on me and only four on
Richard: now I was taking over for the younger children.

Elizabeth and Priscilla

In many ways I thought of the babies as my children whom I could observe and teach and cultivate. I also wanted to give them everything I had missed. This continued until, when they were eight and ten, I gave them both lockets and discovered that neither of them had ever wanted a locket.

My care for my younger sisters fitted in with the role I chose for myself as a kind of stage manager at family festivals. It was a role that appealed to me. I did not think of myself as pretty and I had no special performing skills. What gave me the greatest pleasure, especially in later years, was arranging the settings within which Priscilla could display her beauty, Dick could sing, and Elizabeth could play and dance for our enjoyment.

During all the years while we were growing up I was fascinated by the contrasts between my sisters. Elizabeth was enthusiastic, loving, and devoted. Priscilla was more self-centered and was devastatingly honest about her motives. She would pay someone a compliment and then remark, "But I only told you that so you would take me along." Except for a brief period in her adolescence when she gained too much weight and became almost plain and had to wear glasses, she had an extraordinary beauty. But she thought of it as a burden—a talent she had to cultivate but never could really enjoy. In many ways she was the most American of us all. As a child she had an intimate friend, the daughter of a clergyman. In describing their relationship, she spoke of her friend as "the unusual child of a usual family, while I am the usual child of an unusual family." It was Elizabeth who was the real changeling in our midst, the child whose imagination illuminated—and often transformed in some very special and personal way—the ordinary facts of the workaday world.

In 1926, at the time when I was returning from my first field trip to Samoa, Grandma took both the little girls to study at the School for Organic Education in Fairhope, Alabama. Priscilla did not take to the program of "organic" freedom and soon rebelled. She insisted, "I am not organic and I want to go to a school where you learn something." So she was allowed to return to Philadelphia and to go to school at Friends Central. She found it hard going, but she did not complain. "You aren't meant to like school," she said, "and I am learning something." In 1928 she graduated with special honors.

Elizabeth, however, stayed on at Fairhope. When she worked in the pottery room, she smuggled in hairpins, for the use of every kind of tool was forbidden in this unusual school, which was a precursor of the 1960's back-to-nature movement. At Fairhope she learned practically nothing at all—except how to teach, how to waken children to enthusiasm, and how to treat each individual as a person. This she has carried all through her life with her own gifted children, with the other children on the block where she lived in Greenwich Village, and with all her later pupils—crippled children, mothers at Vassar Summer Institutes, old ladies gathered in an experimental old-age group at Cold Spring, the terribly deprived children in Harlem high schools, where in one year some 2,500 youngsters came into her art room—a room without running water or any other facility and in which the floor was so rotten that a third of the room had to be fenced off for safety—and today at Lesley College, the girls she is teaching to become teachers of young children.

Both my sisters were left-handed, and Grandma, who believed in experts, took them to Philadelphia to consult an eminent University of Pennsylvania psychologist. In the best tradition of the day, he advised her to teach them to use their right hands. She herself, a far better practical psychologist through her years of teaching young children, wondered whether it might not be better to let them follow their natural, inborn preference. But the psychologist pointed out that this would interfere with their social adjustment; for example, it would be awkward for them to use the "wrong" hand at meals and always risk colliding with their left-side neighbor's elbow. So Grandma, who respected intellectual authority, took the little girls home and made them learn to use their right hands.

Priscilla learned to write a copperplate hand and became the winning speller in a state-wide New Jersey spelling contest. Elizabeth wrote a frightful hand and misspelled every second word. In college, when she decided to study architecture, she began sketching with her left hand and then drawing the finishing lines with her trained and disciplined right hand—and she began to stutter. By that time we knew something about the relationship between handedness and stuttering, and I persuaded Elizabeth to learn to use her left hand—and the stuttering stopped.

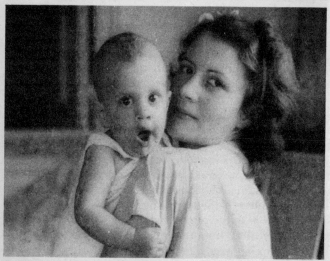

TOP Elizabeth with her daughter Lucy
ABOVE Priscilla with her son Philip

But I wondered, as I always have wondered, what made the difference. Why did one child take the painfully enforced learning, which violated both her neurological makeup and her earlier learning experiences, as a challenge she had to meet and transcend, while the other was simply hampered and impaired by her effort to conform to an externally imposed standard?

In thinking about all four of us, mulling over and over and over my own early memories and the family lore that grew up around each child, as it does in all articulate families, I continually tried to formulate my observations. The differences among the three girls could not be attributed to sex. There was, of course, order of birth. Elizabeth was neither the eldest nor the youngest, and she used to remark bitingly, "When I die I am going to leave everything to the next-to-youngest." Priscilla had Mother's mind; like Mother, she was less given to a search for originality than to the development of competence in whatever task came to hand. Like Mother, also, she lacked buoyancy and any deep sensory enjoyment of life.

Like Priscilla, Richard had Mother's mind, and neither of them cared very much for their most personal gifts. Priscilla was not made happy by her beauty, and Dick, in the end, made little of his beautiful tenor voice. Although he studied for several years and, after college, spent a year in New York working under a very good teacher, a musical career did not appeal to him. Instead, he went back to graduate school and, like his father, became a professor.

Only Elizabeth was an artist to her fingertips, and whichever of her talents she used, she used it differently from all the rest of us. Her perceptions, so different from ours, have nourished me through the years. Her understanding of what has gone on in schools has provided depth and life to my own observations on American education. And her paintings have made every place I have lived in my home. I have the first watercolor she ever painted and a painting of the New York Stock Exchange building she made for Father. I have a painting of Grandma, Priscilla, and herself, dressed for church, standing by the gate to our house in Holicong, and another of the view from our windows in Philadelphia. Still another painting shows the façade of an Italian house in which each door and window plays on the imagination. Recently, when I changed the colors in my room, I found a painting by Elizabeth that gathers up the light, and now, hanging beside it, I have a new painting by Elizabeth's daughter, Lucy Steig.

All my life I have felt that a painting or a poem composed by someone I know is far more meaningful to me than work by a greater artist or poet whom I do not know. I like to have my experiences buried deep in a personal context—my experiences of knowing the life of the artist or of being in the company of someone I love while I see—and later remember—a particular play or hear a favorite opera.

Of course, I see a work of art also as part of the culture which produced the artist, and the more I know about the culture, the more meaningful a painting, a poem, or a novel becomes for me, until finally, knowing the culture, intellectually and schematically, takes something away from my perception of the single, individually created work. But the tie to my own personal experience —my knowledge of the day a poem was written or of the dream that preceded the poem, my memory of the room, the particular room in one of our many high-ceilinged houses, that Elizabeth is recreating in a painting—this always gives me a greater aesthetic delight.

Thinking about the contrasts between my sisters led me also to think about the other women in my mother's family and of the way in which, generation after generations, pairs of sisters have been close friends. In this they exemplify one of the basic characteristics of American kinship relations. Sisters, while they are growing up, tend to be very rivalrous and as young mothers they are given to continual rivalrous comparisons of their several children. But once the children grow older, sisters draw closer together and often, in old age, they become each other's chosen and most happy companions. In addition to their shared memories of childhood and of their relationships to each other's children, they share memories of the same home, the same homemaking style, and the same small prejudices about housekeeping that carry the echoes of their mother's voice as she admonished them, "Never fill the tea-kettle from the hot-water faucet," and "Wash the egg off the silver spoons at once," and "Dry the glasses first." But above all, perhaps, sisters who have grown up close to one another know how their daydreams have been interwoven with their life experiences.

One of the happiest memories of my younger sisters' girlhood is of a Christmas when they drove home from Chicago in a blinding snowstorm and we celebrated together, enjoying all the food that was, for once, richly and generously on hand. I have a picture taken on that Christmas Day, the only occasion, after we had grown up, that all three of us were together.

My mother's next younger sister, Fanny, is now a very fragile old lady. She lives in a nursing home where she still entertains her friends and relatives at cocktails. Occasionally, she complains that some modern book she is reading—a book by Claude Lévi-Strauss, for example—is difficult. She is ninety-five, and seeing her so gay and so aware of the world around her gives an extraordinary pleasure to her nieces, her grandnieces, and her great-grandnieces. But she still laments that her sister Emily, my mother, is not with her to share her last years.

7 In and Out of School

Some years we went to school. Other years we stayed at home and Grandma taught us. That is one way of describing my schooling. Another way is to explain that between the ages of five and seventeen I spent two years in kindergarten, one year—but only half-days—in the fourth grade, and six years in high school. If I had not very much wanted to go to school or if I had been a sickly child, probably I would have spent even less time in school.

It is curious that a family of teachers—for Mother, too, had taught before I was born—should have had such paradoxical views about schools. As a family we took an active interest in schools wherever we lived, and many of our frequent moves to a new place for the winter months were made with the expectation of finding a particular kind of school. However, my family deeply disapproved of any school that kept children chained to their desks, indoors, for long hours every day.

Kindergarten—the one I attended was a private kindergarten in the home of well-to-do people with a large house—was an expression of the most modern ideas about education. The training of eye and hand, learning about color and form and pattern by sewing with bright wools, cutting and pasting, and stringing brightly colored beads made of different materials, and singing in time to rhythmic play—these were all activities that my grandmother and mother and father regarded as good for children. Father appreciated the precision, the command over my fingers, and the ability to make things I learned in kindergarten; Grandma and Mother were more interested in the freedom to move. In their minds these two things went together. They were complementary, not contradictory—as is so often the case when one examines what underlies the more recent belief that children can be, simultaneously, spontaneous and obedient.

Looking back, my memories of learning precise skills, memorizing long stretches of poetry, and manipulating paper are interwoven with memories of running—running in the wind, running through meadows, and running along country roads—picking flowers, hunting for nuts, and weaving together old stories and new events into myths about a tree or a rock. And there were long intervals, too, that were filled with reading, reading as many hours a day as I could manage between playing outdoors and doing formal lessons. Of course, reading was a good thing, but too much reading was believed to be bad for a child. And so it became, in part, a secret pleasure I indulged in at night when I was supposed to be asleep or in the daytime hours I spent curled up in a hollow at the roots of a tree while I was supposed to be off on some more active quest.

From the time I was six, the question was not when does school open, but what, if anything, is to be done about school. We lived in a different house in a different place each year—first in Lansdowne, then in Philadelphia on the edge of Fairmont Park, near the zoo, in an apartment house managed by a distant relative of my grandmother's, then for two years in Swarthmore—one year "on the hill" where the college people lived and one year at the edge of town. The owner of that second house lived in a smaller house, and we used to steal corn from his corncrib and feed it to his chickens. Prank-stealing was a part of life that was pickled in songs and stories, and we had to act it out. In all that time I had only one period of formal schooling—and then I was allowed to go to school for only half a day. I was envied by the other children, but the teacher was annoyed—and I was, too, for I felt singled out and forced to be different. But that one year, the winter of my ninth birthday, gave me a clear idea of what school was like. Before that I had known only about kindergarten, a kind of school from which I had never wanted to come home. In the first month of that fourth-grade class I failed dismally in arithmetic. But by the third month I had worked my way up to 90 percent in arithmetic and had discovered that school was a system you had to learn about, just as you had to learn about each new house and garden and explore the possibilities of each new town.

Mother thought about every place we lived not only in terms of its school, but also as a more or less promising source of "lessons." Whatever form such lessons took— drawing, painting, carving, modeling, or basketry—she thought of them as a supplement to formal education

Play group: Buckingham Climbers Club

within the context of the most advanced educational theories. In Hammonton I had music lessons and also lessons in carving, because the only artist the town boasted was a skillful wood-carver. In Swarthmore we were taught by an all-round manual training teacher under whose tutelage I even built a small loom. In Bucks County I had painting lessons from a local artist and later from an artist in New Hope. And one year Mother had a local carpenter teach Dick and me woodworking. She was completely eclectic about what we were taught in these lessons, provided the person who was teaching us was highly skilled.

Looking back, it seems to me that this way of organizing teaching and learning around special skills provided

The farm in Holicong

me with a model for the way I have organized work,
whether it has involved organizing a research team, a
staff of assistants, or the available informants in a native
village. In every case I try to find out what each person is
good at doing and then I fit them together in a group
that forms some kind of whole.

Wherever we lived, Mother also sought actively for
suitable playmates for us, an obligation, as she saw it,
that she carried out with a very sturdy sense of egalitari-
anism. In Landsdowne we played with the children of a
coachman and with a child whose mother, a Christian
Scientist, had warned her never to talk about religion
with other children. In Swarthmore we played with a
group of small girls that centered on the nursery of a

wealthy neighbor. In Bucks County, where we were paired with the Gardys, the only other family of city people, our friendships were much more diversified. But the core group was the club which Julian Gardy and I organized and which had some sixteen members, first in the country and later in Doylestown, where we all finally moved to finish high school. Julian, who was a year older, and I built up a firm, non-sentimental friendship, the first of a great many friendships based on collaboration in a long series of enterprises in which I have had some part.

Mother had found the farm in the Buckingham Valley on the long walks she took with Father while she was in the country recovering from her illness, and she had fallen in love with it because it had a ravine. There had also been five acres of primary forest which the owner sold before we bought the farm, and all the first year we heard the sound of crashing trees. This disturbed me so much that old Judge Fell, whose father had owned the farm, bought me a single tall tree that remained standing when all the others had fallen.

The ravine, too, was spared. Our brook, on the banks of which I found every kind of spring flower, tumbled down the ravine and then ran under the little bridge between the upper and the lower orchard, where the threshing machine used to be taken for water, and down through the deep meadows carpeted with wild blue hyacinths and bordered with watercress to the narrow tree-lined road we called Rabbit Run.

The farm had 107 acres with fields planted in wheat and rye and oats and usually two fields of maize. It had a huge, three-storied barn with a haymow floor just the right height for giving plays and chutes to jump down in games of hide-and-go-seek. There was a windmill, which sometimes stood still and then there was no water in the tank, a corncrib, some empty pigeon lofts, a dairy barn, and an old carriage house filled with odd remnants of earlier lives, including the things that Father bought at sales and that Mother did not like. In the farmyard there was a bull, and once the child of our current cook painted

his nose with green paint through the bars of the barn-
yard fence.

Living on the farm—and we were told that we lived
there because Grandma believed every child had a right
to grow up on a farm—opened our eyes to great diversity
of experience. There was always another family in the
farmer's house, and we often had maids with little children. When the threshers came, there were twenty to sit
down in the farmer's kitchen, and we all helped. My
father taught me how to top off shocks of wheat as it
was done in Ohio and then left me with the task of
showing the men how to do it without making them
mad.

We had six horses—two pairs of farm horses and two
carriage horses. One we believed had been a racehorse,
and the other, an old mare, was said to be pregnant when
we bought her, but after sixteen months, while Mother
drove her very considerately, no colt arrived. We were
allowed to drive ourselves but not to ride. Still, with our
buggies and the Gardys' pony, we got around the countryside as very few eleven- and twelve-year-old children do
today. We were followed only by the telephone, and when
it rang we would call out, "If that's my mother, say I've
left!"

The last year in Swarthmore, when again I did not go
to school because all of us had whooping cough that
winter, I gained forty pounds and grew from the size of
a seven-year-old child to my present height. Then, the
first year on the farm, where I continued to do my lessons
at home, I reached puberty. Mother treated this as an
important event and told me that I was now grown up
and could have childen. She herself had always resented
menstruation, which she called the Curse, and her careful
efforts to have me accept it as something good did not
preclude my learning to expect very bad cramps, and so
I called menstruation Cramps.

But I still kept my eleven-year-old stance. I was warned
that I might injure my body by being hit, for example,
by a baseball, and so I insisted on wearing corsets that
girded me about like armor—and went on playing vigor-

ous games. This is why, I suppose, I kept the movement style of an eleven-year-old and never acquired the staid walk and manner of girls who mature at a later age.

The years between Landsdowne and our move to the farm were years in which I searched for some kind of religious anchorage. Grandma had been a devout Methodist, but partly because it might have meant conflict with Mother, who had been a Unitarian before she gave up religion, and partly, I think, out of boredom, she had given up going to church when I was quite small. I was allowed to explore Sunday schools with neighbors and I also attended a wide variety of church services with our immigrant maids. When we lived in Swarthmore, I joined our Quaker neighbors in attending Meeting and suffered a good deal of badinage through my father's anti-Quaker jokes. When we moved to the farm, I was disappointed by the Buckingham Meeting, where a very few old wealthy people sat in absolute silence.

So I shifted with enthusiasm to the little Episcopal church in Buckingham when the English-born rector, Mr. Bell, and his daughter, Miss Lucia, came to call on us. Almost at once I felt that the rituals of the Episcopal church were the form of religious expression for which I had been seeking. I had not been looking for something to believe in, for it seemed to me that a relationship to God should be based not on what you believed, but rather on what you felt. My mother's overcognitive approach to religion—she had made me try to read the story of the Nativity in German when I was seven, in order to demonstrate to me the crudity of the story of the Incarnation—simply failed; all it did was to make me regard credibility as irrelevant. What I wanted was a form of religion that gave expression to an already existing faith.

From the first I also found a place for myself in the rectory. Miss Lucia was the loveliest, the most humanly sensitive person I had ever known. She took me into her life, as her father's daughter in the little country parish, and I shared her engagement and, finally her determina-ation to break it off. I can still feel the anguish that came over me as I looked at the lovely golden sunset on my way home on the day Miss Lucia told me that she had broken her engagement because her fiancé was too dependent on his mother. I felt the world had no right to be beautiful when Miss Lucia was so unhappy. For years, almost up to the time of her death, I used to ask her advice about my occasionally worrying problems. What should I do, I once asked her, about a definitely suicidal secretary at the Museum, a woman who had a bad skin and an unpleasant disposition and whom I did not like at all? I can still hear her answer, "Somebody ought to make friends with her—but not you."

Miss Lucia, Mr. Bell, the little church, the rectory, and later the religious books which I sent away for, all became part of a life of my own that I shared only with my two godmothers—Miss Lucia and Isabel Lord, a High Church friend of my mother's—both of whom I had chosen for myself. I enjoyed prayer. I enjoyed church. I worried over the small size of our congregation. The other children I knew thought all of this was odd. They went to church when they were told to do so, and they rolled pennies in their hats or pinched each other during the sermon.

After the years of lessons with Grandma, which seldom took more than an hour a day and left me with too much time on my hands while the other children were in school, I was finally sent to school when I was eleven. The Buckingham Friends School in Lahaska was a famous old foundation where, it was said, a number of Chief Justices of the Pennsylvania courts had attended school. In 1911, however, the foundation yielded so little money that there were funds only for one teacher and three grades—the eighth grade and two years of high school. The upper story of the building was rented to the township for the elementary school, where Miss Mary Johnson had taught for decades. We had the downstairs room and sat at desks that opened up and provided shelter for doing other things besides lessons.

We ranged in age from about ten to twenty. There were two children younger than I, little wispy creatures, and almost from the beginning I took it upon myself to shield the little girls from the merciless teasing of a large, much older, bullying girl. There were also big gangling boys and girls, some of whom came from a nearby farm whose owner boarded charity children while others came from a school for disturbed children in the same village.

All our books were at least two generations old. We studied Latin from the same grammar that my grandmother had studied and were taught by a teacher who had never passed Vergil. Thirty years later the school was rehabilitated and now it has become a well-known private school for the children of the many city people who live in Bucks County. But when I was a student, most of what I learned I learned from the old-fashioned schoolbooks themselves or from Grandma, who continued to help us with our lessons.

The war in Europe broke out while I was at the Buckingham Friends School. At first it meant mainly tales of German atrocities in Belgium, and I used to close my eyes and imagine the Germans marching through our wheat fields. My daydreams became war oriented, too, and I pictured myself as the leader of a group of Spanish spies who were working inside Germany for the downfall of the Kaiser. Although discussions of the war at home were realistic, it all seemed very far away and I think I was trying to make it more real, even if it meant nightmares about Germans advancing through our wheat fields.

In the spring of 1915, four of us graduated with all the paraphernalia of valedictorian, salutatorian, class historian, and class poet. I called my graduating address "IF Germany Had . . ." in which I suggested how different the fate of Europe might have been had Germany adopted another course of action. That same spring we had to make up for the various blank spots in our education by cramming for the eighth-grade examination given by the county so that we could go to the new public high school. I read the required books and briefed my classmates on the plots, and we all memorized the capitals

TOP Buckingham Friends School, 1914; Margaret,
middle row, on the left
ABOVE Trinity Church, Buckingham

of states and countries and learned such things as the trade route from Odessa to New York or to Sydney, Australia, while Grandma told us about the singing geography classes of her childhood.

The following year I went to the public high school two miles in the other direction from our farm, miles that I had already walked twice a week for painting lessons. I was given these lessons only on condition that I do a lot of posing for my teacher, Pemberton Ginther, a writer and illustrator of girls' books, for heroines named Beth Anne and Miss Pat, and so I spent many weary hours looking at drawing and painting not as an artist but as the subject of the artist's work.

The next winter we moved to Doylestown, and for two years I went to a quiet good small-town high school where the teachers were college graduates, the standards of teaching were high and the books modern, and my parents were far less critical of the education I was receiving. Nevertheless, in my own eyes, there continued to be an odd quality about school. Going to school offered no challenge. No one had to study very hard, and if there was good ice and a bright moon, we all went ice skating. But there was something else as well. In all the schools I had attended so far I felt as if I were in some way taking part in a theatrical performance in which I had a role to play and had to find actors to take the other parts. I wanted to live out every experience that went with schooling, and so I made a best friend out of the most likely candidate, fell sentimentally in love with one of the boys, attached myself to a teacher, and organized, as far as it was possible to do so, every kind of game, play, performance, May Day dance, Valentine party, and, together with Julian Gardy, a succession of clubs, in one of which we debated such subjects as "Who was greater, Washington or Lincoln?" In all these projects we were given generous backing by my mother and the other mothers she drew into the circle. In the summer of 1915, with the help of a dance and drama teacher Mother brought out from the city, we gave a big Shakespeare festival—with our front porch as the stage—in which we performed the casket scene from *The Merchant of Venice* and sang madrigals.

During all these years of informal education and occasional hit-or-miss inappropriate schooling, which served to educate me in American culture but did little to prepare me for formal academic work, I had ample time to practice writing. I began to write poetry when I was nine and the next year, when we moved to the farm, I kept a diary and wrote long letters to my Swarthmore friends, a correspondence I kept up through high school. I also had two pen pals whose names I got through *St. Nicholas Magazine*. One girl answered my voluminous letters with frank and honest accounts of her life in Pottstown, Pennsylvania, but the other wrote fantasies about a variety of identities. Writing letters has always been a very real part of my life, especially in the years I have been in the field. For then letters home, letters to colleagues—particularly Ruth Benedict and Geoffrey Gorer—and bulletin letters to a widening circle of family and friends have linked my life to theirs in a way that is disappearing from a world in which most people communicate by telephone and, very occasionally, by tape recordings.

I also began trying to write seriously. I began a novel. I reported on lectures given in a Lyceum series in the winter of 1915 for *The Intelligencer*. I wrote short plays for school occasions. And in Doylestown I helped to start a school magazine, wrote for it in various styles, and learned how to organize copy and to manage the intricacies of printing in the local newspaper office. Writing was what my parents did, and writing was as much a part of my life as gardening and canning were in the life of a farmer's daughter of that day. Yet it was something much more special—something other people around us did not do.

In school I always felt that I was special and different, set apart in a way that could not be attributed to any gift I had, but only to my background—to the education given me by my grandmother and to the explicit academic interests of my parents. I felt that I had to work hard to become part of the life around me. But at the same time I searched for a greater intensity than the world around me offered and speculated about a career. At different times I wanted to become a lawyer, a nun, a writer, or a minister's wife with six children. Looking to my grandmother and my mother for models, I expected to be both a professional woman and a wife and mother.

In some ways my upbringing was well ahead of my time—perhaps as much as two generations ahead. Mother's advanced ideas, the way in which all children in our home were treated as persons, the kind of books I read—ranging from the children's books of my grandmother's generation to the most modern plays that my mother sent for to read with a group of friends—and the way all I read was placed in historical perspective, and above all, the continuous running commentary by my family on schools, on education, on the way teachers were treated by the community, and on the relationship between good schools and much needed higher taxes—for I never heard taxes mentioned except in terms of their being too low— all these things represented an extraordinary sophistication and a view of children that was rare in my childhood.

But in other ways those years in Bucks County gave me a view of a much earlier life-style, one that corresponded with my grandmother's girlhood. There was the beautiful old eighteen-room house in which we lived, with its low windows under the eaves, deep cellar to keep the milk cool, and woodshed where the kerosene was kept to light the lamps for the eighteen rooms. When we bought the house, it was innocent of plumbing, and we spent the first year making it over so that we had a kitchen and bathroom with running water, and a furnace, and the old fireplaces were opened again. We saw it all, the way it was and the way it became.

Moreover, nothing was taken wholly for granted. Opening up the old fireplaces, or making butter, which Grandma had to learn to do, or setting out a great iron kettle to make apple butter in the fall—all this was part of an experience of a way of life that was compared and commented upon, on the one hand, against the background of my grandmother's childhood and, on the other, in the light of our experience of living in a modern city where people drove cars and rode in power-driven streetcars. The farm represented one way of living, but only one of many ways.

Quite early I also became aware of great discrepancies of attitude. At home the facts of life were presented to me seriously and realistically, but in a very abstract way. At the same time, in school, I continually heard about the startling and brutal events in the lives of our neighbors. At about the time my mother explained to me why it was that many readers had discontinued their subscriptions to a magazine when a statue of a white slave was pictured on the cover, I also learned from my schoolmates how a hired girl had been savagely raped within the hearing of her blind mistress, a woman held in high esteem in the community, and how she had not lifted a hand to help the girl. Listening to my mother's outspoken, modern views and to the crude, open gossip of the countryside left me little to find out in books. But I did discover through reading novels what an abortion was and what illegitimacy meant.

Our move to Doylestown put an end to the extreme contrasts and discrepancies between home and school and church that had characterized the years in the country. It also meant a setback in school. Since I was only fourteen, the principal admitted me to the high school on the condition that I repeat the third year. I had to study *L'Allegro* and *Il Penseroso* for the third time and Cicero for the second time—but at least they were better taught. The Gardys, with whom we had played all the years before, also moved to Doylestown, and once more Julian and I organized a club so that the members could dance in our house on Saturday nights. That spring the United States entered the war. There were community sings and we began to hear about men going away to fight.

In June, when we had already moved back to the farm, my science teacher, George Cressman, was asked to give the graduation address at the high school in Buckingham.

I asked Mother to invite him to dinner, and when he explained that his younger brother Luther was visiting him, she invited him, too. I drove all the way to Furlong to meet them at the Interurban station. That night we danced and danced at the high school. And then, later that same night, I had an acute attack of appendicitis. That occupied the whole summer as I had first to recuperate and then undergo an operation.

I did not see Luther again, but he sent me his yearbook. In the fall, together with another girl, I visited the Cressmans—six boys, the sons of a country doctor, of whom George Cressman was the eldest. When we were children, we had played at having beaux and Valentine choices, and Julian Gardy and my cousin Philip had invented a club all of whose members listed in order of choice the ten girls or boys they liked best. Nine places were counters that allowed each of us to threaten, "I'll take you off my list!" But we kept the first place for a stranger to the group—someone whom no one else knew. In high school in Doylestown we still kept up this game—and Luther Cressman filled the role of the "stranger" on my list.

Luther was four years older than I and a senior in college. He was studying Latin and Greek, and he gave me books of poetry with dedications in verse that he himself wrote. He was tall and slender and well built. He could drive a car and shoot a gun with great skill and he took beautiful photographs. He danced magnificently. He had an engaging grin and a wry sense of humor, yet he took life seriously and, like my mother, was willing to see life whole.

At Christmas, on another visit, Luther and I became engaged. And at this time his tentative plan to enter the ministry began to crystallize—it was what his mother had always wanted him to do, and a minister's wife was what I wanted to be.

That year Luther finished college at Pennsylvania State College and went from ROTC training to officer's training camp. Community wartime activities, the expectation that Luther would be sent overseas, and finishing high school made an uncertain mix in my life. I missed Luther's graduation, the one big college event I could have attended, because my brother and I came down with German measles. Then there was my own graduation.

Once again the war, which had come so much closer to us now, was the central theme. This time I planned to give a speech on the war in posters, illustrated by five posters that I intended to hang up in the assembly hall. But it was the future, not the war itself, I talked about:

Posters (I wrote) are like flashlights. They are designed to illuminate only a certain part of a particular moment. But as with a flashlight we can find the lock of a closed door in which to put the key, so with war posters we can throw light on the closed doors that lead to the result of this war. These five posters throw light on five of these doors, the doors that lead to internationalism, a new status for womanhood, a greater value for childhood, a more real religion, and a greater vision.

But I had some doubts about the reactions of our high school principal, an intense, vivid Italian-American, who taught civics and American history as only an inspired first-generation immigrant could. So I left town at the end of school and returned only in time for graduation when it was too late for him to raise any objections or to insist on any changes.

That last summer of the war was hard. I had not yet told my parents that I was engaged, but I wrote Luther a letter every day—four pages in small, fine handwriting. My main occupation was being a wartime homemaker on the farm, where Dick was also working hard to increase the harvest. Our last cook left us to sing for the soldiers, and Mother knew nothing about cooking. And so, with only the help of a very small black girl and her mother, who washed for us on Mondays, I cooked for eight people on a three-burner kerosene stove, making do with all the strange substitute flours we were asked to buy with every pound of wheat flour. Every morning I cooked two meals. Twice a week in the afternoons I went to roll bandages at the local Red Cross, and the other afternoons I knitted

and read aloud to the younger children and my two
sparring grandmothers. In the evenings I wrote my long
letters to Luther, filled with poetry.

In the autumn of 1918, the whole family moved again,
this time to New Hope, where the Holmquist School, a
new and very special school, had opened. Doylestown
High School had discontinued teaching German, and I
needed another year of German or three years of French
in preparation for Wellesley. In addition, Elizabeth and
Priscilla, who had never gone to school at all, could
attend the children's section of this private school set in
the midst of the famous old artists' colony. There were
almost as many teachers as students, and we had a
precious diet of exciting teaching and religious exploration under one of the founders who also taught religion
at Bryn Mawr. As the only help we had at home was a
high-school girl, I did the cooking and, in between,
learned trigonometry and worked my way through three
years of French. When the war was over, Luther came
home from camp and I told my parents that I was engaged to him. This was, of course, kept a deep secret from
the other girls in school, who were still living out their
romantic daydreams by reading forbidden books.

In the spring my father suffered a lot of losses in one
of his private business ventures. This precipitated a crisis
over my going to college. Hoping to get someone to back
up his new view that I need not go to college, he called
in our local physician, who said, "Look at those useless
little hands! Never did a day's work in their life and
never will! You'd maybe make a good mistress, but a
poor wife. You'd better study nursing!" Hearing this, I
exploded in one of the few fits of feminist rage I have
ever had. At that moment I was not only carrying a
heavy school program and making all the costumes for
a play, but was also keeping house for the whole family.
However, what really infuriated me was the totally contradictory notion that although I was not strong enough
to study for a degree, I was strong enough to become a
nurse.

Margaret and Luther, Doylestown, 1918

In the end, using tactics that were wholly alien to her transparent honesty, Mother persuaded Father to send me to DePauw. This was his college, and the idea captured his interest. I was accepted at DePauw—and all my studying that year had been unnecessary. Luther, who had taught the half year after he was demobilized, was accepted at the General Theological Seminary in New York.

I spent the summer in the home of the woman who had been my English teacher in Doylestown and whose husband was head of the Daily Vacation Bible Schools in Philadelphia. I took care of their baby and was the principal of a Bible school with three teachers and 150 pupils—truly an arduous introduction to teaching. That summer I really learned about the possibilities of twelve-year-old boys, all of whom seemed determined to catch me out. Later in the field, I was to find twelve-year-old boys my principal resource and I decided that museums should be designed for boys of this age, who were at the height of their intellectual curiosity and skepticism. But that summer, especially after the one male teacher of handicrafts dropped out, I managed to keep just one step ahead of them.

Although I was tired at the end of the summer, I had my mother's stories of the free and democratic "West"— the West she had known in her girlhood—to buoy me up, and I packed for DePauw with enthusiasm. Mother let me plan my own clothes for a dressmaker who came to the house to make them. I designed an evening dress that was to represent a field of wheat with poppies against a blue sky with white clouds. The skirt, made of a stiff silver-green material, was accordion pleated and decorated with poppies; the blouse was made of blue and white Georgette crepe. The idea was romantic, but the dress was dreadful. However, Mother had done her duty by letting me plan it for myself. The dressmaker also made me little smocked-over blouses in crepe de Chine to wear for dinner. But I did not have a single garment that resembled anything the girls at DePauw actually wore.

I also planned my college room carefully. I picked the material for the curtains—the room was to be done in old rose and blue—and chose pictures to go on the walls, among them a picture of Rabindranath Tagore and a portrait of Catherine Bushovka, the "little grandmother" of the Russian Revolution. (Mother had danced for joy at the outbreak of the Revolution, when word came that the Russians, who had been enslaved by the evil czars, were free at last.) And of course I packed many boxes of books—poetry, novels, and essays.

My father said, "Of course you will be a Theta." Several of his fraternity brothers were on the campus at Greencastle. They had married Thetas, and he would write them. I found this all quite mysterious. I knew that Mother had belonged to Shakespeare at Wellesley and that Aunt Beth had been Mortarboard at the University of Chicago, but I had never heard of Greek-letter societies. During the summer I began to receive letters from an effusive girl who lived in the town where Aunt Beth, married to a very successful businessman, was living as a young social matron. The girl explained that she was a Kappa from DePauw and that she was looking forward to inviting me to a Kappa party when I arrived at college.

I was seventeen. I was engaged to be married. But above all else I was eager to enter the academic world for which all my life had prepared me.

8 *College: DePauw*

American families differ greatly in their expectations about what going to college will mean in their children's lives. In the intellectual community to which my parents belonged, college was as necessary as learning to read. It was an intellectual experience and the gateway to the rest of life. All my life I expected to go to college, and I was prepared to enjoy it.

My mother had included drawing lessons in the advantages she had wrested for me out of the various strange environments in which we lived, and I had enough talent to be encouraged to become a painter. However, when I was told by my artist cousins that in order to become a painter I should go to art school and skip college, I gave up the idea. For me, not to go to college was, in a sense, not to become a full human being.

This did not mean, of course, that all the children in the family felt as I did. My brother very dutifully went to college and took a Ph.D. But he never cared much for reading books. Instead, he fastened on the applied aspects of my father's essentially very intellectual but very concrete interests. What interested Richard primarily were the business aspects of the ongoing world—such matters as the relationship of highway legislation to bus lines and trucking, or working out the best locations for chain stores, or the uses of coal. Had he come from a different kind of family, he might have gone very contentedly straight into business. As it was, he became for most of his life a college professor in schools of business concerned with the kinds of projects in which he himself did consulting. He exemplified in his own person one of the things that has happened in America as higher education has become instrumental in business, industry, and agriculture, as well as in professions like law and medicine which once had their own exclusive forms of preparation.

For my sister Elizabeth, college never was more than a background—and not a very relevant background at that—for the development of her gifts. She willingly left college to go to Italy with my mother and spent a happy year in Rome studying architecture. Afterward she continued to study architecture at the University of Pennsylvania and Columbia University and, still later, took courses both in fine arts and in education at New York University. When it was necessary to write papers, she wrote them. When it was necessary to read books, she read them and knew how to get a great deal out of them. Although her delight in painting and music and dancing made her seem to be a changeling in our midst, she too received the family intellectual imprint and she became a teacher and only secondarily— and sometimes and still with delight—a painter. And she married William Steig, an artist from a family of artists, who left college after one semester and made a name for himself as a cartoonist, one of the most ironic and compassionate of our time.

And there was my youngest sister, Priscilla, who was so responsive to the standards of the wider society. Having begun to read at five, she read what she chose, reached out for science fiction and formulas of dissent and assent, and used her reading as a weapon against the rest of the family. By the time she was ready for college, she was entrancingly beautiful; she was also competent and had a mind that could do anything asked of it. I decided, then, that if she were to resist the temptation to become a well-bred, well-dressed young woman who could talk intelligently about any subject but who cared really deeply about none, she would have to have an overdose of the kind of social life that at Vassar or Smith College would have been tempered by her relationships with fine women teachers who were using their own minds and hoped that some students would become intellectually active. So I helped her choose the University of Wisconsin, saw to it that she had the right introductions and the right clothes, made the right sorority, and was showered with the attentions to which her looks entitled her. She herself decided that she would make Phi Beta Kappa in three years. When she succeeded in this, she left the fraternity-sorority life of the Wisconsin campus behind, took what she had gained from the good teaching of professors who cared about their subject, and, in her own phrasing, went to the University of Chicago to learn something. In the same spirit, she resisted the attractions of young men with impeccable Ivy League backgrounds. Instead, she married Leo Rosten, a brilliant young political scientist who had worked his way through college by giving lectures on Great Literature to women's clubs and by teaching English to immigrants, an experience that he later utilized in *The Education of Hyman Kaplan*. Throughout her married life she restrained the exuberant imagination of her gifted husband by periodically advocating the kind of economies my mother had insisted on when she had made my father return the lapis lazuli necklace because the money should be given to a fellowship fund. In the last years of her life, she was studying to become a social worker.

So the overriding academic ethos shaped all our lives. This was tempered by my mother's sense of responsibility for society, by my father's greater interest in real processes than in theoretical abstractions, and by my grandmother's interest in real children, in chickens, and in how to

At DePauw, 1920

season stewed tomatoes with toasted bread. But at the heart of their lives, the enjoyment of the intellect as mediated by words in books was central, and I was the child who could make the most of this—the child who was not asked to constrain or distort some other gift.

And so, even though it was decided that I was to go to DePauw rather than Bryn Mawr or Wellesley, I approached the idea of college with the expectation of taking part in an intellectual feast. I looked forward to studying fascinating subjects taught by people who understood what they were talking about. I imagined meeting brilliant students, students who would challenge me to stretch my mind and work instead of going skating with my lessons done well enough so that I led my classmates who hated what they were studying. In college, in some way that I devoutly believed in but could not explain, I expected to become a person.

At DePauw in 1919 I found students who were, for the most part, the first generation to go to college and whose parents appeared at Class Day poorly dressed while their daughters wore the raccoon or the muskrat coats that were appropriate to the sorority they had made. It was a college to which students had come for fraternity life, for football games, and for establishing the kind of rapport with other people that would make them good Rotarians in later life and their wives good members of the garden club.

I arrived with books of poetry, portraits of great personalities to hang on the wall, and the snobberies of the East, such as the expectation that one dressed in the evening for the members of one's own family. And I was confronted by the snobbery and cruelty of the sorority system at its worst, with rules against rushing that prevented the women who had gone to college with my father and who had married my father's fraternity brothers from ever speaking to me or inviting me to their homes—rules made by the Panhellenic Association in order to control competition that was so harsh and so unashamed that the very rules designed to control it made it even worse. This was my first and only real experience of discrimination—mild enough in all conscience.

It is very difficult to know how to evaluate how essential it is to have one's soul seared by the great injustices of one's own time—being born a serf or slave, a woman believed to have no mind or no soul, a black man or woman in a white man's world, a Jew among Christians who make a virtue of anti-Semitism, a miner among those who thought it good sport to hire Pinkertons to shoot down miners on strike. Such experiences sear the soul. They make their victims ache with bitterness and rage, with compassion for fellow sufferers or with blind determination to escape even on the backs of fellow sufferers. Such experiences can breed the desire to fight unrelentingly against the injustice that has let one's mother die because no doctor would attend her or let one's brother work in a mine because there was no school to recognize his talents—an injustice that substitutes arbitrary social categories for the recognition of humanity. Injustice experienced in the flesh, in deeply wounded flesh, is the stuff out of which change explodes. But the passionate fight for humanity—the fight to free slaves, free colonies, free women and children—also has been carried by those who have never experienced, and in the case of whites fighting for blacks or men for women, never could experience in their own persons the depths of injustice against which they have fought.

There is a great deal of talk today about the inexperience of the suburban children of affluent middle-class families, who have never seen an open wound, or a baby born, or anyone die, whose conceptions of humiliation, deprivation, and suffering are drawn wholly from films and television. But such discussions do not take into account the different kinds of fighters, all of whom are needed in any case—both those who know at first hand the searing effects of discrimination and those who are shocked to the core by their encounters with the tragedies that are part of others' everyday experience.

The point of John Howard Griffin's book, *Black Like Me,* was precisely that he was not black. For a brief period he experienced the humiliation and hostility that a black man can expect to experience daily—and throughout his life in the United States. But Griffin experienced this *not* as a black man but as a white man with temporarily blackened skin, a white man who had been reared to expect something else and who suddenly drew back from his own image when he called his own wife—white and far away at the other end of a telephone line—by an endearing term. Out of his experience, Griffin was able to tell men and women in the white world things that no black individual had ever thought to tell them. And I think it is no accident that some of the most impassioned statements about woman's rights have been made by men, or that anti-imperialist movements in colonial countries have been inspired and even led by Europeans who were outraged by the consequences of social arrangements through which they, as members of a privileged group, had never suffered.

Yet it is very difficult to draw a line. Certainly, positions of privilege can breed a kind of hardened insensitivity, an utter inability to imagine what it is to be an outsider, an individual who is treated with contempt or repulsion for reasons of skin color, or sex, or religion, or nationality, or the occupation of his parents and grandparents. Some kind of experience is necessary to open one's eyes and so to loosen the ties of unimaginative conformity. It can come from a terrible shock—through the brutal experience of having a close companion ejected from a restaurant or even shot down in the street. But there is another kind of initiation into humiliation—through the experience of hardship in some petty caricature of the real world which, by its very pettiness, engages one's emotions and enlarges one's consciousness of the destructive effects of every kind of social injustice.

All my life I had been a leader in children's groups that were democratically constituted. In our family, my mother's idealistic altruism and egalitarian principles meant that the children of farm laborers were treated with no less—and perhaps even more—gentleness and consideration than were the children of educated, professional parents. From this position of security, I believed that I could dictate egalitarian behavior. I had been brought up to the American standard of good breeding, based on the assumption that a well-bred person never intentionally hurt anyone—an assumption that reverses the English conception of a well-bred person as someone who is never rude unintentionally. My father sometimes paraphrased Chesterfield's admonition to be considerate of one's inferiors, courteous to one's equals, and stiff with one's superiors. But no one suggested that we had any superiors, only people who had more money or who were more interested in validating their social position. My father refused to make social efforts and my mother's position was, therefore, related to her own associations with other women who were equally concerned with good works. My mother used to complain because my father would not make the effort, but no one suggested that he would not have succeeded had he wanted to.

In some ways I was in the position of a child who is brought up in a leading family in a sequestered minority group, in the position, for example, of the daughter of the rabbi in a Jewish community or of the pastor in a segregated black community, a girl who has never questioned her privileged status but who has absorbed an ethic that is deeply critical of injustice in the world. In *Ex-Prodigy,* Norbert Wiener describes how he was reared, in a setting of anti-Semitism, with an attributed superiority as a Russian. When he discovered that he himself was Jewish, he could not identify only with Jews but had to identify with all oppressed peoples. The stigmata of privilege remained.

When I arrived at DePauw, I found that I had two roommates. One was a girl who had come to college to join a sorority, and this had been arranged in advance; the other expected to be rushed by a sorority that had little prestige. I soon learned that no one belonging to a sorority could speak to an unpledged freshman. This, of course, explained why I heard nothing from the effusive girl who had written me so many letters during the sum-

mer. When the invitations came out, I was invited to the
Kappa rushing party. But when I arrived wearing my
unusual and unfashionable dress that was designed to
look like a wheat field with poppies blooming in it, my
correspondent turned her back on me and never spoke
to me again. I found the whole evening strangely con-
fusing. I could not know, of course, that everyone had
been given the signal that inviting me had been a mistake. Afterward, my two roommates got the bids they expected, but I did not get a bid.

It still took a little time for me to realize the full implications of what it meant to be an unpledged freshman
in a college where everything was organized around the
fraternities and sororities. For one thing, I had no dates;
these were all arranged through commands to the freshman pledges of certain fraternities to date the freshman
pledges of certain sororities. Although all freshmen had
to live in dormitories, it meant also that there was a
widening gulf between the pledges, who spent a lot of
time at their sorority houses being disciplined and shaped
up, and the unpledged freshmen and the few upperclassmen in the dormitories.

With a very few exceptions, these upperclassmen were
pretty dismal. But there was Katharine Rothenberger,
who became my lifelong friend; she had transferred from
a college where she had turned down a sorority bid because it was too expensive. And there was an English girl,
very tall and very serious, also a transfer, who in later
life became a very well-known missionary. By and large,
however, the girls who were, by sorority standards, ineligible were less attractive and less sparkling than their
classmates who were among the chosen. Moreover, all
those who still hoped had one characteristic in common—
their fear of making friends with others of their own
kind. Although I was experiencing the bitter injustice
of being excluded, on grounds that I did not respect, I
experienced also what I have come to regard as a principal reason for abolishing such exclusive institutions,
that is, the damage done to the arbitrarily excluded who

With Katharine Rothenberger

continue to believe that one day they still may enter the ranks of the chosen.

It also took some little time for me to discover that previously rejected students might nevertheless be accepted later if they displayed some special ability that would help a chapter keep up the kind of competitive records that were cherished by rival chapters on the campus or within the intrafraternity and sorority rivalries that were fostered by the national Greek-letter societies. So a student could continue to hope that the members of a chapter would eventually recognize in him—or her—some sign of high scholarship or an outstanding ability in some extracurricular field or a strong political potential and then, overlooking the initial disability, they would invite the girl or boy to join the chapter and perhaps even make some effort to like the person who once had been so harshly excluded.

It was many years before liberal white Americans came

to realize that what they offered Negro Americans was not so very different from this. In the period between the two wars, Negro physicians, lawyers, scientists, and men with other recognized talents and outstanding abilities were admitted to the fraternal relationships of occupations that hitherto had been closed to them and they were treated almost as though they had been accepted by the group they had joined.

During the next forty years, before fraternities and clubs lost almost all their power on campuses in the general rejection of elitism that developed in the 1960's, various efforts were made to democratize an institution that was essentially incapable of democratization—for the only point of exclusiveness is that someone is excluded. But the main result of such efforts was that they strengthened the conviction of members of Greek-letter societies that students who were left out had not wanted to join or could not afford to do so. And the unchosen seldom talked.

The blandness with which the privileged accept their status was illustrated when the Panhellenic Association of Syracuse University, during World War II, invited me to be a dinner speaker on "Democracy," a topic that was particularly fashionable at that time. The organizers had not bothered to find out whether I had ever attended a college where there was Greek-letter societies. So they heard a lot of stories they had previously been protected from hearing.

During the year I studied at DePauw, I did not deny that I was hurt, nor did I pretend to myself that I would have refused the chance to be accepted by a sorority. The truth is, I would not have known enough to refuse. And once inside, it is quite possible that I would have been as unseeing as the rest. As it was, what particularly offended me as the year wore on was the contrast between the vaunted democracy of the Middle West and the blatant, strident artificiality of the Greek-letter societies on that midwestern campus, the harshness of the rules that prevented my father's classmates from ever addressing a hospitable word to me, and, more than anything else, the lack of loyalty that rejection engendered among the unchosen.

I discovered, too, that simple rejection was not enough. It had to be rubbed in. At that time it was fashionable for girls to wear what were called Peter Thompson suits —tailored middy suits in dark-colored wool or pastel-colored linen. In the spring, when I too acquired a Peter Thompson suit, a prominent Theta, meeting me on the campus, roughly turned down my collar to look at the label, certainly expecting to find that my new dress was not authentic—as it was.

My unusual clothing was not all that was held against me. There was my room with its carefully planned color scheme, my books and pictures, and, above all, my tea set. And I did not chew gum. Then, as if these things were not enough, there was my accent. The big Freshman English Literature course was taught by a New Englander who conceived it to be his principal task to educate provincial Americans. The very first day he glared around the room and asked, "Does anyone in this class know how to pronounce c-a-l-f?" I volunteered, and when I used the broad *a* he commented, "Oh, you come from the East, don't you? Out here they say 'calf,'" and mockingly drew out the flat *a* sound. A third of the freshman class heard that doubtful compliment. There were two other students from the East. One was the daughter of a Methodist bishop who had formerly been the president of DePauw; the other was her close friend. That saved them. But I was branded. After a while some of my friends thought it was fun to get me to say, "I have been there," using the Bryn Mawr pronunciation, "bean," instead of the Middle Western "bin." This usually happened when mothers came to visit and the girls wanted to show off the local curiosities.

And, although the sorority rejection was the sharper blow, there was another. I found out that I was also ineligible to belong to the Y.W.C.A. because, as an Episcopalian, I did not belong to an Evangelical religion. There were five of us at DePauw who were religious rejects—myself, one Roman Catholic, one Greek Orthodox, one Lutheran, and one Jew. The Jew was David Lilienthal. On one occasion he was asked to give a talk to the Methodist Sunday School on the Jewish conception of Jesus. The rest of us were simply beyond the pale.

So I was confronted, for the first time in my life, with being thoroughly unacceptable to almost everyone and on grounds in which I had previously been taught to take pride. I responded by setting out to see what I could do within this system, which I found sufficiently uncongenial so that I spent no time lamenting my exclusion.

I wrote a stunt that was performed by the freshman dormitory, Mansfield Hall, as part of a competition in which we challenged the senior dormitory and the sororities—the first time this was done. I set to work to make the English honors society, Tusitala, which was the Samoan name that had been given Robert Louis Stevenson. I wrote and directed the pageant that the entire feminine student body, under the direction of the Department of Physical Education, gave each year. I also designed the freshman float for this occasion. And finally, I went into the political arena and succeeded in getting Katharine Rothenberger elected vice-president of the class by setting the sororities against one another. I was satisfied that by the end of the year I would have received a bid to join a sorority—probably at least two. For although no sorority might want to have me, each one would be afraid that I might become the property of a rival.

The teaching at DePauw was far less disappointing than the college social organization. In my catalogue I had marked courses totaling over 200 hours, even though 120 hours was all that a student could take in four years. I thoroughly enjoyed the magnificent teaching given by men who were first and foremost teachers, interested in their students and unharassed by the demand that they "publish or perish," an attitude that later came to haunt even small colleges like DePauw. The training in writing given me by Professor Pence was never equaled by anyone else. At DePauw I was introduced to discussions of the Old Testament prophets and the Social Gospel, and

Katharine and Margaret: King
and Queen of the pageant

this firmly established association between the Old and
the New Testament and the demands of social justice
provided me with an ethical background up to the time
of the development of ecumenicism and Vatican II. These
courses were taught by deeply religious men who regarded
it a privilege to be teaching where they were.

At DePauw, too, I took a course in History as Past
Ethics, to which I still refer. However, there were only
two girls and a couple of dozen boys in that class, and the
two girls received the highest marks. As long as I was in
high school, the greater maturity of adolescent girls had

not struck me. But in the setting of this coeducational college it became perfectly clear both that bright girls could do better than bright boys and that they would suffer for it.

This made me feel that coeducation was thoroughly unattractive. I neither wanted to do bad work in order to make myself attractive to boys nor did I want them to dislike me for doing good work. It seemed to me that it would be much simpler to go to a girl's college where one could work as hard as one pleased.

This preference foreshadowed, I suppose, my anthropological field choices—not to compete with men in male fields, but instead to concentrate on the kinds of work that are better done by women. Actually, there are two kinds of field work that women can do better than men. One is working with women and children in situations in which male investigators are likely to be suspected and resented by the men of a society. The other is working with both men and women as an older woman, using a woman's postmenopausal high status to achieve an understanding of the different parts of a culture, particularly in those cultures in which women past the reproductive period are free from the constraints and taboos that constrict the lives of younger women. The first choice can be effectively exercised only in a situation in which the culture is being studied by a male-female pair or a team. For when a woman explicitly classifies herself with excluded women and uninitiated children, she does not have access to the rest of the culture. The second role is very practical for an older woman who is working alone in a culture that has already been explored by a male and female pair.

Nevertheless, as long as I remained at DePauw, I felt I was an exile. I used to sit in the library and read the drama reviews in *The New York Times*. Like so many other aspiring American intellectuals and artists, I developed the feeling that American small towns were essentially unfriendly to the life of the mind and the senses. I believed that the center of life was in New York City, where Mencken and George Jean Nathan were publish-

ing *Smart Set,* where *The Freeman, The New Republic,*
and *The Nation* flourished, where F.P.A. and Heywood
Broun were writing their diatribes, and where the theater
was a living world of contending ideas.

And Luther Cressman was in New York. I had had
enough of the consolation of knowing that I was engaged, so that all the nonsense about having dates—or not
having dates—was irrelevant. I wanted a life that demon-
strated in a more real and dramatic form that I was not
among the rejected and unchosen. And so, at the end of
the year, I persuaded my father to let me leave DePauw
and enter Barnard College.

What did I learn from this essentially very mild
experience of being treated as an outsider and a reject
from my own society? Just enough to know more clearly
than ever that this is not the way to organize society—
that those who reject or those who are rejected, and
usually both, suffer irreversible character damage. It is
true that sometimes one or the other may show magnificent character traits. I believe that the ideal of the
English gentleman, embodied in the belief that he alone
—and no one else—can destroy his position, is valuable.
Equally, the position of the Jews, steadily persecuted
but sustained by their conception of themselves as a
chosen people, has produced an enormous number of
highly intelligent, humanly sensitized, valuable men and
women. But the reciprocal, the belief of the Nazis that
they were the proper heirs of European civilization, from
which all whom they regarded as lesser men should be
excluded, was an evil that the world cannot face again.
Whatever advantages may have arisen, in the past, out of
the existence of a specially favored and highly privileged
aristocracy, it is clear to me that today no argument can
stand that supports unequal opportunity or any intrinsic
disqualification for sharing in the whole of life.

By the very contrast that it provided, DePauw clarified
my picture of the kind of college at which I wanted to
be a student—a place where people were intellectually
stirred and excited by ideas, where people stayed up all
night talking about things that mattered, where one

would meet one's peers and, still more important, people with different and superior minds, and, not least, where one would find out what one could do in life.

I left DePauw, sorry only to leave Katharine Rothenberger. At the time, I hardly realized how lasting some of my impressions would be. I never again went to a football game as a partisan, but more than twenty-five years later, when I was asked to lecture at Wabash College, the college that was DePauw's football rival, I felt a little like a traitor.

Even now, when I lecture in the Middle West, if I want my voice to be free of a carping note, I have to think myself back into the world of my grandmother and my mother—the Middle West as they presented it to me—and will myself to omit my own experience of DePauw in 1920. The dream glowed; the reality had been more than disappointing.

9 College: Barnard

In the autumn of 1920, I came to Barnard, where I found —and in some measure created—the kind of student life that matched my earlier dreams. In the course of those three undergraduate years friendships were founded that have endured a lifetime of change, and by the end of those years I knew what I could do in life.

At that time Barnard had only one large dormitory, and during preceding years one group of students had been permitted to live in an apartment and do cooperative housekeeping. They were unusual girls, most of whom became well known in later life—Margaret Myers, Dorothy Swaine Thomas, Betsy Anne Schellhase, Agnes Piel, and Léonie Adams. When I arrived on the scene the group had dispersed and the Coop had been abolished, but the overflow of students still was housed in apartments. Although the space in which we lived was usually very confined, the fact that the cost of rooms varied—the kitchen and the maid's room were the least expensive—meant that a group with unequal financial resources could live together.

In our group Léonie Adams provided a link to the old Coop group and their ethos; out of this we developed our own ideas of unity, based on common tastes and a respect for diversity. Most of the group we formed lived together, in three successive apartments, throughout college. There were always accidents—girls added who turned out not to fit, but we included them, wept with them, and supported them when they dropped out for reasons of their own or were expelled for spending the night in Greenwich Village.

Each year we adopted as a group name some derogatory and abusive phrase that was hurled at us in particular or at the students at large. The first year Miss Abbott, the head of the dormitory apartments, described us as "a mental and moral muss," and we accepted this with a kind of wicked glee. The second year we adopted the phrase "Communist morons," from the angry words of a commencement speaker. "Ash Can Cats," the name that finally stuck, was an epithet bestowed on us by our most popular professor, the vivid, colloquial, contemporary-minded Minor W. Latham, after whom Barnard's theater is named. We all took the course in drama in which she brought together, with a fine human relevance and a contempt for historical sequence, Greek plays, the contemporary Broadway theater, and miracle plays, and we were her partisans against the more conventional members of the English Department, critics ever, who admired creativity only when the creator was dead.

Sophisticated as we were, we were still remarkably innocent about practical matters relating to sex. During that first year, the sixteen-year-old daughter of a friend of my mother's was found in bed with a boarder and was forced by her mother to get married. We knew that she ought not have a baby yet, and I compiled a five-page typed list of home remedies that could be used as a douche. However, our young friend in due course had a baby, and she taught him to sit still on the piano while she practiced. Meanwhile the paint peeled off the plaster wall in the outer living room of our dormitory apartment, and she painted an enormous cartoon on it, in which a huge grinning world invited in a very small miss in cap and gown. The inscription read: "Come in and learn the rest of the alphabet."

But we knew about Freud. Agnes Piel was being analyzed and, although overnight visitors were not allowed and had to be hidden when Miss Abbott pounced, Ag occasionally spent the night with us. The first time she came, I made up her bed for her. Accustomed to being the eldest, that was the kind of thing I always did. Ag looked at me and said, "Well, the man you marry will certainly have an Oedipus fixation on you, which will be all right if it isn't joined to an incest complex."

We learned about the existence of homosexuality, too, mainly from the occasional covert stories that drifted down to us through our more sophisticated alumnae friends and through upperclassmen who were close to some members of the faculty. Allegations were made against faculty members, and we worried and thought over affectionate episodes in our past relationships with girls and wondered whether they had been incipient examples.

We knew that repression was a bad thing, and one of our friends—not a member of the inner circle—described how she and her fiancé had made up a set of topics to talk about on dates so that they would not be frustrated. When she heard that I had been engaged for two years and did not intend to get married for three years more, she exclaimed, "No wonder your arm hurts!"

Toward the end of my first year at Barnard, I myself, my grandmother, and my sister Elizabeth all developed extreme muscle pains which were then diagnosed as neuritis. One day, while I was going through a routine physical checkup and my grip was being tested, I discovered

Three Ash Can Cats: Léonie Adams, Margaret Mead,
and Eleanor Pelham Kortheuer

that all the strength had gone out of my right hand. That
spring I wore my arm in a sling, took my examinations
orally, and learned—as did my grandmother—to write
with my left hand. It was then that my father, short of
ready cash, again threatened to keep me home from
college.

The pain stayed with me all through college, and I
have always been subject to muscle pains of various sorts
—in my neck and in my arms and legs. In later years I
learned to play with the pain by concentrating on some
other part of my body. Still later, Janet Travell's method
of treating pain by inserting a needle at the trigger point
—so reminiscent of the Chinese method of acupuncture—
used to ease the periodic strains. But at the time when
the pain first lamed my arm, it appeared to us that I

might have suffered some unknown "affectively toned trauma." We liked the phrase, and I wrote a poem called "The Pencil Lines of Pain," which was published in *The Barnacle,* the new freshman paper.

We thought of ourselves as radicals—in terms of our sentiments rather than our adherence to any radical ideology. But there were always staunch conservatives in our midst. Among them were Muriel Mosher, a devoted medievalist, and Viola Corrigan, a Catholic, who found her first year in our group very hard going. Then there were Virginia Huey and K. Wright, two girls from the the South, who found very disturbing what they heard in sociology courses about mine workers and Negroes. At the same time Mary Anne McCall, known as Bunny, who was the perfect flapper of the early 1920's, provided us with a running commentary on a way of life that was quite alien to the rest of us, either because we were too old-fashioned or because we were too intellectual and ideal-istic.

The core of our group lived in the dormitory-apart-ment on West 116th Street, but we provided a center, too, for commuters whom we called, inelegantly, "parasites," because they hung up their hats in our quarters. Of these, two remained lifelong members of the group. One is Eleanor Phillips, with whom I have carried on running battles, based on our temperamental differences, for fifty years. It was Eleanor Phillips who said that Shelley was not always Shelley to me, while, from her viewpoint, the poet was always, under any circumstances, the poet. The other is Leah Josephson Hanna, who has, I think, a special gift for friendship and who provided all of us with warmth as she listened to us with never-failing, sophisticated sympathy.

Our group was half Jewish and half Gentile. Looking back, it seems to me that the Gentile families were, on the whole, a little more receptive to their daughters' friendships than were the more tightly knit Jewish fami-lies. I had enjoyed the few Jewish children I had known earlier, and during college summers I often got very bored with the slower intellectual pace of the Gentile world.

In that first apartment, Léonie had the only single room, which had a swinging door through which we used to push her when, after endless days of *not* doing a piece of work, the date for completion of a paper became too imminent. The second year she and I shared a room and pinned a sign on the door: "We don't believe in private property, please keep yours out." Each of us chose as a motto lines from a poem in Edna St. Vincent Millay's recently published book, *A Few Figs from Thistles*. The choice Léonie and I made was:

Safe upon the solid rock the ugly houses stand:
Come and see my shining palace built upon the sand!

But we liked equally well the three poems that begin "My candle burns at both ends," and "Cut if you will, with Sleep's dull knife," and "Was it for this I kicked the stairs . . ."

When we first began living together I invented a kinship system for the group. Deborah Kaplan, Léonie Adams, and I were the "parents," and Viola Corrigan and Eleanor Pelham Kortheuer—who had an extraordinary gift for sensitive and humorous insights—were the "children." In 1922 we added "grandchildren," only one of whom, Louise Rosenblatt, has remained part of the group and finally, in 1923, we added a "great-grandchild," Hannah Kahn, whom we called David because of her resemblance to "the shepherd lad." Léonie graduated in 1922. During the third year we lived in a much more imposing apartment at 29 Claremont Avenue.

Throughout the three years our lives were filled with theatrical and literary events. We went to the theater often—to see Robert Edmond Jones' staging of *Macbeth* and to admire Katharine Cornell when she stole the show in *A Bill of Divorcement*. We shared a baby by baby-sitting, in turn, for the daughter of a professor—as much, I think, because we wanted to keep in touch with a world with babies in it as for the money each of us earned. Sometimes we read aloud long sections of Milton. Or we worried about whether the new Freudian insights, which seemed to strip life of mystery, could be assimilated and sunk into the unconscious, so that spontaneity in art would again be possible.

Deborah Kaplan became the president of the Hebrew Culture Society and I the president of the Sunday Night Club, which was the only organization on the campus through which young people of both sexes could meet to hear liberal speakers. Before meetings, Deb and I used to buy huge pieces of cardboard that we cut in half to make our posters, and we used to argue vigorously as to whether or not Jews had a "chromosome" for social justice.

All of us took part in a mass meeting for Sacco and Vanzetti during the period of their trial in the spring of 1921. When this netted only $25, Léonie, as editor of *The Barnard Bulletin,* was moved to write an editorial, "Cheer Up, Mr. Coolidge"—her answer to an article the Vice-President had written, "Are the 'Reds' Stalking Our College Women?" for *Delineator.* At different times we also made forays into radical activities, walking on a picket line or stuffing envelopes for the Amalgamated Clothing Workers. We also took a course on the contemporary labor movement with Sylvia Kopald, a brilliant young economist, whose lectures were so elaborately organized that I could outline a point down to 1^{15} in the system with which I was experimenting.

But the most exciting events centered around Léonie's poetry, for while she was still an undergraduate she was already having poems accepted and published. Because we all were interested in literature, we recognized that Léonie was a real poet, whereas none of the rest of us was a real anything as yet; indeed, we were not sure where we were going.

The presence of one highly gifted person whose talent is recognized has an enormous effect on everyone belonging to a group. It makes for a very different affirmation of the values that are being taught in courses and discussed by critics. It also affects one's estimation of one's own talents. I too had been writing verse and I continued to do so for several years, but it became an avocation—

an enjoyable way of translating experience for myself and of communicating with friends who were poets. But because Léonie was there, it ceased to be a serious ambition. Without her, I might have gone on much longer, fancying that a slight talent was a real gift. It meant, too, that we had to look at the choices we made in other fields in much stricter terms, evaluating our respective gifts much more critically than we would have been able to do otherwise. And the relationship was not all one-sided; we made a protective and enjoyable shield around Léonie and supported her in whatever she chose to do. This included editing *The Barnard Bulletin;* I followed her, and Louise Rosenblatt followed me. It saddened us when Léonie failed to obtain the Caroline Duror Fellowship, Barnard's only graduate fellowship. I too failed to win it, but finally Louise, as an alternate, received it.

We were a happily captivated audience for Léonie's long narrative anecdotes, many of which are as vivid today in my memory as they were when she told them. I saw myself as a kind of production manager, helping to keep our shifting groups organized around Léonie. I believed that cross-generational continuity among college students, which characterized our own group and which was the one good thing I had perceived in the sorority system at DePauw, was essential to correct the narrow age typing that is so common in American colleges. But I had very little sense that I myself provided a focus for the group, and I remember the surprise I felt, at a college tea during senior year, when I found a group listening to what I said and laughing. I had always been told that I had no sense of humor, and I still don't know how the shift came about so that I could make others laugh, instead of being part of the laughing audience.

Although we were bound together by ties of temperament and congeniality and by a common interest in literature, some—but not all—of us also were children of our period and true descendants of the group of girls who had lived in the Coop. We belonged to a generation of young women who felt extraordinarily free—free from the demand to marry unless we chose to do so, free to postpone marriage while we did other things, free from the need to bargain and hedge that had burdened and restricted women of earlier generations. We laughed at the idea that a woman could be an old maid at the age of twenty-five, and we rejoiced at the new medical care that made it possible for a woman to have a child at forty.

We did not bargain with men. After college many of us fell in love with an older man, someone who was an outstanding figure in one of the fields in which we were working, but none of these love affairs led to marriage. Schooled in an older ethic, the men were perplexed by us and vacillated between a willingness to take the love that was offered so generously and uncalculatingly and a feeling that to do so was to play the part of a wicked seducer. Later most of us married men who were closer to our own age and style of living, but it was a curious period in which girls who were too proud to ask for any hostage to fate confused the men they chose to love.

At the same time we firmly established a style of relationships to other women. "Never break a date with a girl for a man" was one of our mottoes in a period when women's loyalty to women usually was—as it usually still is—subordinate to their possible relationships to men. We learned loyalty to women, pleasure in conversation with women, and enjoyment of the way in which we complemented one another in terms of our differences in temperament, which we found as interesting as the complementarity that is produced by the difference of sex. Throughout extraordinarily different career lines we have continued to enjoy one another, and although meeting becomes more difficult as we scatter in retirement, we continue to meet and take delight in one another's minds.

In college, as in earlier years, I had several sets of friends. Although I never tried to keep the Ash Can Cats and other groups in separate compartments, their interests were not the same and often the different groups were mutually incompatible. There was, for instance, a group of girls who liked dancing and who used to go to tea

Marie Eichelberger   Louise Rosenblatt

dances, girls for whom I sometimes provided extra dancing partners from among Luther's friends. And there was Marie Eichelberger, who looked younger than many freshmen but who, in fact, came to college very late after curing a severe tuberculosis infection she had contracted in high school. We became close friends and later her home became a focal point in my life. During her college years she remained peripheral to the Ash Can Cats, but afterward many of them became her friends also.

When I went to DePauw, I intended to be a writer, and when I transferred to Barnard I continued to major in English. But the experience was disappointing. Billy Brewster, with whom I took Daily Themes, said I would

never be a writer. I took a course on the novel and
learned less than I could get out of reading novels by
myself. So, although I had been deeply bored by my
course in Introductory Psychology, I went on to take the
necessary hours for a second major, in psychology.

But I was still uncertain. The experience of knowing
Léonie had given me new insight into my talents. Although I could write well, I realized that creative writing
would not provide a central focus for my life. I was also
interested in politics, especially in bringing about change
in the world, and I became a collegiate debater, but I
early rejected debating as dishonest. In active politics,
debate essentially provides a means of exploiting any
weakness in one's opponent and of seizing on any argument, strong or weak, that will bolster one's own position.
I had known Scott Nearing as a child and while I was in
college I went to hear him debate with the popular radical minister of the Community Church, John Haynes
Holmes. Holmes only wanted to win; Scott cared about
the issues. I was fairly certain that I could succeed in
politics. I could speak well, I had a good memory for
people, and I could plan—but I felt that political success
was both too short term and too exigent.

Later, by the time the state of the world might have
provided a different rationale, I was effectively debarred
from political life because I had been divorced twice.
Therefore, during World War II, when my friends suggested that I should aim for some political appointment,
I could always answer that I was too vulnerable since I
might damage any cause I would be expected to promote
or defend.

In a curious way this has both protected me and permitted me a kind of single-minded pursuit of the things
I have valued, just as being a woman has protected me
from having to accept administrative posts. Otherwise,
with my propensity for letting life call the shots, I might
easily have been diverted by the argument that it was
necessary for me to play a political role. As it was, as
long as I did not put myself in the position of being a
political target, my private life was not a liability and,

At Barnard, 1922

in fact, rapidly faded from most people's memories. Today, occasionally, I receive letters attacking me as a
spinster without any right to discuss questions of family
life. Almost invariably, advocacy of causes on which
society is polarized produces the kind of hostility that
seizes on any real or apparent vulnerability. Today when
I advocate some unpopular point of view, my age is used
as target and some fanatic is likely to denounce me as
senile.

But I definitely decided, while I was still in college,
that I would not make a career out of politics. At the
same time my experience with painting and writing had
convinced me that I did not have the superlative talent
that might not have been necessary in an earlier age but
that was crucial for success in the contemporary world.
America in the 1920's had no place for the kind of artist

Luther Cressman
at the General
Theological Seminary

who could paint an angel's wing and would leave the painting of the angel's face to someone with a greater gift.

I wanted to make a contribution. It seemed to me then—as it still does—that science is an activity in which there is room for many degrees, as well as many kinds, of giftedness. It is an activity in which any individual, by finding his own level, can make a true contribution. So I chose science—and to me that meant one of the social sciences. My problem then was which of the social sciences?

I entered my senior year committed to psychology, but I also took a course on psychological aspects of culture given by William Fielding Ogburn, one of the first courses in which Freudian psychology was treated with respect. I had also to choose between the two most distinguished courses open to seniors—a philosophy course given by William Pepperell Montague and the course in anthropology given by Franz Boas. I chose anthropology.

I had absorbed many of the premises of anthropology at home as they lay back of what my mother had learned at Bryn Mawr under Caseby and what both my parents had learned from Veblen. I was accustomed to regard all the races of man as equal and to look at all human cultures as comparable. What was new to me was the vista that was opened up by discussions of the development of men from their earliest beginnings. The reconstructions of Stone Age men with bundles of sticks in their arms had a tremendous power to move me, as they evoked a sense of the millennia it had taken man to take the first groping steps toward civilization and of the many thousands of years the slender flakes from the cores men made into hammerstones had lain unused in paleolithic workshops.

Boas was a surprising and somewhat frightening teacher. He had a bad side and a good side of his face. On one side there was a long dueling scar from his student days in Germany—an unusual pursuit for a Jewish student—on which his eyelid drooped and teared from a recent stroke. But seen from the other side, his face showed him to be as handsome as he had been as a young man. His lectures were polished and clear. Occasionally he would look around and ask a rhetorical question which no one would venture to answer. I got into the habit of writing down an answer and nodding when it turned out to be right. At the end of the semester I and another girl whom I did not know but whose name rhymed with mine were excused from taking the examination for "helpful participation in class discussion."

Ruth Benedict was Boas' teaching assistant. She was tentative and shy and always wore the same dress. She spoke so hesitatingly that many students were put off by her manner, but Marie Bloomfield and I were increasingly fascinated. On Museum trips we would ride down and back on the Broadway streetcar with her. Her comments humanized Boas' formal lectures, as she would remark how like a communist státe the Inca Empire had been or satirize the way the Crow Indians invested in visions. She invited Marie and me to the graduate seminar, where we were embarrassed by her shy, inarticulate report on John Dewey's *Human Nature and Conduct*. But we kept on going to the seminar. By the end of the first term I had decided to attend everything Boas taught, as Ruth Benedict said he might retire at the end of the year. I also propagandized the course so thoroughly at Barnard that it doubled in size the second semester and this made it possible for Boas to persuade the Barnard administration to appoint an instructor rather than paying Columbia for each student.

By the spring I was actively considering the possibility of entering anthropology, but I was already launched on my Master's essay in psychology. Then one day, when I was at lunch with Ruth Benedict and was discussing with her whether to go into sociology, as Ogburn wanted me to do, or into psychology, as I had already planned to do, she said, "Professor Boas and I have nothing to offer but an opportunity to do work that matters." That settled it for me. Anthropology had to be done *now*. Other things could wait.

I was slowly getting to know Ruth Benedict when, during the break between semesters, the tragic death of Marie Bloomfield precipitated us into a much closer relationship. Marie, who was the orphaned younger sister of the linguist Leonard Bloomfield, was an awkward girl, intellectually eager but stiff and unresponsive to any kind of physical affection. Although we were not especially congenial, I was moved by her loneliness. And so, when I realized that there was no one to bring her back from the hospital where she had been confined for six weeks with the measles, I felt that I had to take some responsibility for her. I knew how gloomy an empty dormitory could be, especially for someone as isolated as Marie. So I brought her clothes down to the hospital, and when we returned to the dormitory, I installed her in her room.

After that I had to leave her, at least for the time. I had agreed to have lunch with another friend who was taking a physics examination. She emerged from her exam hysterically blind. What was I to do? There was no one to turn to; everyone in the college would be away until Sunday night. This was Friday. I had to make a conscious choice—and I chose to take care of the girl who had gone blind and was in need of immediate help. She got her sight back, but on Monday, when Marie did not come down to dinner, we had to break into her room and found that she had taken cyanide. Of course, I could not know what would have happened to the other girl had she been left alone, but I felt that if I had been able to stay with Marie, she might not have been driven by such desperation. All my life, since then, I have been hypersensitive to the possibility of suicide.

Marie's death was spread all over the newspapers. Her face stared up at us from trampled newspapers on the subway floor. Understandably, the college administration was frantic and was determined to convince me—so that I would convince others—that Marie had been insane. I resisted this, feeling very much embattled against the adult world of doctors and deans who cared nothing at all about Marie Bloomfield's plight, but only about keeping the college community quiet.

The one exception was Ruth Benedict. She wrote me a little note and I went to see her. She was the one person who understood that suicide might be a noble and conscious choice. As a child, she herself had wondered why the Roman Cato had been hailed as noble, while in the upstate New York countryside where she grew up, suicides were repudiated. From that time I began to know her not only as a teacher but also as a friend. I continued to call her "Mrs. Benedict" until I got my degree and then, almost imperceptibly, our relationship became one of colleagues and close friends. Nevertheless, I was always aware of the fifteen years' difference in our ages; I always feared that one day I would find a gulf I could not bridge.

By electing anthropology as a career, I was also electing a closer relationship to Ruth, a friendship that lasted until her death in 1948. When I was away, she took on my varied responsibilities for other people; when she was away, I took on hers. We read and reread each other's work, wrote poems in answer to poems, shared our hopes and worries about Boas, about Sapir, about anthropology, and in later years about the world. When she died, I had read everything she had ever written and she had read everything I had ever written. No one else had, and no one else has.

So I came to the end of my years at Barnard. I was engaged to be married in the fall. I was committed to taking my Master's degree in psychology and to finishing the work for this during the summer. I had accepted an assistantship to Ogburn in economics and sociology for the next autumn, when I would also begin my graduate work in anthropology.

At the senior dance Luther and I danced all night and in the damp dawn, which took all the curl out of my small ostrich feather fan, we walked along Riverside Drive, watching the sky brighten over the river.

10 Student Marriage and Graduate School

In September, 1923, Luther and I were married in the little Episcopal church in Buckingham where I had been baptized of my own choice with godmothers summoned by myself. Father Pomeroy, who had been Luther's favorite professor at the seminary, came to celebrate an early Mass. The ceremony itself was performed by the Reverend Mr. Hollah, for my godmother insisted that one must stick by one's parish priest, however uncongenial his theology and liturgical behavior—even Mr. Hollah, who objected to marrying anyone on daylight saving time instead of God's time. By train and by car, everyone came to the wedding and out to the farm, which many of them had never seen. At the reception, Dr. Ostrolenk, one of my father's collaborators, spilled coffee down the front of my dress. Later I could recall this as a good story and feel sorry for the wedding guest who spilled coffee on the bride.

In very modern fashion we waited until the last bit of confetti had been thrown and then I sent for a whisk broom to brush it out of the car before we took off, cool and unfrantic. We had borrowed Luther's brother's car and drove up through the Poconos and the Berkshires, bright with autumn foliage, to a cottage on Cape Cod that had been lent us by my mother's brother.

It was pleasant to sit and talk over breakfast with a sense of great leisure we had not known before and were seldom to know again, as we were both plunging into lives that combined study and a great deal of hard work. Our enjoyment of these long lazy hours did not mean that even after an engagement of five years there were not moments of strangeness and disappointment to overcome. We had read so many books written by the sex specialists of the 1920's, who believed that sex was a matter of proper technique—that men should learn to play on women's bodies as if they were musical instruments, but without including in their calculations the idea that women must be very good musical instruments in order to please the men who played on them.

I had decided to keep my own name. This made a flutter in the press, partly because I had stated my decision as a matter of preference rather than principle. I had got the idea from an angry cousin of my mother's; in describing what an impractically idealistic young woman Mother had been, she had said, "If your mother were getting married today, she'd even keep her own name!" I resented the tone in which she was putting my mother down, and I said to myself, "Why not?" Keeping my own name, in which Luther concurred, led to endless explanations, on and on through life. But I was merely acting on my mother's belief that women should keep their own identity and not be submerged, a belief that had made her give her daughters only one given name, so that they would keep their surnames after marriage.

The apartment Luther had found was small enough for the furniture we had: a strong round folding table, four old Dutch chairs that my mother had bought at a sale for twenty-five cents each and that my brother had refinished for me, Luther's mission-style desk and a handsome mahogany screen from his bachelor years at the seminary that hid the narrow kitchenette, a couch for which I made a handsome linen cover to match the curtains, bookcases I myself made in a last tribute to the days when Mother had made us learn capentry, a filing cabinet left over from the Consumers Cooperative that Father had tried to start, the bureau from my room at the farm—another of Mother's finds, beautiful but without handles so that the drawers, which stuck, had to be opened with a buttonhook—two new beds with woven covers made by the weavers of Appalachia, and a strange, Gothic-style mission chair that had belonged to Marie Bloomfield and that I still possess today. The apartment had only two tiny rooms with a vestibule in between, from which the bathroom opened off, and, in the kitchenette, a two-burner stove that sat on the miniature refrigerator.

Here we gave dinners for four, even when I was on crutches for part of that first winter. I amused and annoyed Ruth by speaking of them as "formal dinners," which she thought showed a lack of knowledge of the ways of the world. In fact, we usually could afford only hamburgers, cooked in different styles, for the years 1923–1925 were a period of inflation, during which the cost of everything skyrocketed. Nevertheless, we invited Lewis Mumford to dinner and, on another occasion, W. I. Thomas, because Luther was the president of the Graduate Sociology Club.

However, we seldom went out to dinner. There was no one to ask us, because almost everyone else lived in

Wedding in Holicong,
1923

ABOVE The wedding party:
Priscilla, Richard,
Charles Cressman,
Margaret, Luther,
Léonie Adams,
Morris Cressman,
Elizabeth

LEFT With my
grandmother

some odd arrangement or in a dormitory. So our apartment became a kind of center and hardly a week passed when no one was sleeping on the couch. I had all the enjoyment of being an unchallenged, if somewhat inexperienced, hostess. In fact, it was not until the late 1950's, when I invited all the members of Section H of the American Association for the Advancement of Science to our house, that I ever had the experience of prying hostile eyes that so many women have to live through when they entertain their husband's business friends. We never invited anyone we did not enjoy having in our apartment and so, unburdened by reciprocity, we found hospitality only a pleasure.

Luther had a graduate fellowship and he was the parttime pastor of a little church in East New York, a church to which I went only occasionally, because I was burdened with the jobs I had taken on so that we could make ends meet. When I refused my father's offer of money to travel around the world, instead of getting married, he withdrew his support of my graduate work. But then, in the spring of 1923, I received a note from Ruth Benedict that read: "First Award No Red Tape Fellowship, $300." At about the same time, Professor Ogburn asked me to be his assistant in the Barnard Department of Economics and Sociology and, in addition, his editorial assistant on the *Journal of the American Statistical Association*. I remember that he asked me how much I could manage to live on and pieced the money out so that it fit.

I did not know shorthand, but I could write very rapidly and I learned proofreading as I went along. Ogburn was such a shy and considerate employer that often he went to extremes to protect my feelings. Once when I had addressed a manuscript to ourselves instead of the Rumford Press in Maine, he hid it under a pile of mail so that I would find it without knowing that he had already seen it. And once I sat and watched him pace the floor, while I agonized, sure that I was going to be fired, until he got up the courage to ask whether I would call for his child at school that day!

I had never been fired—I never have been fired—and I had never been called to the principal's office. Yet many years later, when I came into the Museum from lunch one day and the telephone operator told me that the assistant director wanted to see me at once, the fear of something that had never happened—but that I had learned could happen—clutched at my stomach. What had I done? In fact, the assistant director simply wanted to ask me to serve on a special advisory committee for a science book club.

My only real experience of having to face a possibly punitive authority happened when I was about two. I had picked a violet in a little park in Philadelphia, and Mother made me walk across the park to show it to a policeman—who only smiled. But that one little exercise in fear has lasted me all my life. I do not like receiving letters from the Department of Justice, even though I am only being asked to attend some conference, and my foreboding seemed to be fulfilled in 1947, when I received a cable about my daughter from the Department of State that read: "Mary Catherine Bateson's visa revoked. Please return passport at once." It had been discovered that she was only seven years old, and so was too young to be admitted as a student at a seminar that was to be held in Austria, still an occupied country. It took weeks to get the visa reissued.

We often forget, I think, that children may experience indirectly the impact of all the customary horrors that their culture provides, even though they may have almost no personal experience of them. When my daughter was two, she would return from the park and beat her doll to the great indignation of her nurse, who had never raised her hand to her. But she had seen mothers and nurses in the park hit the children in their charge. And it was a most revealing experience to me, as a mother, when Cathy decided to give up her painting lessons and I found out—but only after an intensive interview with her—that she had made this decision because she was afraid to tell her very much loved teacher that she did not like painting in oils!

I suffered a second unreal trauma that first year of graduate study on the day I gave my initial seminar report, a comparative study of Polynesian tattooing. I had made beautiful enlarged reproductions to place all around the seminar room for this, my first full-dress performance. At the end of the seminar, Ruth said with one of her strange, distant smiles, "I learned a lot." For some reason I decided that she was expressing disappointment, and I was deeply distressed. Finally, Luther went to ask Ruth whether she really had been as disappointed as I thought—and found out, of course, that I had imagined it.

But I did not really learn from that experience either. Three years later, after my return from Samoa, when I submitted my manuscript of *Coming of Age in Samoa* to Boas, he turned to me at a Department lunch and said, "About that manuscript. Come to lunch with me next Tuesday." Then, turning to Ruth, he added, "You had better come, too." I was devastated by his tone. "What is he going to do?" I asked Ruth. "Make you bowdlerize it," was her response.

On the fatal Tuesday morning I paced my office floor—there was room to pace in those days when it was still nearly empty—saying to myself, "I have betrayed him, like everybody else." But at last we went to lunch, and after a lot of aimless talk he turned to me, brows beetling ferociously, and remarked, "You haven't made clear the difference between passionate and romantic love." That was the only criticism he ever made of it.

But the sense that one may somehow, someday, let down those who have put their faith in one does not go away—fortunately, I suppose. I have no anxiety as a public speaker unless some special responsibility rests on my shoulders, such as getting a new organization started, or making the participants in a group feel that their work has been worthwhile. This happened at the first Congress of the World Federation for Mental Health in 1948, when people who had worked very hard for a year came to London to learn about the results of all their efforts. Then I worried. I sat in every part of the great barnlike hall beforehand, I studied the effect of simultaneous translation, and I gave a personal paper earlier as a trial run. And recently, after James Baldwin and I had had the discussions that led to *A Rap on Race,* I worried because I did not hear from him until the day on which we were to appear on television to talk about the finished book. Had I turned into a monster in his mind? We had known each other so briefly, and here I was, forever in the middle of his book. One look into his loving, luminous eyes was enough to dispel that nightmare, but I voiced it just the same, as a final precaution.

During that first year of graduate work I was not only preparing to take a Ph.D. in anthropology but also completing my Master's essay in psychology. There were many tiresome statistics to do, as I correlated the scores on intelligence tests made by the Hammonton Italian children with the amount of Italian spoken in their homes. Luther had given me a beautiful slide rule, and I did the final statistics sitting on the bank of the Hudson —there was no West Side Highway then—feeling the spring. The problem on which I was working had been suggested by Boas. At the same time he became interested in having my mother do some measurements for him. In this way his original study of changes in the head form of the children of Italian immigrants as a function of the length of time they were in this country during childhood—a breakthrough study of the effect of environment on traits that had been believed to be unalterable—met, through me, the research my mother had carried out on the cultural changes wrought in the Italian group as a result of their immigration from southern Italy to the United States. My Master's essay, "Intelligence Tests of Italian and American Children" concluded my relationship to psychology.

Luther's and my marriage was an ideal student marriage, unclouded by the fear of pregnancy. The pressure to have children was not great enough to make those who wavered in their determination careless, as so often happened in the 1950's. We both enjoyed our graduate work. Luther suffered no pangs of betrayed masculinity as he shared in the household chores, and we pooled our money for our expenses.

He enjoyed my friends, especially the freedom with which they sat at our breakfast table and explored the intricacies of their disturbing love affairs. I think he liked women better than men, as people; perhaps this was a reaction to his childhood spent with five brothers and an intense and gifted mother. He did not grudge my friendships, nor did he question what I did with my time, although occasionally he joked about having to make an appointment to see me. We were free from the pressures of mate-seeking, pressures that inevitably are disturbing whether they come from within and are a search for love and sex or come from without and are a search for role and status. All that, for us, was settled.

We could get on with life and we still expected our life to center around the church. Luther had completed his studies at the seminary a year before I finished college. He then began graduate work in sociology, a field that attracted him because of his interest in problems of human relations. We planned to finish our graduate work at the same time. The church as a vocation was slipping away, but neither of us quite knew it yet. We never quarreled and never had a misunderstanding even of the kind roommates often have over leaving the light on or keeping the bathroom tidy. They were two eminently peaceful years, broken only by other people's troubles or by outside events, such as my being run over and having to spend two months on crutches. I had what I had thought I wanted—a marriage that contrasted sharply with my mother's, a marriage in which there seemed to be no obstacles to being myself.

Yet the short stories and poems I was writing were curiously contrapuntal to my expressed contentment. One poem began, "Throttled by sullen weeds I lie"; in another, in which I compared myself to quicksilver, I exclaimed, "My soul you can shatter/Ne'er hold in your hand." I felt that I had accepted a too easy felicity, a feeling that was most openly expressed in "Rose Tree of Assisi," a poem published in *The Measure*:

And you could bear to keep the thorns
Where no rose would ever grow,
Accept the power to wound and still
The blossoming forego?

It was a gentle saint whose blood
Set three rubies on your leaf;
Your swift retreating thorns had been
Clear witness to your grief.

And as the last white petals fell,
Was he not seen to stand,
Ready to strip you of your thorns
With kind, still-bleeding hand?

So that, denied the power to bloom,
No sharpness might remain
To torture precious flesh in which
You could not ease the pain.

It was a gentle saint, but you
Were loyal to the listening wind,
Accepting no release from thorns,
Heraldic of your kind.

And while the slanting rain of God
Pushes your blood-traced leaves apart
No tears of mine fall to caress
The thorn-stripped rose tree in my heart.

Spring came, the spring of 1924, and then the summer.
One evening we looked at each other realizing that, just
for once, there was no undone task waiting to be done.
"Let's go for a walk," I said. But when we went downstairs we found a telegram informing us that a broken-
hearted friend was arriving in an hour, in search for comfort.

That summer Ruth spent in the Southwest, working
with the Zuñi Indians. At the end of the summer I went
to the meeting of the British Association for the Advance-

ment of Science in Toronto. As there were only a handful of us, we saw a great deal of everyone who came. Edward Sapir and A. A. Goldenweiser argued about Jung's recently published theory of psychological types. Erna Gunther, who had made an avant-garde "contract marriage" with Leslie Spier, had her young son with her. Diamond Jenness discussed the work he was beginning in the Arctic. T. F. McIlwraith talked about his work with the Bella Bella, whom he had had to help reconstruct old ceremonies so that he could study them. Everyone there had a field of his own, each had a "people" to whom he referred in his discussions. I had entered anthropology with the expectation of working with immigrant groups in the United States and perhaps of doing some research on American Indian groups, among which I had not yet learned to distinguish very sharply. At Toronto I learned the delight of intellectual arguments among peers. I, too, wanted to have a "people" on whom I could base my own intellectual life.

By the time I returned from Toronto, I knew that I wanted to do field work as soon as I had my degree. Fortunately, the library work for my dissertation was already well under way. Luther proposed working out an adaptation that would allow him to pursue futher studies that were open to him, and at the same time, allow me to go to the field. He would get a European travel fellowship for the next year, 1925–1926, and I would get a fellowship to take me to the field. It was not said that this was a choice that was less relevant to continued parish work. We saw it as a way of broadening the preparatory period of our lives.

That second year, when I had my eyes firmly fixed on getting into the field, the pace of life quickened. Sapir was in New York for part of the year, enjoying the poets he met and developing a new interest in pattern, an outgrowth of our interest in Gestalt psychology. I read and lent him Koffka's *Growth of the Mind*. We were all still writing poetry with almost as much intensity as we were working on anthropology.

Franz Boas. *Photograph by Martin Vos*

The choice of a field and a people and a problem on which to start work—all this was much more difficult. I wanted to work on change: on the way in which new customs in a new country or new ways of life in an old country were related to older ones. This idea had grown directly out of my dissertation, in which I had worked on the question of whether technical processes—such as a method of building a canoe, thatching a roof, or making the black pigment for tattooing—were more stable, that is, more enduring, than the religious and social practices in which such processes were imbedded. This had been a purely cultural problem, based on the assertions of other ethnologists about what the "oldest" or the "most unchanging" traits were—whether they were the kinds of tools a people used and the techniques for making them or the form of the family and a people's beliefs about the supernatural world.

I had been exposed to a type of psychology in which the practitioners were emulating the "scientific" standards of physics, so that measurement was important. A new technique of measuring the galvanic skin response had recently been invented, and psychologists hoped that this would provide a discriminating tool for measuring the individual's emotional responses to a given subject. I had intended to use this device in the field, but it turned out that the instrument, far from making fine discriminations, simply recorded massive changes in emotional tone. Fifty years later, the so-called "lie detector" is still neither fine enough in its discriminations nor technically constructed for use in the field.

The choice of where I went to the field and what problem I would work on was not mine alone to make. The final decision rested with Boas, and he wanted me to study adolescence.

He had reached one of those watersheds that occur in the lives of statesmen-scientists who are mapping out the whole course of a discipline. He felt that sufficient work had gone into demonstrating that peoples borrowed from one another, that no society evolved in isolation, but was continually influenced in its development by other peoples, other cultures, and other, differing levels of technology. He decided that the time had come to tackle the set of problems that linked the development of individuals to what was distinctive in the culture in which they were reared. In the summer of 1924, when Ruth Bunzel said she wanted to go to Zuñi, he suggested that she work on the role of the individual artist. Now he wanted me to work on adolescence, on the adolescent girl, to test out, on the one hand, the extent to which the troubles of adolescence, called in German *Sturm und Drang* and *Weltschmerz*, depended upon the attitudes of a particular culture and, on the other hand, the extent to which they were inherent in the adolescent stage of psychobiological development with all its discrepancies, uneven growth, and new impulses.

Scientists who are building a new discipline have to keep in mind the necessary next steps. In Boas' case, there were two additional considerations: first, the materials on which the new science depended were fast vanishing, and forever. The last primitive peoples were being contacted, missionized, given new tools and new ideas. Their primitive cultures would soon become changed beyond recovery. Among many American Indian groups, the last old women who spoke a language that had developed over thousands of years were already senile and babbling in their cups; the last man who had ever been on a buffalo hunt would soon die. The time to do the work was *now*. And secondly, there were few sources of funds and very few people to do the work. In 1924 there were four graduate students in anthropology at Columbia and a mere handful in other universities. He had to plan—much as if he were a general with only a handful of troops available to save a whole country—where to place each student most strategically, so that each piece of work would count and nothing would be wasted and no piece of work would have to be done over.

Boas had a keen eye for the capabilities of his students, although he confounded them by devoting his time to those whom he found least promising. As long as a student was doing well, he paid almost no attention to him at all. This was a loss. For good students it meant little person-to-person contact with Boas, and in some cases it led to serious errors in a student's self-estimate. With the exception of an occasional course taught by an outsider from another institution, Boas taught everything. This meant that I saw him in classes every day. But I had only a few rare interviews with him. The first was when I told him that I wanted to do graduate work in anthropology and he advised me to go to Harvard. The second took place when I chose my thesis subject and he suggested that I compare different cultures within an area: I could work on Siberia (that would mean learning Chinese and Russian), or on the Low Countries (for which I would have to have a command of French, Dutch, German, and medieval Latin), or on Polynesia ("which you could do with only French and German"). I chose Polynesia. I gave a seminar report on one section of my work, and when I turned in my dissertation I was told to add another paragraph or so to the introduction. That was all. But now there was the question of field work.

Boas was profoundly human in his concern for students who had no money to live on. There was no question of rewarding those who did good work by giving them grants or appointments. Those who had enough money he did nothing for. The few jobs that were at his disposal went to those who needed them most. But research was a different matter. He assigned problems to those who could handle them, alone or with his help. In a way it was an ideal world where

> . . . no one shall work for money and no one shall work for fame,
> But each for the joy of working, and each, in his separate star,
> Shall draw the Thing as he sees It for the God of Things as They are!

It was said that in those last years of his teaching he was softening. We heard stories of how, in earlier years, he would assign a topic to be reported on within a couple of weeks in a language the student did not read. The generation of our elders—Kroeber, Lowie, Goldenweiser, Radin, Sapir, and others—had had a hard time. But he treated us rather like grandchildren, and we called him "Papa Franz." Still, he was very definite about what he wanted done.

I was equally definite. I wanted to go to Polynesia, the area on which I had read so extensively. He thought it was too dangerous, and recited a sort of litany of young men who had died or been killed while they were working outside the United States. He wanted me to work among American Indians.

I wanted to study culture change, a subject that was not yet on his agenda, although it was soon to be. He wanted me to study adolescence.

Today a student would chafe against the restrictions with which we had to contend. Even then, some of my older contemporaries did chafe when Boas wanted them to work on the problems he thought came next, instead of following their own interests, like will-o'-the-wisps, wherever they led. But going to the field at all depended on his approval, for the only way to do it was to get one of the newly inaugurated graduate fellowships.

I was determined to go to Polynesia, but I was willing to compromise and study the adolescent girl, especially as the technology I had hoped to use in studying change had proved to be disappointingly inadequate. So I did what I had learned to do when I had to work things out with my father. I knew that there was one thing that mattered more to Boas than the direction taken by anthropological research. This was that he should behave like a liberal, democratic, modern man, not like a Prussian autocrat. It was enough to accuse him obliquely of exercising inappropriate authority to have him draw back. So I repeated over and over that by insisting that I work with American Indians he was preventing me from going where I wanted to work. Unable to bear the implied accusation that he was bullying me, Boas gave in. But he refused to let me go to the remote Tuamotu Islands; I must choose an island to which a ship came regularly—at least every three weeks. This was a restriction I could accept.

From that point on Boas gave me his firm support. He fully backed up my application for the National Research Council fellowship I needed in order to do the field work, and he resisted Sapir's argument that I was not strong enough to survive in the field. His concern and the grounds on which he stood by his decision, once he had made up his mind, come out clearly in the letter he wrote Ruth Benedict a few weeks before I left for the field:

My dear Ruth:

Sapir had a long talk with me about Margaret Mead. You know that I myself am not very pleased with this idea of her going to the tropics for a long stay. It seems to my mind, however, and it has seemed to my mind ever since I prevented her going to the Tuamotu, that it would be much worse to put obstacles in her way that prevented her from doing a piece of work on which she had set her heart, than to let her run a certain amount of risk. . . . Of course, I know that Margaret is high strung and emotional, but I also believe that nothing would depress her more than inability on account of her physical makeup and her mental characteristics to do the work she wants to do. In my opinion an attempt to compel her now to give up the trip—and that is all Sapir has in mind—would be disastrous. Besides it is entirely against my point of view to interfere in such a radical way with the future of a person for his or her own sake,—unless there is actual disease that needs control. Of course, Sapir takes that point of view, but if he were right, then who should not be restrained?

At the same time, while I was bargaining with Boas, I told my father that Boas was trying to make me work with American Indians, already heavily contacted, instead of letting me go where things were interesting. My father, rivalrous as men often are in situations in which someone else seems to be controlling a person whom they believe they have the right—and may also have failed—to control, backed me up to the point of saying he would give me the money for a trip around the world. The trip he always wanted to take he now offered me so that I could do what I wanted to do. In the end, although he played with the idea of going to Florence to study the banking practices of the Medici, he never even went to Europe.

We had not then begun to discuss the ethics of manipulation of other individuals, groups, or whole societies, much less manipulation of ourselves. That same spring it appeared to me that the safest way to save the self-respect of a man who had fallen in love with me was to let him find a reason for rejecting me by letting his imagination, so ready to project disappointments on others,

Ruth Benedict, 1924. *Photograph by Stanley Benedict*

brand me as unworthy of his love. This plan, which I hoped would protect him, gave me a sense of great virtue. Ruth Benedict did not disapprove; she only commented, "I don't know anyone for whom that would be a harder thing to do," for she knew how much I valued being understood.

Later, when I seriously turned my attention to the whole question of manipulation, I began to understand that one should not use either a person's strength or his weakness against him. As I see it now, the only course that is ethically justified is an appeal to strength—not in order to throw one's opponent by means of his own strength, but on the grounds that reliance on strength will work for the good. Ruth never had this kind of trust. In many ways she expected the worst from people and steeled herself against it. In later years I had to fight for what I believed people were capable of at their best, while she acted in terms of the expected worst.

I do not advocate a philosophy of blind and naïve trust. Occasionally it is clear that a person in a position of power will, if he can, block or destroy something of great value. In such circumstances it is necessary to be politic; this means, essentially, using the strengths and weaknesses of other persons or groups for one's own ends. In the same way, in wartime, a nation plays on the weaknesses—and even on the strengths—of the enemy. But there is always a price to pay later, an erosion of the capacity for trust, a kind of damage that persists after the war and makes the reestablishment of working relationships much more difficult.

But in 1925, when both Boas and my father let me have my way, I was simply gleeful. That was the year in which I wrote "Of So Great Glee," a verse in which I expressed the sense I had of being invulnerable as long as I was moving in the right direction:

> She used to skip when she was small
> Till all her frocks were tattered,
> But Mother gently gathered up
> The dishes that she shattered.
>
> Her skipping rope got caught in trees
> And shook their blossoms down,
> But her step was so lighthearted
> That the dryads could not frown.
>
> And when at last she tore a star
> Out of the studded sky,
> God only smiled at one whose glee
> Could fling a rope so high.

I walked with a light step, the light step of a small, determined eleven-year-old, with no weight on my shoulders, and Ruth said, "One of the reasons people criticize you is the way you walk." Years later, when Gregory Bateson read that poem, he remarked sagely that it was a mistake to confuse one's husband with God. But that poem was not about husbands, although it may have included my feeling that if I could skip as I went along, I would be able to work in a world that had not been constructed for a woman to work in. I was beginning to realize that the freedom to work as one wished was the important thing.

It was a hectic spring. Luther had to finish his thesis on the social composition of the rural population in the United States. I dictated my own thesis, complete with ten or twelve footnotes to the page, to a young man who was earning his living as a typist while he studied for the ministry. It was a feat of typing very few typists could manage today. In addition, the *Journal of the American Statistical Association* had to be sent to press every quarter. But at the end of the term Ogburn was leaving for a sabbatical year in France, and if I got my fellowship, I would be going to the South Seas—to Samoa because, among all the less spoiled Polynesian islands, a steamer went there every three weeks.

On May Day Eve the news came that I had been awarded the fellowship. The Ash Can Cats celebrated in the midst of preparations for another ritual—we were planning to hang a May basket, woven of willow withes and filled with wild flowers, on the doorknob of Edna St. Vincent Millay's house in Greenwich Village. This, although our ages ranged from twenty-one to twenty-six! We loitered near her house, watching while her husband walked up and down the little court in the moonlight, until at last he went indoors. Edna Millay called out to us from a high window and, feeling safe, we lingered on in the court. But having set her sister in her place, she ran down the steep stairs and caught us and asked our names. "Léonie Adams I know," she said, holding out

On the eve of departure, 1925

her hand to her. Later, that May basket was mentioned in F.P.A.'s column.

The summer was given over to preparations. I made one trip to New York in response to Pliny Earle Goddard's invitation to discuss a job at the American Museum of Natural History. On the same visit, I had lunch with Eleanor Steele, who had just been told that she had tuberculosis, and dinner with Edward Sapir. However, most of my time was given over to getting inoculations and frantically assembling my field equipment—spare glasses, cotton dresses, a camera, pencils, and notebooks.

Nowadays preparations for a comparable trip take many months and involve not some twenty objects but, more likely, two thousand, including all the spare gadgets for tape recorders and various kinds of cameras, materials to mend typewriters, containers for protecting precious objects from dust and moisture, and other containers for mailing out film, color charts, and projective tests. But then my preparations, which in retrospect were so simple, seemed fairly strenuous. And in spite of all the differences between assembling that simple collection of materials and the complex field equipment necessary today, the aura of the last few days before a field trip remains very much the same.

Now, as then, it is necessary to survive all kinds of hazards—having the inoculations that make you feel clumsy and feverish (in 1971, I had five sets all in one day, and afterward crushed my finger in a door and bruised my knee getting out of a taxi); breaking your glasses; falling in love or having someone fall in love with you; trouble about passports and funds (in 1925, the Committee for the Biological Sciences of the National Research Council held a special meeting to decide whether they could advance $450 of my stipend, because communications with Samoa were so difficult); clothes that do not get finished and things that have been ordered but have not come. In those days, however, everything went on the same ship with you. Today, field equipment is sent off three or four months in advance and you wait at home, hoping to receive the news that it has arrived safely, and then you fly to your destination.

At the end of the summer, when every problem had finally been solved, Luther and I had a last vacation together. Once more we borrowed his brother's car and my aunt lent us a cottage in Rhode Island for a week. On the way we spent a few days at Lake Winnepesaukee, where we visited Ruth and Stanley Benedict, the only occasion I ever spent any time with him.

Then I set off for Samoa and Luther sailed for Europe.

PART TWO

11 Samoa: The Adolescent Girl

When I sailed for Samoa, I realized only very vaguely what a commitment to field work and writing about field work meant. My decision to become an anthropologist was based in part on my belief that a scientist, even one who had no great and special gift such as a great artist must have, could make a useful contribution to knowledge. I had responded also to the sense of urgency that had been conveyed to me by Professor Boas and Ruth Benedict. Even in remote parts of the world ways of life about which nothing was known were vanishing before the onslaught of modern civilization. The work of recording these unknown ways of life had to be done now—*now* —or they would be lost forever. Other things could wait, but not this most urgent task. All this came to a head at the Toronto meetings in 1924, where I was the youngest participant and everyone else had talked about "my people" and I had no people to talk about. From that time on I was determined to go to the field, not at some leisurely chosen later date, but immediately—as soon as I had completed the necessary preliminary steps.

But I really did not know much about field work. The course on methods that Professor Boas taught was not about field work. It was about theory—how material could be organized to support or to call in question some theoretical point. Ruth Benedict had spent a summer working with a group of quite acculturated Indians in California, where she had taken her mother along for a vacation, and she had worked in Zuñi. I had read Ruth's descriptions of the landscape, of how the Zuñi looked, of the fierceness of the bedbugs and the difficulties of managing food, but I knew little about how she went about her work. Professor Boas always spoke of the Kwakiutl as "my dear friends," but this was not followed by anything that helped me to know what it was like to live among them.

When I agreed to study the adolescent girl and Professor Boas consented to my doing this field work in Samoa, I had a half hour's instruction in which Professor Boas told me that I must be willing to seem to waste time just sitting about and listening but that I must not waste time doing ethnography, that is, studying the culture as a whole. Fortunately, many people—missionaries, jurists, government officials, and old-fashioned ethnographers—had been to Samoa, and so the temptation to "waste time" on ethnography would be less. During the summer he also wrote me a letter in which he once more cautioned me to be careful of my health and discussed the problem he had set me:

I am sure you have thought over the question very carefully, but there are one or two points which I have in mind and to which I would like to call your attention, even if you have thought of them before.

One question that interests me very much is how the young girls react to the restraints of custom. We find very often among ourselves during the period of adolescence a strong rebellious spirit that may be expressed in sullenness or in sudden outbursts. In other individuals there is a weak submission which is accompanied, however, by a suppressed rebellion that may make itself felt in peculiar ways, perhaps in a desire for solitude which is really an expression of desire for freedom, or otherwise in forced participation in social affairs in order to drown the mental troubles. I am not at all clear in my mind in how far similar conditions may occur in primitive society and in how far the desire for independence may be simply due to our modern conditions and to a more strongly developed individualism.

Another point in which I am interested is the excessive bashfulness of girls in primitive society. I do not know whether you will find it there. It is characteristic of Indian girls of most tribes, and often not only in their relations to outsiders, but frequently within the narrow circle of the family. They are often afraid to talk and are very retiring before older people.

Another interesting problem is that of crushes among girls. For the older ones you might give special attention to the occurrence of romantic love, which is not by any means absent as far as I have been able to observe, and which, of course, appears most strongly where the parents or society impose marriages which the girls may not want.

. . . Stick to individual and pattern, problems like Ruth Bunzel on art in Pueblos and Haeberlin on Northwest Coast. I believe you have read Malinowski's paper in *Psyche* on the behavior of individuals in the family in New Guinea. I think he is much too influenced by Freudians, but the problem he had in mind is one of those which I have in mind.

For the rest, there was G. Stanley Hall, who had written a huge book on adolescence in which, equating stages of growth with stages of culture, he had discussed his belief that each growing child recapitulated the history of the human race. There were also the assumptions set forth in textbooks, mainly derived from German theory, about puberty as a period of storm and stress. At that time puberty and adolescence were firmly equated in everyone's thinking. Only much later, students of child development began to say that there was perhaps a "first adolescence" around the age of six and a second crisis at puberty and that adolescence could be prolonged into the twenties and might in some sense reappear in adults in their forties.

My training in psychology had given me ideas about the use of samples, tests, and systematic inventories of behavior. I had also some very slight experience of social case work. My aunt Fanny was working at the Juvenile Protective Association at Hull House, in Chicago, and

one summer I had sat on the floor and read their records.
This had given me an idea of what the social context of
individual behavior was—how one had to look at the
household and place the household in the setting of the
community.

I knew that I would have to learn the language. But I
did not know anyone who was colloquially proficient in
the language of the people they studied except missionaries, or the children of missionaries, turned ethnologists.
I had read only one essay by Malinowski and did not
know how he had used the Trobriand language. I myself had never learned a foreign language; I had only
"studied" Latin and French and German in high school.
Our training in linguistics had consisted of short demon-
strations of extremely exotic languages in the course of
which we were confronted, without previous preparation,
with phrases like these:

"Adë'," në'x·lata NEmö'guis lăxis ts'ă'yē Lö'La'watsa; "3oă'LEla sEns
"Friend,"   he said   NEmö'guis to his younger Lö'La'watsa;   do not   us
                                   brother   let
hēquä'lē yā'wix·'idag·a x·ins qa yā'yats'ē sEns xunö'kuëx."
go on in   let us act   us   to   go on the   our   son this."
this way   sea

In a way this was an excellent method of teaching. It
prepared us—as our classes on forms of kinship and religious belief also did—to expect almost anything, however strange, unaccountable, and bizarre it might seem
to us. This is, of course, the first lesson the field anthropologist must learn: that he may well meet up with new,
unheard-of, unthought-of ways of organizing human behavior.

The expectation that we may at any time be confronted by some as yet unrecorded mode of behavior is
the basis on which anthropologists often clash with psychologists, whose theories have developed out of their
efforts to be "scientific" and out of their skepticism about
philosophical constructs. It is also the basis of our clash
with economists, political scientists, and sociologists, to
the extent that they use the model of our own social
arrangements in their studies of other societies.

The tough treatment given us by Professor Boas shook us up, prepared us for the unexpected, and be it said, the extremely difficult. But we did not learn how to organize work on a strange new language to the point at which a grammar could be worked out on the basis of which we could learn to speak the language. Sapir remarked parenthetically on the immorality of learning foreign languages; one was never really honest, he said, except in one's mother tongue.

There was, in fact, no *how* in our education. What we learned was *what* to look for. Years later, Camilla Wedgwood, on her first field trip to Manam Island, reflected on this point when she wrote in her first letter back: "How anyone knows who is anybody's mother's brother, only God and Malinowski know." Lowie, too, illustrated the startling differences between his field methods and mine when he inquired, "How does anyone know who is whose mother's brother unless somebody tells you?"

Our training equipped us with a sense of respect for the people we would study. They were full human beings with a way of life that could be compared with our own and with the culture of any other people. No one spoke of the Kwakiutl or the Zuñi—or any other people—as savages or barbarians. They were, it was true, primitive; that is, their culture had developed without script and was maintained without the use of script. That was all the term "primitive" meant to us. We were carefully taught that there was no regular progression from simple "primitive" languages to complex "civilized" languages; that, in fact, many primitive languages were far more complex than some written ones. We were taught also that whereas some art styles had been elaborated from simple designs, other art styles were reduced to simpler forms from originally more elaborate ones.

We had, of course, had lectures on evolution. We knew that it had taken millions of years for the first human-like creatures to develop language, to make tools, to work out forms of social organization that could be taught to the next generation, for all these things, once acquired, had to be taught and learned. But we went to the field not to look for earlier forms of human life, but for forms that were different from those known to us—different because particular groups of primitive people had lived in isolation from the mainstreams of the great civilizations. We did not make the mistake of thinking, as Freud, for example, was misled into thinking, that the primitive peoples living on remote atolls, in desert places, in the depths of jungles, or in the Arctic north were equivalent to our ancestors. True, we might learn from them how long it took to chop down a tree with a stone axe or even how much of the food supply women may have contributed in societies based on male hunting. But these isolated peoples were not in the line of our ancestors. Obviously our ancestors had been located at various crossroads where peoples met and exchanged ideas and traded goods. They had crossed mountains, they had sailed the seas and returned. They had borrowed and copied. They had stimulated and had been stimulated by the discoveries and inventions of other peoples to an extent that was not possible among peoples who lived in much greater isolation.

We knew that in our field work we could expect to find differences—differences far greater than those we would expect to find among the related cultures of the Western world or in the lives of people at different periods in our own history. The record of what we found out about the way of life of each primitive people we studied was to be our principal contribution to the accumulating store of exact knowledge about the world.

As far as anthropology was concerned, this was my intellectual equipment. I had, of course, acquired some knowledge of the techniques in use for categorizing, for example, the uses a people made of their natural resources or the forms of social organizations they had developed. And I had some practice in analyzing the observations that had been made by other fieldworkers.

But nobody really asked what were the young fieldworker's skills and aptitudes—whether he had, for instance, the ability to observe and record accurately or the intellectual discipline to keep at the job, day after day, when there was no one to supervise, no one to compare notes with, to confess delinquencies to, or even to boast to on an especially successful day. Sapir's letters to Ruth Benedict and Malinowski's private diary are filled with self-flagellating confessions of idleness written at a time when, as we also know, they were doing prodigious work. No one considered whether we could stand loneliness. No one inquired how we would get along with the colonial or military or Indian Service officials through whom we would have to work; and no one offered us any advice.

The style, set early in the century, of giving a student a good theoretical orientation and then sending him off to live among a primitive people with the expectation that he would work everything out for himself survives to this day. In 1933, when I gave a girl student who was setting out for Africa some basic instructions on how to cope with the drinking habits of British officials, anthropologists in London sneered. And in 1952, when I arranged for Theodore Schwartz to spend a year learning the new technologies—running a generator, making tape recordings, and working with cameras—that we intended to use in the field, his professors at the University of Pennsylvania thought this was ridiculous. Men who are now professors teach their students as their professors taught them, and if young fieldworkers do not give up in despair, go mad, ruin their health, or die, they do, after a fashion, become anthropologists.

But it is a wasteful system, a system I have no time for. I try to work against it by giving students a chance to work over my own field preparations and notes, by encouraging them to work at photography, and by creating field situations for my class, in which they have to work out a real problem and face up to the difficulties of an actual situation in which there are unknown elements. For only in this way can they find out what kind of recording they do well—or very badly—or how they react when they discover they have missed a clue or have forgotten to take the lens cap off the camera for a critical picture.

But I am also constantly defeated. A year's training in how to protect every object so that it will withstand humidity or being dropped in the river or the sea does not keep a young fieldworker from turning up with a unique copy of a manuscript wrapped in brown paper, or with her passport and money in a flimsy handbag, or without an airtight container for a valuable and essential camera. Yet students in other disciplines do learn; chemists learn laboratory procedure and psychologists learn to use a stopwatch and to write protocols.

The fact that anthropologists insist on learning everything over again for themselves, often including all the theory they have been taught, is, I think, an occupational disease that may well be inseparable from field work itself. For field work is a very difficult thing to do: To do it well, one has to sweep one's mind clear of every presupposition, even those about other cultures in the same part of the world in which one is working. Ideally, even the appearance of a house should come to one as a new, fresh impression. In a sense it should come to one as a surprise that there are houses and that they are square or round or oval, that they do or do not have walls, that they let in the sun or keep out the wind or rain, that people do or do not cook or eat in a dwelling house. In the field one can take nothing for granted. For as soon as one does, one cannot see what is before one's eyes as fresh and distinctive, and when one treats what is new merely as a variant of something already known, this may lead one far astray. Seeing a house as bigger or smaller, grander or meaner, more or less watertight than some other kind of house one already knows about cuts one off from discovering what *this* house is in the minds of those who live in it. Later, when one has come to know the new culture, everything has to be reassimilated into what is already known about other peoples living in that area, into our knowledge about primitive peoples, and into our knowledge about all human beings, *so far*. But the point of going to the field at all is to extend further what is already known, and so there is little value merely in identifying new versions of the familiar when we might, instead, find something wholly new. But to clear one's mind of presuppositions is a very hard thing to do and, without years of practice, all but impossible when one is working in one's own culture or in another that is very close to it.

On one's first field trip one doesn't know all this. All one knows is that there is a tremendous job ahead—that it will be a struggle to learn the language well enough to hear and speak it, to find out who everyone is, to understand a myriad of acts, words, glances, and silences as they are integrated into a pattern one has no way of working out as yet, and finally, to "get" the structure of the whole culture.

Before I started out for Samoa I was warned that the terms in which others had written about the culture were anything but fresh and uncontaminated. The recorded grammar was contaminated by the ideas of Indo-European grammar and the descriptions of local chiefs by European notions about rank and status. I knew I would have to thread my way through this maze of partial understandings and partial distortions. In addition, I had been given the task of studying a new problem, one on which no work had been done and for which I had no guidelines.

But in essence this is true of every worthwhile field trip. Today students sometimes are sent into the field to work on a small problem that does not involve much more than making the observations necessary to fill out a prearranged questionnaire or giving a few specific tests. Where the questions are unsuitable or the tests are wholly uncongenial to the unwilling subjects, these may not be the easiest things to do. But if the culture has already been properly studied, this kind of work may do as little harm as it does good. But it is not the same thing as being charged with getting the whole configuration of the culture down correctly.

But at the same time one has always to remember that the pattern one discerns is only one of many that might be worked out through different approaches to the same human situation. The grammar you work out is not *the* grammar but *a* grammar of the language. But as it may be the only grammar anyone will ever make, it is crucial that you listen and record as minutely and as carefully as you can and, as far as possible, without reference to the grammar you are tentatively putting into shape.

All this is important, but it gives no sense of what the day-to-day tasks will be. For there is no way of knowing in advance what the people will be like or even what they will look like. There may be photographs of them, but by the time one arrives they may look different. The summer I worked among the Omaha Indians, the girls were getting their first permanent waves—something I could not have foreseen. One doesn't know what the particular officials, the planters, the police, the missionaries, or the traders will be like. One doesn't know where one will live or what there will be to eat or whether it will turn out to be a good thing to have rubber boots, mosquito boots, sandals that keep one's feet cool, or woolen socks to absorb the sweat. So there is a great tendency—and when fieldworkers were poor there was a greater tendency—to take along as little as possible and to make very few plans.

When I set out for Samoa I had half a dozen cotton dresses (including two very pretty ones) for I had been told that silk rotted in the tropics. But when I arrived, I found that the Navy wives dressed in silk. I had a small strongbox in which to keep my money and papers, a small Kodak, and a portable typewriter. Although I had been married for two years, I had never stayed alone in a hotel and I had made only short journeys by train as far as the Middle West. Living in cities and small towns and in the Pennsylvania countryside, I had known a good many different kinds of Americans, but I had no idea of the kind of men who enlisted in the United States Navy in peacetime, nor did I know anything about the etiquette of naval life on an outstation. I had never been to sea.

At a party in Berkeley, where I stopped briefly on my way out, Professor Kroeber came and sat next to me on the floor and asked in a firmly sympathetic voice, "Have you got a good lamp?" I did not have any lamp at all. I had six large fat notebooks, some typing and carbon paper, and a flashlight. But no lamp.

When I arrived in Honolulu I was met by May Dillingham Freer, a Wellesley friend of my mother's. She and her husband and daughter were living in their house up in the mountains, where it was cooler, but she said I could live in Arcadia, their beautiful big house in the town. The fact that my mother had known May Dillingham and her sister-in-law Constance Freer at Wellesley made all the difference in my comings and goings in Honolulu for many years. May Dillingham was the daughter of one of the original missionary families, and her husband Walter Freer had been governor of the Hawaiian Islands. She herself was strangely out of place in her great, extensive, wealthy family; she was full of delicate sentimentalities and was childlike in her approach to life. But she was able to command any resources she needed and her influence, which extended even to Samoa, smoothed my path in a hundred ways. Under her guidance everything was arranged. The Bishop Museum made me an honorary member of the staff; Montague Cook, a member of another old Honolulu family, drove me to the Museum every day; and E. Craighill Handy gave up a week of his vacation to give me daily lessons in Marquesan, a language related to Samoan. A friend of "Mother May"—as I immediately named her—gave me a hundred littles squares of torn old muslin "to wipe the children's noses," and she herself gave me a silk boudoir pillow in response to one of the few bits of practical advice I was given, in this case by a biologist who said, "Always take a little pillow and you can lie on anything." Someone else took me to visit two part-Samoan children in school; this meant that their family would be on hand to help me in Samoa.

It was all extremely pleasant. Basking in the Freer and Dillingham prestige, I could not have had a more felicitous beginning to my field trip. But this I only vaguely realized, for I did not know how to sort out the effects of influence and the courtesies that were entirely routine.

But many a young fieldworker has known heartbreak in those first weeks. He has been made to feel so miserable, so unwelcomed, and so maligned—perhaps in terms of another anthropologist who got everyone's back up—that his whole field trip has been ruined before he has really got under way. These are the incalculable risks from which one can only try to protect one's students. But the factor of accident is great. Mrs. Freer might have been away from Honolulu when I arrived. Just that.

After two weeks I left, weighed down with flower leis, which in those days we threw from the ship's deck into the sea. Nowadays the Samoans give shell leis, because the admission of flowers and fruits into other ports is forbidden, and they bring a plastic bag in which to carry the leis home. But in those other days the ship's wake was bright with floating flowers.

And so I arrived in Samoa. Remembering Stevenson's rhapsodies, I was up at dawn to see with my own eyes how this, my first South Sea island, swam up over the horizon and came into view.

In Pago Pago there was no one to meet me. I had a letter of introduction from the Surgeon General of the Navy, who had been a fellow student of Luther's father at medical school. But that day everyone was too busy to pay attention to me. I found a room at the ramshackle hotel and hurried back to the square to watch the dances that had been arranged for the visitors from the ship. Everywhere there were black umbrellas. Most of the Samoans wore cotton clothes—the men were dressed in standard style and the women in heavy, unbecoming overblouses. Only the dancers wore Samoan dress. The chaplain, thinking I was a tourist with whom he could take liberties, turned over my Phi Beta Kappa key to look for my name. I said, "It isn't mine." And this confused things for many months afterward.

Then came the period that young fieldworkers find so trying, even today, no matter how hard we try to prepare them for it. I was in Samoa. I had a room in the hotel—the hotel that had been the scene of Somerset Maugham's story and play, *Rain*, which I had seen performed in New

York. I had letters of introduction. But I still had to establish some kind of base for my work. I called on the governor, an elderly and disgruntled man who had failed to attain the rank of admiral. When he told me that he had not learned the language and that I would not learn it either, I incautiously said that it was harder to learn languages after one was twenty-seven. That did not help.

Without the letter from the Surgeon General I do not know whether I would have been able to work as I wished. But that letter opened the doors of the Medical Department. The chief nurse, Miss Hodgeson, assigned a young Samoan nurse, G. F. Pepe, who had been in the United States and spoke excellent English, to work with me an hour a day.

I then had to design a way of working the rest of the time. I was very conscious of being on my own and yet of being responsible to the Fellowship Committee whose members had objected to giving me three months' stipend in advance. As there was no other way of measuring how hard I was working, I decided that I must at least work for eight hours a day. For one hour I was tutored by Pepe. The other seven I spent memorizing vocabulary and so, by accident, hit on the best way to learn a language, which is to learn as much of it as fast as possible so that each piece of learning reinforces each other piece.

I sat in the old hotel and ate the dreadful meals prepared by Fa'alavelave—whose name meant Misfortune—which were supposed to accustom me to Samoan food. Occasionally I was asked up to the hospital or to the home of one of the medical staff. The National Research Council had insisted on mailing my checks to me, and the next boat overcarried the mail. This meant that for six weeks I had no money and could not plan to leave until I had paid my hotel bill. Every day I walked about the port town and tried out Samoan phrases on the children, but it was not an atmosphere in which I could do field work.

Finally the boat arrived again. And now, with the help of the mother of the half-Samoan children I had met in Honolulu, I was able to move to a village. She arranged

In Vaitogi: in Samoan dress, with Fa'amotu

for me to spend ten days in Vaitogi and to live in the household of a chief who enjoyed entertaining visitors. It was there I had all my essential training in how to manage Samoan etiquette. His daughter Fa'amotu was my constant companion. We slept together on a pile of mats at the end of the sleeping house. We were given privacy from the rest of the family by a tapa curtain, but of course the house was open to the eyes of the whole village. When I bathed I had to learn to wear a sarong-like garment which I could slip off under the village shower as I slipped a dry one on in full view of the staring crowds of children and passing adults.

I learned to eat and to enjoy Samoan food and to feel unabashed when, as a guest, I was served first and the whole family sat about sedately waiting for me to finish so that they, in turn, could eat. I learned the complex courtesy phrases and how to pass kava—something I never did as it is only appropriate for an unmarried woman to do so. However, in Vaitogi I did not tell them that I was married; I knew too little about what the consequences might be in the roles that would be assigned to me. Day after day I grew easier in the language, sat more correctly, and suffered less pain in my legs. In the evenings there was dancing and I had my first dancing lessons.

It was a beautiful village with its swept plaza and tall, round, thatched guesthouses against the pillars of which the chiefs sat on formal occasions. I learned to recognize the leaves and plants used for weaving mats and making tapa. I learned how to relate to other people in terms of their rank and how to reply in terms of the rank they accorded me.

There was only one difficult moment when a visiting talking-chief from British Samoa started a conversation based on his experience with the freer sex world in the port of Apia. Still struggling with the new language, I explained that marriage would not be fitting owing to our respective ranks. He accepted the phrasing, but added regretfully, "White women have such nice fat legs."

At the end of the ten days, which were as delightful and satisfying as the previous six weeks had been laborious and frustrating, I returned to Pago Pago to prepare to go to the island of Tau in the Manu'a group. Everyone agreed that the Manu'an islands were much more old-fashioned and were, therefore, much better for my purposes. There was a medical post on Tau, and Ruth Holt, the wife of Chief Pharmacist's Mate Edward R. Holt, who was in charge of the post, was in Pago Pago having a baby. The chief medical officer arranged that I would live on the post, and I crossed over with Mrs. Holt and the new baby on a minesweeper that had temporarily replaced the station ship. In the dangerous landing through the reef a whaleboat carrying schoolchildren upset, and Mr. Holt was relieved to get his new baby, named Moana, safely ashore.

My living quarters were set up on the back veranda of the dispensary. A lattice separated my bed from the dispensary porch and I looked out across a small yard into the village. There was a Samoan-type house in front of the dispensary where I was to work with my adolescents. A Samoan pastor in the next village presented me with a girl who was to be my constant companion, as it would have been unsuitable for me ever to be alone. I set about working out living arrangements with the Holts, who also had a little boy, Arthur, who was not quite two years old and spoke both Samoan and English.

I soon found that having my base in the dispensary household was very useful, for had I lived in a Samoan household I could have had nothing to do with children. I was too important for that. People knew that when the fleet came in to Pago Pago I had dined on the admiral's flagship; that had established my rank. Reciprocally, I insisted that the Samoans call Mrs. Holt *faletua,* so that there would be no questions about where and with whom I ate.

Living in the dispensary, I could do things that otherwise would have been wholly inappropriate. The adolescent girls, and later the smaller girls whom I found I had also to study, came and filled my screen-room day after day and night after night. Later I borrowed a schoolhouse to give "examinations," and under that heading I was able to give a few simple tests and interview each girl alone. Away from the dispensary I could wander freely about the village or go on fishing trips or stop at a house where a woman was weaving. Gradually I built up a census of the whole village and worked out the background of each of the girls I was studying. Incidentally, of course, I learned a great deal of ethnology, but I never had any political participation in village life.

My field work was terribly complicated by a severe hurricane that knocked the front veranda off the dispensary, knocked down the house I was to have had as a workroom, and destroyed every house in the village and ruined the crops. Village ceremonies were almost completely halted while the village was being rebuilt and, after I had painfully learned to eat Samoan food, everyone had to live on rice and salmon sent over by the Red Cross. The Navy chaplain who was sent over to supervise the food distribution added to the crowding of our small house. In addition, his presence was deeply resented by Mr. Holt, who was only a chief pharmacist's mate because he had refused to go to college; now he smarted under every display of rank.

In all those months I had almost nothing to read, but it did not matter very much because I worked as many hours a day as I could stay awake. My only relief was writing letters. My accounts of life in family bulletins were fairly evenly balanced between pain and pleasure, but in my letters to friends I laid such heavy stress on points of difficulty that Ruth concluded I was having a hard and disappointing time. The truth was that I had no idea whether I was using the right methods. What were the right methods? There were no precedents to fall back on. I wrote to Professor Boas just before I left Pago Pago, outlining my plans. His reassuring answer arrived after I had finished my work on Tau and was ready to leave!

Still, it is letters that bring back to life that distant scene, and in one I wrote:

In Vaitogi: with Paulo

The pleasantest time of day here is at sunset. Then accompanied by some fifteen girls and little children I walk through the village to the end of Siufaga, where we stand on an iron bound point and watch the waves splash us in the face, while the sun goes down, over the sea and at the same time behind the cocoanut covered hills. Most of the adult population is going into the sea to bathe, clad in lavalavas with buckets for water borne along on shoulder poles. All the heads of families are seated in the *faletele* (village guesthouse) making kava. At one point a group of women are filling a small canoe with a solution of native starch (arrowroot). And perhaps, just as we reach the store, the curfew-angelus will stop us, a wooden bell will clang mellowly through the village: The children must all scurry to cover, if we're near the store, it's the store steps, and sit tight until the bell sounds again. Prayer is over. Sometimes we are all back safely in my room when the bell sounds, and then the Lord's Prayer must be said in English, while flowers are all taken out of their hair and the siva song stopped in the middle. But once the bell sounds again, solemnity, never of a very reliable depth, is sloughed off, the flowers replaced in the girls' hair, the siva song replaces the hymn, and they begin to dance, by no means in a puritan fashion. Their supper comes about eight and sometimes I have a breathing spell, but usually the supper hours don't jibe well enough for that. They dance for me a great deal; they love it and it is an excellent index to temperament, as the dance is so individualistic, and the audience thinks it is its business to keep up incessant comment. Between dances they look at my pictures. I am going to have to put Dr. Boas much higher on the wall, his picture fascinates them. . . .

The times I remember with most pleasure are the expeditions we made to other villages, to the other Manu'an islands, and to the other village on Tau, Fitiuta, where I lived like a visiting young village princess. I could summon informants to teach me anything I wanted to know; as a return courtesy, I danced every night. These expeditions came at the end of my field work, after I felt I had completed my project and so could "waste time" on ethnology by bringing up to date all the detail on ways in which Manu'a differed from the other islands.

On all my later field trips when I was working on cultures about which nothing was known, I had the more satisfactory task of learning the culture first and only afterward working on a special problem. In Samoa this was not necessary, and this is one reason why I was able to carry out my work on the life of the adolescent girl in nine months.

By studying the pre-adolescent girls I invented a cross-sectional method that can be used when one cannot stay many years in the field but wants to give a dynamic picture of how human beings develop. In Samoa I went back only one step. Later I went back to small children and then to infancy, realizing that I needed to include all the stages of growth. But in Samoa I was still under the influence of the psychology I had been taught, and I used case histories and tests that I invented, such as a picture-naming test, using pictures someone had sent me from a magazine story about Flaherty's *Moana of the South Seas,* and a color-naming test, for which I painted the hundred little squares.

When I wrote *Coming of Age in Samoa* I carefully disguised all the names, sometimes using double disguises so that the actual individuals could never be identified. In the introductions I wrote to new editions I did not include the girls I had studied among the readers for whom I was writing; it seemed extremely unlikely that any of them would ever learn to read English. Today, however, the children and grandchildren of girls like the ones I knew in Tau are attending American colleges—for nowadays half the Samoan population lives in the United States—and as their classmates read about the Samoans of fifty years ago, they wonder how what I have said applies to them.

12 Return from the Field

In June, 1926, I returned to Tutuila and two weeks later boarded a small ship in Pago Pago. These last weeks in Samoa were deeply nostalgic. I went back to Vaitogi, the village where I had first learned to sleep on a pile of mats and where Ufuti, the gentle chief who enjoyed entertaining visiting Americans, had presided over my learning how to pass kava correctly and how to pronounce the all-important courtesy speeches. My adopted family welcomed me as if I had been away for many years, and I had the sensation of returning home from a long voyage. Coming back to Vaitogi, I realized how homesick I had been and how starved for affection, a need that had been met only in part when I held the Holt children in my arms or played with the Samoan babies. It is the babies who keep me alive in contexts in which otherwise my sense of touch is seldom exercised. As Gregory Bateson phrased it later, it is not frustrated sex, it is frustrated gentleness that is so hard to bear when one is working for long months alone in the field. Some fieldworkers adopt a dog or a kitten; I much prefer babies. I realized now how lonely I had been, how much I wanted to be where someone else wanted me to be just because I was myself.

My adopted family comforted me, and I realized that they would gladly have cared for me for the rest of my life. Fa'amotu, my "sister," was planning to be married, and because I had remarked in some earlier, flowery speech that whereas Samoa excelled in courtesy, France excelled in making beautiful clothes, Fa'amotu wanted a wedding dress from Paris. That summer I bought it for her, in the Galerie Lafayette, but by the time it arrived, she had to write to me, "Makelita, make your heart smooth, do not be angry, but something awkward has happened, my fiancé has married someone else."

By the time I had spent a week in Vaitogi one part of my homesickness had been assuaged. I had come home again, albeit to a home I had not known a year ago. This made me all the more aware of a far more fierce longing—longing for conversation and contact with people of my own kind, people who had read the same books and would understand my allusions, people who would understand my work, people with whom I could discuss what I had been doing and would give me some perspective on whether I had actually done what I had been sent out to do. I had had to invent every method I used, even the tests I had tried to give, and I had no way of knowing whether what I had done was good or not.

When I left Pago Pago I was setting out on a six-week ocean voyage to Europe. When I arrived there, I would no longer be alone. Luther, who had spent an interesting but somewhat lonely year traveling and trying to understand a world that was new to him, would be waiting for me. Ruth Benedict, who was accompanying her husband to a conference in Scandinavia, planned to meet me in Paris. Louise Rosenblatt, my college roommate, had spent a year at the University of Grenoble and also was coming to Paris. But meanwhile the letters that had descended on me in the field in intermittent downpours, sometimes seventy or eighty at a time, would cease. There could be no more correspondence; letters would have traveled at the same slow pace as mine. All this made me feel extraordinarily alone.

During the voyage from Pago Pago to Sydney we weathered one of the worst storms that had struck the South Pacific for many decades. Eleven ships were lost at sea. On our ship the waves poured over the top deck and the passengers went down like ninepins, deathly ill. There were several interesting people on board, including one of the ship's officers, who had been an officer on the *Titanic* and who now lived like a man without a country, far from home. But there was also a miserable, under-nourished missionary couple from Western Samoa, who had a two-year-old child and a tiny baby. Like almost everyone else, the parents went down speechless with seasickness. A woman of doubtful reputation, who had brightly dyed hair, shared the care of the baby with her assorted men friends. I took charge of the two-year-old, who spoke no English and would certainly have been traumatized by the experience of having no one understand a word he said. I felt somewhat sorry for myself, miraculously not seasick and so ready for a little gaiety, when, instead, I found myself tied down with the care of a small child. But from this experience I learned what it must mean to a young child to be abruptly separated from everyone who can understand what it has just learned to say, whether this is because other adults do not speak the same language or because there has been so much private family slang in the early learning. What the desperation must be of children who are orphaned by war and then are adopted half the world away, it is hard even to guess for those who have never experienced such total estrangement. Almost fifty years later I can still hear that mournful, distressed little voice saying, *"Ua pau le famau, Makelita, au pau le famau"*—the button has fallen off.

When at last we arrived at Sydney, I was met by cousins of a friend of Luther's, their arms full of flowers from their own garden. This was my first city after nine months in outstations. They took me to hear the Don Cossacks and the Vatican choir. Then, two days later, I boarded the P. and O. luxury liner, the S.S. *Chitral*, sailing on her maiden voyage to England.

Of course, I can never know how differently that whole trip—and so my own life—might have turned out had the *Chitral* sailed to Tasmania, as planned, to pick up a cargo of apples. However, there was a dock strike in England, so apples were an unsafe cargo. Instead of sailing to Tasmania and then proceeding directly to England, the

Chitral loitered several days in Sydney Harbor, while most of the passengers stayed ashore and the dining room was all but empty. But a few passengers, people like myself who had little money and no reason for staying in the city, did board the ship. Among them was a young New Zealand psychologist, Reo Fortune, who had just won a two-year fellowship to Cambridge University as a prize for an essay he had written on dreams. The chief steward, noticing that we enjoyed each other's company, suggested that we might like a table to ourselves. For we were talking so eagerly that the miscellaneous others at a larger table were simply an impediment. We accepted the offer happily. Coming as I did from a world in which intellectual exchange did not automatically imply an affair, I had no idea how this move would be viewed by the Australian passengers.

Both Reo and I were in a state of profound excitement. He was going to England to meet people who would understand what he was talking about, and I, just emerging from the field, was hungering and thirsting for communication. In many ways innocent and inexperienced, Reo was unlike anyone I had ever known. He had never seen a play professionally performed; he had never seen an original painting by a great artist or heard music played by a symphony orchestra. But to make up for the isolation in which New Zealanders lived in the days before modern communications, he had read deeply and with delight, ranging through the whole of English literature, and he had eagerly taken hold of whatever he could find on psychoanalysis. It was like meeting a stranger from another planet, but a stranger with whom I had a great deal in common.

Reo had saturated himself in the work of W. H. R. Rivers, the Cambridge don whose work in physiology, psychoanalysis, and ethnology had excited people right around the world. I had never met Rivers and, of course, neither had Reo. But we both knew he was the man under whom we would like to have studied—a shared and impossible daydream, because he had died in 1922. Rivers had been interested in evolution and in the unconscious mind and its early origins in man's precursors. He had been fascinated by Freud, but was critical of his theories. With the kind of insight that was so characteristic of him, Reo had pointed out in his prize-winning essay that what Rivers had done was to stand Freud on his head, without changing the premises, by making fear, instead of libido, the driving force in man.

Reo had studied sleep, all by himself, by sleeping in the psychology laboratory and waking himself to test whether the first hours of a stretch of sleep were, or were not, more restful than the later hours. He was interested in the question, raised by Freud, as to whether all the dreams dreamt on one night were on the same theme. Quite early in the voyage I began to dream and to record my dreams for him. I got up to eight in one night with a main theme and two minor themes. One of these dreams, very slightly disguised, appears in his book *The Mind in Sleep*.

The ship loitered on and spent days in every port. In Melbourne we went to the theater. While I was in Samoa, Ruth had written to me about Bronislaw Malinowski's visit to America, and I told Reo about him. Her comments had not been entirely flattering, for Malinowski enjoyed presenting himself in public as a Don Juan, and gossip had added to the repertoire of his own stories. Very likely most of this was a pose, but in Reo's New Zealand eyes, his behavior appeared to be that of a shocking roué.

Argonauts of the Western Pacific, Malinowski's first great book on the Trobriands, was published while I was a graduate student, but I did not read it at that time. A rather inadequate report on the book had been presented in the anthropology graduate seminar, where our discussion had focused on the mechanics of the *kula,* the interisland trading complex analyzed in the book, rather than on Malinowski's theories and methods of field work, which were not as electrifying to Boas' students as they were to students in Britain. However, Ruth's letters had roused my curiosity, and at Adelaide, Reo and I went ashore, found the University library, and read the article on anthropology that Malinowski had contributed to the latest supplement to the *Encyclopaedia Britannica.* I had mentioned that I intended to go to the meeting of the British Association for the Advancement of Science that summer, before the Congress of Americanists in Rome. Reo was already fascinated by Malinowski, but he was also jealously determined that I should not go to the meeting in England, where, he was convinced, Malinowski would certainly seduce me.

The long saga of his one-sided internal debate with Malinowski, a debate that was deeply tinged with oedipal overtones, had begun. Later, on his first lonely field trip to Dobu, an island adjacent to the Trobriands and one of those included in the discussion of the *kula,* Reo pored night after night over *Argonauts,* which had become for him a model for the development of fieldwork techniques, a set of theories to argue over, and a way of dramatizing life. In 1963, in a new introduction to a paperback edition of *Sorcerers of Dobu,* Reo's abidingly valuable first book, he joined the argument again, an argument that gains nothing in clarity from the degree of emotional involvement with which it is laden.

When Reo finished the manuscript of *Sorcerers of Dobu,* I wrote to Malinowski and suggested that it might be politic for him to write an introduction to the book, since otherwise reviewers might well make too much of certain interpretations of the *kula* that differed from his own. Malinowski agreed, and his long, appreciative introduction assured both the book's acceptance by Routledge in England and the immediate interest it roused on publication.

Still, I never met Malinowski until 1939, although he had again come into my life in another way. In 1926, during his American visit, Malinowski had gone out of his way to tell everyone that my field trip to Samoa would come to nothing, that nine months was too short a time to accomplish any serious research, and that I probably would not even learn the language. Then, in 1930, when *Growing Up in New Guinea* was published, he inspired one of his students to write a review in which it was said that I had, of course, not understood the kinship system, which had been mediated by a school-boy interpreter. Whether I would have been half so angry had the criticism come from anyone else, I do not know, but I was so enraged that I got our next field trip postponed for three months while I wrote my monograph, *Kinship in the Admiralty Islands,* to demonstrate the full extent of my knowledge of the subject.

So Malinowski, who did in fact play a role in England that was somewhat similar to the one played by Ruth and myself in the United States, both in making anthropology accessible to a wider public and in relating anthropology to other disciplines, came into our lives through the accident of a meeting on board a ship that was loitering along the coast of Australia and rolling because its hold was empty.

By the time we arrived at Adelaide, most of the passengers had joined the ship. However, owing to the chief steward's maneuver, Reo and I were almost completely isolated. One kindly English naval captain and his sisters talked to me occasionally, but for the most part we were left severely alone.

Then came the fancy dress ball. As neither of us had a costume, we gladly accepted the chief steward's offer to lend us, as costumes, outfits of the lascar crew, specially washed and pressed for the occasion. As a masking device that added verisimilitude to our dress, we blackened our faces. When we arrived in these costumes for the masked dinner, the chief steward gleefully proposed—and we had no way of knowing that this, too, was pure mischief—that he seat us at the captain's table. The friendly English naval officer and his sister also were seated there, and he muttered, "We know who you are!" Otherwise we were frigidly ignored.

After dinner the naval officer made a point of telling us that we owed the captain an apology. It was an intolerable insult, he said, to go to his table dressed as filthy black lascars who did the dirtiest work on the ship. He had also talked with the captain who, apparently, had not known that he had been insulted. Convinced that we

had gone where the chief steward had directed us, Reo
flared up in anger and was against making an apology,
but I smarted as if I had been accused—as in one of
Mother's stories—of eating peas with my knife. I insisted
that of course you apologized for an unintended dis-
courtesy. So we sent our cards up to the captain. When
Reo, looking very handsome, flushed and straight, made
a stiff and unbending apology, the captain, uncertain and
defensive, started to bluster. Clearly, we had reached an
impasse, but when I explained that in the United States
"black face" was an accepted masking role, the captain
subsided. Back in the lounge, the naval officer compli-
mented us for having apologized. This really infuriated
me, and I said so. After that he did not talk with us.

Now we were completely isolated on the big ship,
eating three meals together, so enthralled by what we
were talking about that we had to be shooed away from
the table by the impatient waiters, and spending the
evenings at the very bow of the ship where the spray
came in and the sea sometimes seemed to be on fire. No
doubt everyone on shipboard thought we were having an
affair. We were not, but we were falling in love, with all
the possibility of a relationship that I felt was profoundly
unsuitable. Reo was so young, so inexperienced, so fiercely
ambitious, and so possessively jealous of any fleeting
glance I gave another person.

Reo told me stories about his Irish grandfather who was
said to have locked his wife in the kitchen with a stallion,
telling her, "I hope he damn well stamps you to death!"
This was romantic, possibly not true, but terrifying; it
was certainly not the stuff of which my life had been
made. He was proud of his father who, within a few
years of his retirement as an Anglican clergyman, had
gone to his bishop and said, "My lord, I have lost my
faith," and had left the church to become a pioneering
farmer. He described to me, too, how his father had become passionately attached to the younger sister of his
wife, how this young aunt had comforted Reo when his
younger brother was born, and how terribly he had
suffered when she went away and he felt he had lost her.

He told me also about Eileen, the girl with whom he was in love and for whom he had written a long series of poems. She had refused him, and he was suffering from unrequited love as well as from passionate ambition. He told me that he had thought of going somewhere and reading Blake, nothing but Blake, until he had induced in himself the state of mind in which Blake had created a new mythology.

I talked about anthropology and the kinds of problems anthropology was preparing to investigate. I said that with the grounding I had received from Boas I hoped that in ten years I might add something original to anthropological theory. Reo answered that he meant to add something original immediately.

The weeks wore on. We had a day ashore in Ceylon. We came to Aden. We saw the shores of Sicily. And finally we approached Marseille. Reo was going on to England to stay with an aunt and prepare for Cambridge. But Luther was coming to meet me and I was leaving the ship. When the ship docked, we were still deep in debate and did not realize it. Finally, sensing that the ship was not moving, we walked around the deck and saw Luther standing on the dock, wondering what had happened to me. That is one of the moments I would take back and live differently, if I could. There are not many such moments, but that is one of them.

And so I came to Europe for the first time, not across the stormy Atlantic but the longest way around and after living for nine months in Samoa. Luther wanted to show me the kinds of things he had been exploring. He took me to Provence—to Nîmes, where Louise Rosenblatt joined us, and to Les Baux—and then to Carcassonne. Both Luther and Louise were full of their year in France. I was preoccupied with my field experience, which I found it hard to convey, with the intensity of those shipboard conversations, and with ideas that were not the ones that occupied my companions. But those days remain etched in my mind. Finally, in Carcassonne, I rechose Luther.

From southern France we went to Paris, where Ruth

had come from Sweden and many other friends were spending their holiday. But Luther could not stay in Paris with us. He had finally given up the ministry and had been offered a teaching position at City College, where he had taught earlier. Now he had to return home in order to prepare for his teaching. And in the midst of all our discussions, while we were still catching up with the news, hunting for one another in the cafés, and going to the theater to see *The Captive* and *The Dybbuk,* Reo arrived from England, determined to make me change my mind.

Finally, I went to Rome to meet Ruth again. She had had an unhappy summer. She had been alone part of the time and was deeply depressed. But she had cut her hair and appeared with a silver helmet of white hair, her early beauty restored. We had a week together in Rome, during which we got locked in the Protestant cemetery, sitting by Keats' grave, and had to ring the bell specially made for all the visitors who linger on after sunset. At the Congress of Americanists there was a great fanfare for Mussolini and a sober, subdued greeting for the assembled scientists.

I was to meet Reo in Paris again, but a railroad tunnel was blocked and when we woke up in the morning, our train was still in Italy. However, Reo came to the boat to see me off. Ten days on that slow boat and we were in New York. All my college friends were on the dock to meet me, and I was overwhelmed with news. Léonie had been very unhappy, Pelham had fallen in love, Luther had found us an apartment. Without a pause, I plunged into my first job as Assistant Curator of Ethnology at the American Museum of Natural History.

But things were changed. My trip was romantic and people wanted to hear about it, while Luther had been to Europe—like everyone else. "Is it to be, do you think, a case of Mrs. Browning's husband?" he asked good-naturedly as we came home from a party given for me by Mrs. Ogburn, a party at which she had asked, "But do they have table manners?" and I had answered, "They have finger bowls, Mrs. Ogburn."

It was an odd winter. Luther was teaching anthropology, which meant that I became a resource at breakfast. But we had married with the expectation of having a common vocation working with people within the framework of the church. Now this was gone, and with it much of the sense of a shared purpose. My new job gave me time to write, and I finished *Coming of Age in Samoa*, all but the last two chapters in which I related my findings to American life. I also began to do over the Museum's Maori collection with the help of the New Zealand specialist H. D. Skinner, who was visiting New York.

Reo, in Cambridge, was nominally studying psychology, but he was finding it difficult to relate to the men he was working under, F. C. Bartlett and John T. McCurdy. At Cambridge he also got to know the professor of anthropology, A. C. Haddon, and began to think of shifting to anthropology and working in New Guinea. He wrote me, "Haddon is very kind to me but he gave Gregory Bateson his mosquito net"—which was the first time I heard Gregory's name. Finally, Reo received permission from the executors of his New Zealand fellowship to use the rest of his grant money to publish his newly completed study of dreams, *The Mind in Sleep,* which, being subsidized as a trade publication, never got any scientific hearing at all. He had decided to leave Cambridge and hoped to get an anthropological grant through A. R. Radcliffe-Brown, who was developing a lively research center at the University of Sydney in Australia. He wrote me all this, and our correspondence was punctuated by the verses we wrote each other.

My picture of my own future was changing also. Luther and I had always planned to have a lot of children—six, I thought. It had been our plan to live a life of great frugality in a country rectory with a whole parish of people who needed us and a house full of children of our own. I was confident of the kind of father he would make. But that autumn a gynecologist told me that I never would be able to have children. I had a tipped uterus, a condition that could not be corrected; if I attempted to have a child, I was told, I would always miscarry early.

This changed the whole picture of the future. I had always expected to adjust my professional life to wifehood and motherhood. But if there was to be no motherhood, then a professional partnership of field work with Reo, who was actively interested in the problems I cared about, made more sense than cooperation with Luther in his career of teaching sociology. (In fact, he later became a first-rate archeologist, working in a discipline that brought into play all his skills with physical things as well as his human sensitivity. But that was later.) One of my principal reasons for not wanting to marry Reo was my feeling that he would not make the kind of father I wanted for my children. But if there were to be no children . . .

In the spring Reo wrote to me that he had been awarded a fellowship by the Australian National Research Council to do field work and that he was going to Sydney. I agreed to meet him in Germany, where I could make a study of Oceanic materials in German museums. Our summer meeting was tempestuous, but Reo was filled with exciting ideas and when we parted I had agreed to marry him.

I returned to New York to say good-bye to Luther. We spent a placid week together, unmarred by reproaches or feelings of guilt. At the end of it, he sailed for England to see the girl whom he later married and who became the mother of his daughter.

I went to live with three college friends. We spent an affectionate but troubled winter while all of them struggled with various forms of heartbreak. I continued my interest in dreams, and Léonie told us her dreams that later were transformed into poems. That winter she applied for a Guggenheim Fellowship and I insisted on including in her application the fact that she had 119 hours of A in her college record. Sure enough, when she went for her interview with Henry Allen Moe, who directed the Guggenheim Foundation for so many years, he said, "I was so impressed"—in a tone that made her expect him to add "with your beautiful poem 'Homecoming,'" for this was the poem most likely to evoke that tone, but he sighed—"with your wonderful academic record!", I felt that I was really beginning to learn the culture.

Coming of Age was accepted for publication. I had added two chapters which I based on lectures I gave to a working girls' club, where I had a chance to try out my ideas on a mixed audience. That same winter I wrote *Social Organization of Manu'a,* an ethnographic monograph designed for a technical audience. At the Museum new cases were made for the tower room into which I moved the Maori collection, and I wrote a small guide for it. This gave me the feeling that I was making a modest beginning as a museum curator.

The most difficult task ahead of me was to get funds to go out to New Guinea to work with Reo after our marriage. Such anthropological rendezvous are as complicated to arrange as the storied encounters of separated lovers. Each person has to get separate funds from separate sources and plan life so that the two of you will end up at the same time in the same part of the world with scientific mandates that make it feasible for you to work together in the same place. It takes a fair bit of maneuvering. Reo was already assured a second year of research work on the basis of the reports he was making from Dobu. Now it was up to me.

In reading Freud, Lévy-Bruhl, and Piaget, all of whom assumed that primitives and children had a great deal in common—and Freud added that both were like neurotics —I had become interested in the problem of what primitive *children* were like, if primitive *adults* resembled our children in their thinking. It seemed an obvious problem, but no one had raised the question. While I was struggling with the whole problem of how to apply Freudian hypotheses to primitive behavior, I wrote two articles, "An Ethnologist's Footnote to Totem and Taboo" and "A Lapse of Animism among a Primitive People," a paper in which I discussed the fact that the kind of prelogical thinking that Lévy-Bruhl and Freud were talking about did not occur among the Samoans I had studied. This was a subject that I wanted to pursue in the field, and I applied for a Social Science Research

Fellowship to study "the thought of the pre-school child" in the Admiralty Islands, where Radcliffe-Brown had suggested that Reo and I do our field work. The phrase "pre-school child" sounded very strange when it was applied to children in a primitive group without any schools, but this was the fashionable way of referring to children under five.

In order to marry Reo I had to get a divorce, get the fellowship, and also obtain Goddard's permission to take a year's leave of absence from the Museum. When I confided that this also involved a romance, he cheerfully cooperated with my plans. In addition, I had to prepare for the field. Among many other things, this meant assembling a set of tests and toys for my work with children, something that had to be done from scratch as there were no precedents to draw on.

It was a difficult winter in another way as well. All my friends knew that I intended to marry Reo, but Luther did not want anyone to know that he, too, was remarrying. I saw him frequently to discuss his plans. This shocked my father, who held to the opinion so common in earlier generations that it was revolting—somehow like incest—for a couple who were getting a divorce to spend time together. It shocked my friends, too. They felt that I was exploiting Luther and trifling with his affections, and I found it very hard to live through a situation that was so grossly misinterpreted. The only thing that alleviated it was my knowledge that in the end everyone would know the truth.

Nevertheless I found it difficult to bear the fact that most of my friends, when they had time to spare from their own complicated lives, were accusing me of heartlessness. So I was relieved when our composite household, which in the end contained five of us, was dissolved in June. Ruth was teaching in summer school that year and came to live with me. At the end of the summer she left for the field and I started on the long journey to Manus. When I went away I had seen only a dummy copy of my first book and it was many months before I learned that it had become a best seller.

13 Manus: The Thought of Primitive Children

We had planned to marry in Sydney. But while I was on the way Reo, responding to Radcliffe-Brown's persistent disbelief that I would really marry him, became restive and changed his mind. When my ship docked at Auckland, New Zealand, Reo appeared on board and announced that we were getting married that day. There was no wedding ring small enough and we got one altered just in time to reach the registry office before it closed and to make a dash for the ship before it sailed. So we arrived in Sydney and presented Radcliffe-Brown with a *fait accompli*.

It had been decided that we would work in the Admiralty Islands, among the Manus people, because this was an area where no modern ethnographer had done research. As far as I myself was concerned, I simply wanted to work among some Melanesian people in order to enlarge my experience for the Museum and to study the way in which primitive adults, who were said to think like civilized children, differed from primitive children. Reo had talked with a man who had been a government officer in Manus and he had advised Reo to work with the sea-dwelling people off the south coast of Manus, as life was so much pleasanter there. We found some old Manus texts that had been collected by a German missionary and a short account of the people by the German explorer Richard Parkinson. This was all we knew.

When we arrived in Rabaul, which was then the capital of the Mandated Territory of New Guinea, we were met by the government anthropologist E. P. W. Chinnery, who offered to lend us a Manus schoolboy, Bonyalo, to help us get started with the language. Bonyalo was not at all happy to be sent back to Manus, but he had no choice. From Rabaul we went out to Manus, with Bonyalo in tow, and spent some ten days as guests of the district officer while arrangements were made for us to settle in a village. By chance we heard that Manuwai, another boy from Bonyalo's village, was just finishing his work time. Reo went to interview and recruit him. This gave us two boys from the same village, Peri, and we decided that we would go there to work. Forty years later Manuwai still liked to tell the story of his amazement when the strange young white man appeared and addressed him in the language of his village.

It was arranged that the paramount leader on the south coast would take us and our supplies to Peri in a big canoe. The sea journey, begun in the early morning, took until midnight when, very hungry because Reo had insisted it would embarrass the Manus if we took food along, we poled into the still, moonlit village. The dome-shaped houses stood high on piles in the shallow lagoon amid tiny islands of palm trees. The mainland—Manus—was a dark shadow in the distance.

My first quarterly report was due in New York and so, on that first day, we worked very fast photographing the people—the men with their hair tied up in psyche knots, their arms and legs adorned with beaded bands of paraminium nut gum, and the women with their heads shaven and their earlobes distended, their necks and arms hung about with the hair and bones of the dead. The central lagoon was alive with canoes as people set off with loads of fresh and smoked fish to trade in the market for taro, betel nuts, bananas, and pepper leaves. The Manus, we found, were a trading people whose whole life centered around exchanges—exchanges in markets with the people of distant islands for large objects like tree trunks and turtles and exchange among themselves that focused on marriage payments in which indestructible valuables—

dog's teeth, shell money, and in recent times, beads—were given in return for consumable food and clothing.

Thus began the best field trip we ever had. Reo's Dobuans were a dour group of sorcerers; every man's hand was turned against his closest neighbors and every married person lived during alternate years among in-laws who were hostile and dangerous. So he was delighted with our new people, who were so much more open and unsuspicious. However, it took him a long time to realize that they were not holding back dread secrets. On one occasion we were working at opposite ends of a house—I with the women gathered around a corpse and Reo with the men. Periodically canoe-loads of mourners arrived, ran the length of the house, and threw themselves lamenting on the corpse. The floor of the pile house trembled dangerously and the women implored me to leave; they feared that at any moment the house floor might collapse and we might all fall into the sea. I sent a note to Reo telling him what they proposed. He wrote back, "Stay where you are. They are probably up to something they don't want you to see." So I refused to go. Finally, the people, who had been thinking about my safety and were not up to anything, moved the mourning to another house in which I would be safe.

Each of us had already learned one Oceanic language and now we worked together on the Manus language. Our first informant was Bonyalo, the schoolboy who had been lent us by the government in Rabaul and who spoke a little—a very little—English. Neither of us knew any pidgin English, the lingua franca of the area, and so we had to learn pidgin as we learned Manus, a clumsy and roundabout task. When Bonyalo, who was unbelievably dense, could not explain what *mwelmwel* was—it was, in fact, a whole expensive array of bridal finery made of shell money and dog's teeth—Reo ordered him to go and get one of whatever it was. I can still hear Bonyalo's startled, "Kis em along whosat?" much as one of us might reply had we been ordered to bring in a whole bedroom suite to illustrate a point of grammar.

I was as surprised at the ways in which the Manus were

With Reo Fortune in Peri Village, Manus

Reo Fortune with Ngasu

less pleasant than the Samoans as Reo was surprised at the ways in which they were so much more pleasant than the Dobuans. And neither of us identified with them. They were a puritanical, materialistic, driving people and they were driven relentlessly by their ghostly mentors, who punished them for the slightest sexual misdemeanor, like accidentally brushing against a member of the opposite sex when a house floor collapsed, or for gossiping, as when two women were heard talking about their husbands. The ghosts punished people for not meeting their innumerable economic obligations, and if they had met them, for not contracting new ones. Life for the Manus was very much like continually walking up a down escalator. The men died early; they did not live to see their sons' children born. They tolerated us as long as we had something they wanted and even at times showed a certain amount of solicitude for our well-being. But this did not extend to selling us fish when we ran out of trade tobacco. It was, in fact, a very utilitarian relationship. The children were delightful, but I always had before my eyes the kind of adults they would soon become.

In Manus we were not caught up in the kind of partisanship that results from differences in temperamental fit or misfit, which became so important in our later field work. We competed fairly good-humoredly. Reo had as his main informant Pokanau, a misanthropic intellectual who growled at me, when I came back twenty-five years later, "What did you come for? Why did you come instead of Moeyap?" I had Lalinge, Pokanau's principal rival. He was horrified at the exposed position of a woman alone in a village with no one to turn to but her husband, and volunteered to serve as a brother so that I would have someone to run away to if Reo were to beat me. When we bought artifacts—Reo for the Sydney Museum and I for the American Museum of Natural History —everyone delighted in the rivalry of which specimen went into which pile. But the Manus are not a devious people, and the usual New Guinea style in which house servants play off the master and mistress against each other was less pronounced than it was on other, later trips. Perhaps this was so because our whole staff was under fourteen years old. I found having older boys about the place too complicating, and so we had a kind of kindergarten cookhouse, occasionally enlivened by battles in which our dinner went hurtling into the sea.

It was a hard-working life with almost no pleasures. Reo thought it was a waste of time to make bread, so we had no bread. Our mainstay was smoked fish and taro. Once someone brought us a chicken. which I roasted and put away in the food safe, but a dog broke in and stole it. And once I opened our only precious tin of hors d'oeuvres because the captain of a trading schooner said he was coming to dinner, and then the tide turned and he sailed away. We both had bouts of malaria. In order to

With Ponkiau, Bopau, and Tchokal

avoid the children's continual importunate demands for cigarettes, I said I did not smoke—Reo smoked a pipe—and only late at night when the village was asleep did I occasionally smoke a cigarette, feeling very much like a delinquent schoolgirl. When our camp beds broke, we had to substitute "New Guinea beds"—tubes of heavy cloth through which are thrust poles that are fastened at both ends to crossed sticks. Invariably, these beds sag until you feel as though you were sleeping in a tight bag.

But we enjoyed our work and Reo began to perfect what I later called event analysis—a method of organizing observations around the principal events in the village. Friendly competition between us as to the areas we worked on and the methods of study we used enlivened what was otherwise a very workaday world. Although the lagoons appeal to present-day visitors for their tropical beauty, we shared in the local attitudes. The reef was a constant threat. The distant mountains of the mainland-island seemed gloomy and hostile, either because of the spirits and ghosts in which the people believed or because of the surly living people who inhabited them. The village at night was not a place for dancing and singing as it had been in Samoa, nor was it a place in which sorcery stalked abroad, as in Dobu. It was a place in which moralistic and avenging spirits struck down evil-doers and one household was avenged against another. Girls were kept strictly indoors, and canoe-loads of boys and young men, not yet able to marry because the economics of their marriage exchanges had not been completed, paddled aimlessly about the village beating slit gongs or planning to run away to work for the white man.

Reo concentrated on texts, once he had trained Pokanau to dictate the contents of last night's séance. He took everything down in longhand, and twenty-five years later Pokanau enthusiastically acclaimed the pidgin English typing I had developed. "Much better than waiting for Moeyap's pen," he commented. "Now I will put it all in." The "all" simply meant an incredible number of repetitions, which would certainly have broken even

Reo's indomitable industry if he had had to write them all down in longhand.

Having no way of knowing whether even the very shallow time perspective was accurate, we did not probe deeply into the past. When I returned in 1953, I checked everything—the position of the houses and the alignments of economic combinations as they were in 1928—and found that their memories were so meticulously accurate that I knew it was safe to go back another twenty-five years and fill in more history. But in the short run there is no way of testing the accuracy of the tales told by a people who lack written records.

In 1953, the Manus and I shared the memories of that first stay in the village: how Moeyap had sewed up the great cut in Ngaleap's knee; how we had chartered Master Kramer's little schooner and had gone to visit the islands of Lou and Balowan; how the Lou people had wanted us to sleep in a miserable leaky house; and how our small boys had come back chanting Balowan obscenities with salacious glee. This insistent pickup of some incidental moment and pickling it in a chant is a characteristic of New Guinea children. In 1953, the smallest boys, when they met me, used to chant, *"Aua nat e jo um e jo lau we?"*—You little boys of mine, where is my house? This was a phrase I had once used to them, perhaps with a special emphasis.

Our field work progressed steadily. By June, 1929, when we had been in Manus for six months, we were reasonably well satisfied with the materials we had in hand. The Manus were—and still are—a fishing people. Their lives move in monthly cycles while they wait for the fish to come over the reef and then, during a period of intense activity, they fish and bring in the catch. The rhythm of their life is very different from that of an agricultural people, among whom it is essential to watch the whole annual cycle from seeding to harvest and from harvest to the "time-hungry" when people may be tempted to eat their reserved seed.

We had seen death, and without witnessing a death one cannot feel that one understands very much about a people. Manuwai, our very vain and handsome young cook, had had his ears pierced with much ceremonial ritual. Kiteni, a young girl, had reached puberty and I had taken part in the month-long girls' slumber party that marked this big event, of which she retained as a souvenir—much as debutantes used to save the pictures of their coming-out party—a handsome set of fish skeletons from all the fish that had been caught to feed her and her friends. We had counted and recorded innumerable transactions in dog's teeth and shell money, and the people said, "Now we won't have to quarrel anymore, for the Piyap can write it all down." It was for this reason most of all that, after a few more big feasts, they expected to welcome the Catholic Mission, for then they themselves could learn how to keep written accounts.

I had collected a great mass of materials, of which the most important were children's drawings, 35,000 of them. For when I found, contrary to all expectations, that these "primitive children" showed not a trace of the easy animism of our own children, who draw the man in the moon and houses with faces, it was necessary to collect a very large amount of material. This is one of the problems of field work. As long as what one is looking for is something positive—do a people, for example, have a ceremony that marks a girl's puberty?—it is only necessary to see and record one such ceremony, filled with elaborate detail, to be able to affirm that they do, and not only that they do, but also what kind of thing is done in the course of the ceremony. There will be, of course, many variations that may depend on a thousand things—whether the girl's father is prosperous or poor, whether she has sisters, whether she is the eldest, and—in Manus—how many aunts she has, for they have to be represented in a special ceremony in which the girl is ducked in the sea. But once one has recorded one such ceremony, a great many details about variations can be fitted in from a knowledge of other parts of the culture.

A comparable example would be an account of graduation ceremonies in the United States, perhaps in the year 1970, when college campuses were irritable and nervous.

If the general pattern was known—the caps and gowns, the processional music, the honorary degrees and the portentous commencement speaker, the long line of students coming up for their diplomas, and the relatives breaking out of the crowd to photograph their sons and daughters—then all the special variations characteristic of that year's ceremonies could be fitted into the known pattern. Whether the students refused to wear caps and gowns, or the faculty refused to attend the ceremony because the students had refused to wear caps and gowns, or the students sulkily consented to wear caps and gowns, or the rumor spread that all the new graduates would come nude beneath their gowns—any of this could be treated as a significant variation of an accepted custom. Whether the alma mater was sung, or was not sung, or was sung with tongue in cheek, the customary inclusion of the alma mater was part of it all. So patterns of behavior that are active and positive and involve events that can be photographed and tape-recorded—that can even be photographed and tape-recorded without the presence of an anthropologist to pick and choose—are relatively easy to study.

But it is much more difficult in anthropological field work to deal with a negative case—to study, for example, what happens among a people who give no formal recognition at all to a girl's attainment of puberty. For the inexplicit patterns of behavior that take the place of explicit ceremonial and ritual patterns are much more difficult to get at.

In the same way, it is seldom necessary to collect more than some one hundred drawings in order to show that children draw human beings in the same style as their elders do. But if their elders do not draw human beings at all, it will take thousands of drawings to demonstrate what the children, untaught in any positive way, will do when they are asked to draw a human being. For the Arapesh, the Iatmul, and the Balinese, I have small but adequate collections of children's drawings. In each case—stick figures among the Arapesh, stylized designs among the Iatmul, and, among the Balinese, vivid reproductions of shadow-play puppets, made by the boys, and human figures in a kind of confectionery, made by the girls—the style of children's drawings was congruent with the adult style. But when I found that Manus children, far from seeing the world even in as slightly animated terms as their elders did, drew only the most careful representations of real things, I had to go on and on until, finally, I decided that 35,000 examples were enough. And twenty-five years later, when I asked for drawings from grown men—the men who as small boys had drawn for me day after day with apparent delight, but who never drew again after I left—they reproduced so faithfully their earlier individual versions of the group style that I could have placed any one of them from memory.

At the end of our field work in Manus we intended to go to the United States, where Reo had been awarded a graduate fellowship at Columbia University. The alternative would have been to go to New Zealand where, Reo said, I could write up my field notes while he went to work as a navvy, that is, as an unskilled laborer. This was a kind of romanticism in reverse that I had sense enough not to undertake, even though I had premonitions, after I finally heard how well my first book was doing, that life was going to be uncomfortable for Reo in a country in which I was at home and already well-known, but he was a stranger and had published, in England, a small specialized book that no one in America had read. His Dobuan work—not yet published, of course—would be his first anthropological book, and there was one terrible gap in his material. His camera had broken and was not repaired in time for him to use it. He had no photographs, and an anthropological book without photographs was almost unthinkable. What to do?

When we reached Rabaul and went up to lunch with the hospitable Judge Phillips, who became our firmest anchor in New Guinea for many years, we were still turning over in our minds whether it would be feasible for us to get off the boat at Samarai, where I would stay in a hotel while Reo, now equipped with a working camera, made his way to the tiny Dobuan island of

Tewara and took photographs. Somehow this came up at lunch, and in a matter of minutes Monty Phillips produced a solution. He was looking for someone to write the life of a famous pioneer woman, Mrs. Parkinson. She had been badly victimized by an American adventurer who, after promising to write up her life and quartering his family on her for months, had left without producing a word. This was just the opportunity. I could go down to Sumsum, Mrs. Parkinson's plantation, and Reo, traveling light without a lot of gear, could go to Dobu. By then we had exactly two hours to go down to the harbor, get boxes out of the hold of the ship, and re-sort our belongings. Fortunately, we just made it. Although the sun shone only three days during the six weeks Reo spent in Dobu, he got enough pictures to illustrate his book.

Meanwhile I listened to the story of Phebe Parkinson, one of the most remarkable women of her time. Her father was the nephew of an American bishop; he had married into a Samoan family and became American consul in Western Samoa. In 1881, Phebe had come to New Guinea on a sailing vessel as the young wife of a German engineer and explorer. Richard Parkinson had been reared with the little princes of Luxembourg and was always very particular about having his collars starched and his soup very hot. What little Phebe knew of the world she had learned from the nuns who had educated her; her Samoan contemporaries laughed at her for marrying a man twenty years her senior, who had lost his teeth in a riding accident in Africa.

The Parkinsons were one of the first families to settle on New Britain where, together with other Samoan relatives whom they imported, they built up plantations on which they also grew acres of pineapples for the German navy. Mrs. Parkinson and her formidable sister, "Queen" Emma, who once owned a fleet of steamships that plied back and forth to San Francisco, set the early style of life in the Territory. Richard Parkinson, in addition to running Queen Emma's properties, photographed and collected all over the Territory; his *Dreisig Jahre in der Südsee*, published in 1907, is still a classic.

Home from the field, 1929

Through Mrs. Parkinson's vivid tales, I could piece together the early social life of Europeans in the Territory as only someone could do who knew both Samoa and New Guinea. She explained to me, too, how the harsh penalty—death, in earlier times—for a Samoan titled girl who failed the virginity test at marriage had been fitted into the seemingly pliant and adaptable Samoan culture. I had never seen this ceremony and there had always been something about it that troubled me. Mrs. Parkinson told me that actually only those girls were killed who did not take the precaution of warning the old women that they were not virgins, so that the old women, the guardians of the title's honor, could provide chicken blood for the occasion.

She described to me how life in the Territory had been changing under the rising tensions just before World

War I, when German colonial society was becoming more sophisticated and it was no longer quite the thing to pay court to half-caste women. Then the war came. The Australian soldiers arrived in their heavy, inappropriate uniforms and, overcome by the heat, they lounged about in unmilitary attitudes. Mrs. Parkinson drove into Kokopo just one time, looked at the army of occupation and asked, "Is this war? Is this an army?" and drove home again. But she had a hard time, especially after the war when the characteristically racist attitudes of English-speaking peoples accentuated the mixed ancestry of the group of heroic women who had built up early New Guinea. In her old age she had to do labor recruiting for the plantations to earn her living.

It was a magnificent six weeks, and living there in Sumsum also gave me some insight into the running of a plantation. In fact, I became so interested that Mrs. Parkinson thought she ought to warn me that I was not cut out for that kind of life. Here again I heard about "poor Mr. Bateson," who, when he was working among the Baining back of Sumsum, "didn't eat right and got those terrible tropical ulcers." I came away the wiser, with a great collection of old photographs and a unique account of one aspect of life during the transition between exploration and settlement in the contact of New Guinea with Western peoples. In the end, I wrote a long chapter about Mrs. Parkinson, called "A Weaver of the Border," in a book, *In the Company of Man,* in which a group of anthropologists wrote about significant informants.

Reo joined me on the southbound ship at Samarai and we started on the long journey home—to Hawaii, where Mrs. Freer, my mother's college friend and the wife of the former governor, astonished Reo by offering us only glasses of water at bedtime, and then on to San Francisco. There we stayed with Dr. Jarvis, a physician who had once treated my mother and who was something of a monomaniac in his diagnoses. That year he thought that the sinuses were responsible for every kind of ailment, and he insisted that he could cure my persistent muscle pains, which had variously been attributed to trouble with my teeth, emotional conflict, and overwork. He operated on me and permitted Reo to be an interested spectator—which, as it turned out, was unwise, for something went wrong and I almost died. So the last stretch of the journey across the United States with sixteen pieces of luggage—packed New Guinea style, with each piece, rifle, camera, typewriters, and medicine box, packed separately—was something of a nightmare. But at last we arrived in New York and were caught up in the excitement of meeting my friends, who informed me that I had already achieved a wide reputation as an author-anthropologist, something I vaguely knew but had not yet fully comprehended.

14 *The Years between Field Trips*

My father was always amused, although at times a little embarrassed, by his exotic son-in-law. Reo, striding along hatless, wearing a bright Emmanuel scarf twisted around his throat and a sweater under his jacket instead of an overcoat, and carrying a handsome black carved walking stick from the Trobriands, made a conspicuous companion on a Sunday walk in Philadelphia.

From the beginning our life in New York was not easy. An apartment had been found for us—the fourth-story floor-through of an old brownstone house west of Broadway on 102nd Street, in a neighborhood that was just on the verge of decay. The sister of one of the Ash Can Cats lived on the floor below; as we never invited each other to parties, we borrowed chairs and dishes. Farther downstairs, the owner of the house played the same wrong notes on the piano day after day. Our apartment had four rooms strung along the narrow hall that bordered the open stairwell—a big front room, with a couch on which our frequent overnight visitors slept, the kitchen and bath, and a big bedroom with windows on a dark court. At the far end of the hall was another, smaller room that was cheerful and bright. I proposed that this be set up as Reo's study, for he did not as yet have the necessary seniority in graduate school to be entitled to part of an office at Columbia. And all year Reo complained bitterly that I had shut him out of the living room and relegated him to a horrible back room.

In fact, we did not have much money that year and the only help I had was someone who came in to clean. That meant that I had to make the apartment tidy before I went to work so that I could face it when I came home, my arms full of groceries, to cook dinner. To find the living room, where we also had to eat, strewn from end to end with papers and without a place to rest the eye would have been one more penalty for being a female than I could bear.

In addition, Reo did not like to see me doing the housework, which he did not intend to help me with; yet he felt it was a reproach to him that I had to do it at all. As a result, I became expert at tidying up on Sunday morning while appearing to give complete attention to what he was saying. I would wait for a pause in the conversation to slip out and spread one sheet or wash one cup and then appear again. In this way I managed to get the necessary things done so unobtrusively that later, when Gregory Bateson visited our camp on the Sepik, he remarked that he had never seen me perform a domestic task.

These are the penalties of cross-national marriages, even without any of the complications that have been introduced by the changing roles of men and women. British-bred men expect to make the decisions that American-bred women expect to make—how the house is to be furnished, where to plant the roses on the terrace, and where to go on a holiday. During World War II it was comic to watch the two kinds of marriage. If the wife was American and the husband British, there was a continual tug-of-war over who decided what; but if the wife was British and the husband American, the marriage was likely to bog down because neither thought it was his— or her—business to decide whom to invite to dinner or whether to go to the movies that night.

When we arrived in New York in September, 1929, just before the bank failures that set off the Great Depression in the United States, we found everyone deep in the stock market. I had $5,000 in the bank, the total earnings from my book, which was still a best seller. Stanley and Ruth Benedict were plunging gaily, and Ruth tried to persuade me to invest my royalties in stock. I refused, and everyone thought I was a little mad, probably as a result of living so long in the tropics. My own bank account was still in the little country bank in Doylestown. In those years many small-town banks proved to be safer than some of the bigger ones, and in 1932, when I was in New Guinea again, my father cabled me to put our account back into the Doylestown bank. But Reo opened an account in the Bank of the United States, of which there was a branch at a street corner near us, and this was one of the first banks to fail. Reo was stunned. In New Zealand banks did not fail. The crash came, and ruined brokers leaped from high buildings, having nothing but their insurance to leave to their families. Prices began to topple. The Museum called together the staff and reduced our salaries—mine was only $2,500 to start with—and for years afterward salaries stayed at that reduced level.

Nevertheless, the Depression at first meant very little to me. I had had no sympathy with the frantic gambling on the stock market, especially by academic people who had far too little money anyway to risk losing it. My grandmother had drummed into my ears twice a day as she did my hair, "Always live within your income." I am not a gambler, and perhaps hearing the adage, "Lucky at cards, unlucky at love," also made an impression on me as a child. Then when the crash came I was simply glad that I had not risked my royalties, which would have to serve as a nest egg for future field work. I knew about business cycles, and the bank failures did not worry me unduly because I knew there had been panics and bank failures in the past. And apparently my father was not seriously worried; but as he watched the price of gold, through which it had been possible to predict major wars in western Europe since the sixteenth century, he did say, "Sister, you have ten years before the next war." My response was, "Then let's get our field notes written up as quickly as possible, so we can get back to the field to rescue as many cultures as we can before a war comes that may wipe them out altogether."

During my student days I had been deeply impressed with the dreadful waste of field work as anthropologists piled up hand-written notes that went untranscribed during their lifetime and that no one could read or work over after they died. In New Zealand, Reo and I had called on Elsdon Best, that indefatigable chronicler of the Maori, and we had seen his cabinets full of notes. And every summer Pliny Earle Goddard took another lovely field trip to the Southwest and accumulated more notes that he never wrote up. Even Boas, with his tremendous mass of publications, never got around to writing the summary, synthesizing volume on the Kwakiutl Indians. He would plan to do it, but by the third page of a new manuscript he was entrapped in the description of some detailed technique on which he had notes that he had never had time to transcribe. I vowed that I was not going to do this, that I would write up each trip in full before undertaking the next one.

So there was a kind of double pressure on our lives, for I set the pace, as far as writing up was concerned, for both of us. During the two years we lived in New York, in addition to carrying out our short American Indian field trip, we each wrote three major works. With this much accomplished, we could go back to the Pacific with a reasonably good conscience. That first winter Reo wrote the final version of *Sorcerers of Dobu* and I wrote *Growing Up in New Guinea*. In the evening each would read what the other had done during the day or we would read aloud to each other.

Reo had written a first draft of the Dobu manuscript when he returned from the field, before I came out to marry him. Radcliffe-Brown's response to this had been, "I don't believe it!" His own experience had been with beautifully balanced patrilineal societies, and he found a society as dysphoric as Dobu hard to accept, especially as the passion with which Reo wrote about his sorcerer-informant seemed somehow to match Reo's own passion about life. There are others who think that his account of Dobu is exaggerated, but fieldworkers like Géza Róheim, Ian Hogbin, and Ann Chowning, who have had an opportunity to check the accuracy of his work at first hand, do not. In New York he was able to rewrite and expand his original manuscript in the light of his Manus experience, and if Manus was credible to Radcliffe-Brown, he would have to accept Dobu. But this was unfortunate also, because what should have been attributed to the increased depth of Reo's own ethnological perception was instead, quite erroneously, attributed by Radcliffe-Brown—and others as well—to my influence.

This has happened a good many times in my life. Yet people fail to see what should be attributed to me, that is, my capacity to enjoy and appreciate other people's work in a way that seems to give them something like a transfusion of extra energy to complete a piece of research or finish a book. But the fact is, they are happy under what is called my influence only as long as they are working at the top of their own capacity. When their own drive fails, so that they no longer can draw on my energy, they feel it to be a reproach or an unwelcome goad, and so repudiate it. My influence on *Sorcerers of Dobu* was only that of an enthusiastic, attentive, and highly knowledgeable listener. Later, when Reo became increasingly preoccupied with the personal symbolism of what he was working on and shifted his attention from the study of religious behavior, the area in which he made his greatest contributions, to concentrate on problems of sex and aggression, which seem to have less successfully filtered through his own memories, he became far less productive. After we separated, he wrote only one more monograph, his Arapesh texts, and the Arapesh grammar—and he left that incomplete.

But during those two years we complemented each other in our enthusiasm and energy. We worked hard all day and rewarded each other by listening and discussing in the evening. We went to the theater and had friends to dinner, and we gave house room to various of my friends who were having trouble writing their theses at home or were in difficulties with their husbands or lovers. We were a stable, though rather tempestuous, household in which those who were more troubled could find a refuge.

One of my troubled friends was Eleanor Steele, who was beautiful and amiable and also vulnerable because she was so pliant to other people's wishes. Just out of college she had fallen in love with Howard Scott, the magnetic founder of Technocracy. Howard was married, or so we believed. Later we learned how easy it was for people to make up stories about Howard. In any event, we believed that Howard had a wife, and he did have a mistress, an actress whom we saw perform in a magnificent presentation of *King Lear*, and then there was Eleanor. True to the style of our group, she made no bargains and asked for nothing. But once, two years before, when Luther and I had lent our flat to her and I had gone to work in Ogburn's office for the evening, Eleanor telephoned the wry comment, "When is a date not a date? When your lover's mistress won't let him keep it. Come home, he isn't coming."

By the time Reo and I came to New York, Eleanor had left Howard and was married to a perfectly conventional young man who worked for the telephone company and had installed her in a furnished apartment near the Museum. So Howard, who was just starting Technocracy, was at loose ends and spent a lot of time with us. I owe to those long talks a kind of inoculation against the pre-automation concepts of Marxism. It was from Howard that I learned about automation before the word came into our vocabulary.

He had a vision of a society in which people would work for about fifteen hours a week for twenty years only, a society in which money would take the form of adjusted credits and in which spending money would provide an inventory of consumer needs and wants. He envisaged a house in which chairs would be stacked in a wall; when a visitor arrived he would give the number of his constitutional type and the appropriate chair would pop out. At a time when people were still thinking—as they still are—in terms of the limited resources of politically bounded nation-states, he thought in terms of continental masses and their aggregated resources.

He was an extraordinary person, well over six feet in height, gaunt and rangy, Irish and somehow a man of the frontier, endlessly inventive and prophetic. And very honest. In the terrible winter of 1933, when the banks closed and the country was in a panic, he was invited to speak at a very important dinner with a national radio hookup. Ruth Benedict wrote me what happened. There had been stories about him in the press for days and his name was on every tongue. It appeared that he could have had anything he advocated—and he did not even try. Instead, he made a miserable speech in which he said the time was not ripe. Later Howard explained to me that he knew the kind of society he advocated could not come into being yet. There would have to be experiments by the Left and experiments by the Right before people would give up the idea of an economy based on scarcity and recognize that with modern techniques of production the thing to do was to organize consumption. His estimate that every individual in the country would have a buying power—in services and products—equivalent to some $20,000 a year was an idea that interested my father, who arranged for him to speak at a special meeting of members of the Republican Club. But once again Howard stressed the difficulties and failed to explain how it could be done. This question of how it can be done still agitates knowledgeable bankers and businessmen who continue to think in the old terms of where the money will come from, rather than in terms of how often money changes hands for services.

In December, 1933, while Howard was away on an organizing trip, Eleanor fell seriously ill. I took her to stay with me, but even with the help of nurses I could not provide the kind of care she needed, and her physician would not put her into a hospital. Finally, I invoked the help of a friend who was a professor in a teaching hospital, but he said that if her own physician did not make the decision, nothing could be done, unless. . . . I gathered that if I said I would put her out on the street, then, under such circumstances, the niceties of medical ethics could be waived. We did get her into a hospital and there, a week later, she died of miliary tuberculosis, beautiful and considerate of others to the last. She was the first of our college group to die.

The hospital had found her a most puzzling patient, for her former husband appeared on the scene and made friends with her current lover, while all of us held our breath because Howard was in Chicago to address a mass meeting. She was buried by a long-suffering uncle, and her former husband drove me to the funeral in New Jersey. When Howard got back the day after funeral, we walked all afternoon while I let him talk. About Eleanor, he said grandiloquently, "She was the Joan of Arc of Technocracy."

Two other people were present when Eleanor died, her friend Sara Bachrach and the artist Allen Ullman, to whom Sara had just become engaged. Sara and Allen won my affection forever that afternoon, for Allen did something I have never ceased to value. Coming in as a stranger, he supported Sara without making any of us feel that his presence was not completely appropriate. He had the gift of perfect presence, and he was one of the few men I have known who could take three women out together and make each of them feel contented, honored, and amused.

During the two years Reo and I lived in New York I saw a good deal of Howard Scott, but after that only once again. In the autumn of 1941, when Charles Lind-bergh was holding the attention of many Americans with his prediction that Fascism was the wave of the future, Technocracy suddenly blazed forth with newspaper advertisements showing imposing cars and men in uniform standing at attention. It appeared to many people that Technocracy was turning into a form of Fascism, and I was asked to find out what I could. I invited Howard to dinner in a ground-floor apartment, leaving the shades up and wishing there were someone I could tell what I was doing. Howard talked freely. There was no sinister millionaire behind the movement and its goals were unchanged. The members of the organization had put their combined savings into that one set of huge advertisements in the hope of attracting a larger following. But very few people responded.

Recently I wrote something that caught the attention of the small Technocracy headquarters in Seattle—for the movement still appeals to a group of people in the northwestern United States and Canada—and they sent me a little set of pamphlets dated twenty years ago.

At the height of his notoriety, Howard was attacked as an imposter who made all sorts of false claims about his activities and his training. In fact, he had only completed the ninth grade, but his prevision of the electronic revolution was extraordinary. His lack of mastery of the intermediate steps was one of his great handicaps and perhaps also the very vividness of his accounts of people he had never met, places he had never seen, and dams he had not built. Events that lived in his imagination became real to others, and later those who sought to destroy him accused him of fabrication. But he was not destroyed as a person, for he lived to a ripe old age, sustained by the faith of a few people. Had his education matched the scope of his imagination, would he, I have often wondered, have had a profound effect on the country, or was he a forerunner, a man born before his time?

During those early years, however, he made a great contribution not only to my thinking but also to our marriage. Although there were few people who did not arouse in Reo some echo of his emotion-laden past, this never happened with Howard. He was always welcome when he dropped by, after a hard day of map-making or working on calculations, to spend an evening with us.

On the whole, however, social relations were difficult and the hours after a party were hours of strain. At a big party given by the Society of Woman Geographers, at which everyone knew me and Reo knew no one, he asked Fannie Hurst whether she was the daughter of William Randolph Hearst, and he became furious because she felt quite visibly affronted. He was not an easy public speaker, and the few papers he did give were occasions for post-mortems in which the suggestions I made were quite realistic but entirely unappreciated.

I was always willing to pretend that I never did house-work, and I tried to be good-tempered when, after buying food and carrying the packages for four blocks and, finally, up three flights of stairs, I was greeted with the suggestion, "Let's go out to dinner"—which we could not afford. But when it came to intellectual matters, I was not prepared to make use of feminine wiles. I fully realized that it was essential to respect the sensitivities of men reared in other social settings and other cultures, and that their sense of masculinity could be impaired by be-ing asked to behave in ways they had been taught to regard as feminine. I also had a great respect for tem-perament, and I was resigned to having my friends dis-play varying degrees of neuroticism which I felt was compensated for by their unusual gifts.

But I thought then—as I do now—that if we are to have a world in which women work beside men, a world in which both men and women can contribute their best, women must learn to give up pandering to male sen-sitivities, something at which they succeeded so well as long as it was a woman's primary role, as a wife, to keep her family intact or, as a mistress, to comfort her lover. Because of their age-long training in human relations— for that is what feminine intuition really is—women have a special contribution to make to any group enterprise, and I feel it is up to them to contribute the kinds of awareness that relatively few men—except, for example, child analysts or men who have been intimately reared by women—have incorporated through their education. And so, when Reo thought or spoke or wrote well, I was perhaps his most appreciative audience, but I did not applaud where I felt applause was not due; I criticized in situations in which I thought improvement was possible, and I was silent when I believed nothing could be done. And, of course, Reo's charm and wit carried him a long way.

In the spring of 1930, Dr. Wissler, the chairman of the Anthropology Department at the Museum, asked whether I would do a short piece of field work for which he had obtained a grant from Mrs. Leonard Elmhirst's committee for a study of American Indian women. I was not very interested, but Ruth suggested that if we would go to the Omaha, she could find field funds for Reo, so that he could tackle a problem that had been bothering her for some time. In most American Indian tribes, the folktales contain many accounts of visions, and hearing these stories is one of the ways in which the young are subtly schooled in the content and style of the visions they will later seek. But in the great body of Omaha mythology that had been collected no visions had been recorded. Ruth wanted to know why this was so. Consequently, as Dr. Wissler did not care where I used the little grant of $750, which he did not know what to do with, we went to the Omaha reservation in Nebraska.

It was a devastating experience for both of us. We bought a Ford car, which Reo drove with a fine disregard for caution, so that we sometimes landed in a field beside the dusty dirt road. The fierce dry heat of a Nebraska summer, the character of the landscape in which distances are counted by little hills, the atmosphere of the Indian agency, the quality of life on the reservation—all these things were new to us and very depressing. We had both worked in living cultures where the dress and houses and external life-style of the people were congruent with those parts of their culture, their kinship system, their mythology, and their religious beliefs, which it had been our task to work out. But this was a culture so shrunk from its earlier style, from the time when the Omaha had been buffalo-hunting Plains Indians, that there was very little out of the past that was recognizable and still less in the present that was aesthetically satisfying. The women wore long cotton dresses, distinctive, of course, but modern; when they danced they put trade blankets over their shoulders. They lived in the small, now ramshackle houses that had been built for them in the period in which each man was given 160 acres of land on which to farm. But few men farmed. Instead, they lived on their rents, drove around in battered old cars, and took what comfort they could from meeting to play hand games. But where once the stakes had been horses or buffalo robes, these were now reduced to nickels and dimes.

We had been accustomed to making various repayments to the people whom we studied—in medical care, in attentiveness, and above all in providing sustenance for the intellectuals among them who delighted in having a chance to think far beyond the limits of their own culture. But there was nothing we could offer these reservation Indians. They had medical care, which they often failed to make use of, and they had met anthropologists before, whom they had come to regard primarily as a source of revenue. As one old man said, "We never tell anyone everything. We save something to tell to the next one." A man would refuse to act as an informant until he was given an initial payment of $10 or $15 and then very likely he would still refuse.

We did not, of course, attempt to learn the language, for we had money only for three months' work, and as neither of us had ever worked through interpreters, we found the experience both infuriating and depressing. But Reo became desperate mainly because he doubted that he would even have a chance to unravel the mystery he had been sent there to solve. He became convinced that he had been sent there to fail, that American anthropologists never read anything but American Indian material, and that his reputation in the United States would rest entirely on a field trip during which he had accomplished nothing. How could he accomplish anything in a culture in which all the real ceremonial was defunct and people would talk not out of interest but only for money?

The stance of American Indians, a stance they had cultivated through generations of culture contact, was very alien to us, accustomed as we were to Oceanic peoples who, however dour and glum they might be, were dour and glum in ways that were more intelligible. Then there was the dismal sense that the people themselves were going backward. We got to know two magnificent old people who had been tribal interpreters; they had been educated in eastern Quaker homes and spoke precise and fluent English. But the next generation had been sent to schools for Indians, where children from many different linguistic groups were herded together and were taught by federal employees who knew little, and usually cared less, about their pupils and the cultures from which they came. In the end, students returned to the reservation having far less English than their elders and far more alienated from the traditional culture. Drunkenness was rife. Broken homes, neglected children, and general social disorganization were evident everywhere.

My task was to look at the women, and I had the unrewarding task of discussing a long history of mistakes in American policy toward the Indians and of prophesying a still more disastrous fate for them in the future. Although we realized that culture contact in New Guinea would inevitably bring about great changes, many of them for the worse, dreading the future fate of a people one is learning to value is not like staring disaster in the face every day.

Even by putting my field funds together with Reo's for his work, he had a hard time getting the information he needed and, as if in bitter fulfillment of his most pessimistic fears, he has never received adequate recognition for his success in solving the problem of why there are not accounts of visions in the publicly told myths of the Omaha.

What he found out was that although the Omaha had apparently adopted the same convention as their neighbors on the Plains, namely that every man was free to seek a vision and claim the power it gave, in fact, among the Omaha, membership in the religious societies depended on a hereditary right to secret knowledge. When those who had no hereditary right to a vision fasted and made claims, they were told that the vision was false.

This situation was so unusual, as Ruth had sensed, that Reo's analysis did go unrewarded. Americanists did not appreciate the detective skill, developed in his work with the Melanesian sorcerers, with which Reo had unraveled an unfamiliar fabric. He is given great credit for *Sorcerers of Dobu,* his best-known book, and for *Manus Religion,* but he is given very little for *Omaha Secret Societies,* the book in which he published the work he had the greatest difficulty in doing.

It was a hard, trying summer. The second story of our little frame house was so hot that we could not even try to sleep before two o'clock in the morning. Occasionally we made a trip to the nearby town, where there was a band concert and, on Saturday nights, a chicken was thrown from the roof to be scrambled for by the waiting crowd. Or we even drove to Sioux City to see a movie. But Reo said, and I also felt, that field work is much easier when the outside world is far away and it is impossible to go anywhere even if there is somewhere to go to. In Omaha it was too easy to get into the car and drive away.

At the end of the summer we drove home, swearing that each garage broke something so that the next garage would have something to mend. We stopped off in Cincinnati, and even today, whenever I drive in that city, the nightmare of that first driving in traffic comes back to me. But somehow we survived and reached New York safely but very fatigued.

That winter half an office was found for Reo in the Department at Columbia, so he felt less imprisoned than he had felt when he worked at home. We had a little money, too, so that I was able to turn the big back bedroom into a dining room and Reo's old study into a bedroom, and we were able to entertain more comfortably. I wrote up the summer's work and so did Reo. In the spring he took his doctoral examinations, using *Manus Religion* as his dissertation. It was time to go back to the field.

I was convinced, partly on the basis of the Manus field work, in which we had been relatively complementary and uncompetitive, that field work provided the best situation for us to work together. We told Boas that as I could not have any children, both of us were now expendable in any kind of field work that needed to be done. Moreover, we explained that we would like to work among the Navaho, as an American Indian group whose culture was still alive and intact, not destroyed by the disappearance of the buffalo and the end of warfare, as Omaha culture had been. But this was a period when each "field" was rather possessively claimed by the particular fieldworker who had done the research on the culture, a situation that was complementary to the scarcity of fieldworkers and the necessity of spreading them very thin. Consequently, we were disappointed but not too surprised when Boas told us that the Navaho "belonged" to Gladys Reichard.

We now planned to return to New Guinea. We took the money I had saved out of the royalties from *Coming of Age in Samoa,* and matching sums were given us by the Columbia University Social Science Research Council and by the Museum from the Voss Fund of the Department of Anthropology, a special fund that had been given for anthropological research. We planned to leave in the spring of 1931.

It was just at this time, however, that the review written by one of Malinowski's students appeared in which I was accused of not understanding the Manus kinship system, and I immediately decided that I could not go into the field before I had prepared for publication a technical monograph on the subject, *Kinship in the Admiralty Islands.*

This meant that we had to stay in New York for the

summer. Radcliffe-Brown came to Columbia to teach at summer school. He was always indolent and good at improvising and he had not planned to work very hard. But Reo and I took his course, sat in the front row and, expecting the best, we got it. In the evenings I wore my prettiest dresses and prepared the kind of dinners Radcliffe-Brown enjoyed. At the end of the summer term I had finished my monograph, Radcliffe-Brown departed for Chicago, and we turned over our apartment to Louise Rosenblatt, who had just married Sidney Ratner. We were at last on our way to New Guinea.

15 Arapesh and Mundugumor: Sex Roles in Culture

In December, 1931, we came to Arapesh and began the field work that was to give me a completely new insight into the nature of sex roles in culture and into the ways in which innate differences of temperament and culture are related. These new insights depended on such an extraordinary concatenation of circumstances that no notions of serendipity provide an explanation.

When Reo and I returned to New Guinea we had decided to study the people living on the plain beyond the Torricelli Mountains, the northern coastal range. They were a people who built enormous triangular men's houses, and they were said to have a rich ceremonial life. We thought that we might want to study another tribe later, but we had made no specific plans where to go.

The long climb into the mountains on slippery trails, sometimes up almost perpendicular cliffs and sometimes in riverbeds, was slow and difficult, particularly as I had to be carried, but there was no other way into the interior. When we were part way there, the accident of

Reo's success in attracting carriers from farther inland boomeranged. Our carriers left us stranded with all our gear in a village on a mountaintop with no one to move our six months' supplies in either direction—into the interior or back to the coast. So we had no means of reaching the people we had intended to study and no choice but to settle down, build a house, and work with the simple, impoverished Mountain Arapesh, who had little ritual and less art, among whom we now found ourselves. Earlier, when Reo had made his brief trip into the interior to organize carriers, he had found out, as he put it, that "these people haven't any culture worth speaking of—sisters-in-law are friends!" Now that we were stuck in the mountain village, Alitoa, he decided that he would study the language, which appeared to be complicated.

As in Manus, our personal responses to this new culture were heavily conditioned by our past experiences—by the Samoans, whom I had enjoyed, by the Dobuans, whose culture Reo had passionately disliked, and by the Manus, to whom neither of us had had strong responses and among whom we had been able to do good work without any serious clash of temperament or personality. We were in agreement in our conception of the overriding importance of culture in shaping the ways in which children in a society learn to think and feel and act. Some months later, when Ruth Benedict sent us a first draft of *Patterns of Culture,* Reo commented that it was not enough to say that cultures are different; the point was that they are "incredibly different." It had not yet occurred to us that the difference in our experiences—Reo's with Dobu and mine with Samoa—had nearly as much to do with us, as individuals, as it had to do with the nature of the cultures we studied.

I had, of course, shared Ruth Benedict's earlier discoveries of the ways in which different cultures selectively emphasize certain human potentialities and disallow others. She had recognized, with a sense of revelation, the fundamental differences between those American Indian cultures that emphasize ecstasy (for which she adopted Nietzsche's term Dionysian) and those that emphasize moderation and balance (for which she adopted Nietzsche's term Apollonian). This was while she was in the field in the summer of 1927—the summer I had met Reo in Germany before he went to Dobu. The following winter she worked on the paper in which she first developed this brilliant insight, "Psychological Types in the Cultures of the Southwest." At the same time I was writing *Social Organization of Manu'a,* and we discussed at length the kind of personality that had been institutionalized in Samoan culture.

Even earlier she had made the point that it is those individuals whose innate characteristics are too far removed from the norm of their culture who find their culture deeply uncongenial. In 1925 she wrote to me from the pueblo of Cochiti, "I want to find a really important undiscovered country," and she used to wonder whether she would have been happier had she been born in a different time or place, perhaps ancient Egypt. In our discussions we adopted the word "deviant" for the individual who is a cultural misfit, and in *Coming of Age in Samoa* I wrote a chapter called "The Deviant," in which I described girls whose temperament—defined as an extra intensity of response—combined with their life situation and experience had made them deviants from the expected Samoan personality.

However, the idea of native endowment—or constitutional-psychological types—was not yet really integrated in my thinking. I had read C. G. Seligman's significant paper, "Anthropology and Psychology: A Study of Some Points of Contact," and in 1924, in the breathtaking excitement of the meeting of the British Association in Toronto, Sapir had talked about the ways in which cultures emphasized particular styles of behavior, including styles of posture and gesture. I had wondered occasionally what was the basis of my own apparent deviance from the accepted style of the career-minded women I had met; it was clear to me that I was a deviant in the sense that I had a much greater interest in the kinds of things in which most women, not committed to careers, were interested. I had puzzled also about what seemed to me to be contrasts in the innate endowments of my brother and sisters and in their very different responses to shared experiences. And I puzzled about the contrasts between Ruth and myself, especially when she made what seemed to me contradictory remarks, such as that it was quite impossible to imagine me as a man and that "you'd make a better father than a mother."

When I phrased the problem with which I came to the field this time as an attempt to define the way in which culture stylizes the roles of men and women, it was with the declared intention of developing a new approach to the basic question of biological differences that are sex-linked. For until one had got out of the way the problem of the effects of cultural stylization on feminine and masculine personalities, it seemed to be futile to raise questions about biologically given sex differences.

So, in 1931, my problem, which I had declared to be central to the research I was undertaking, was to study the different ways in which cultures patterned the expected behavior of males and females. It had not been necessary for me to spell this out elaborately, for this field trip had not depended on my getting a fellowship grant through a committee that would have insisted on the presentation of a well-developed hypothesis. Instead, my field money came from Museum funds, and for the Museum it was sufficient to say that one wanted to go to one's chosen area and do some field work.

I did, of course, have the problem of sex differences very much in mind, and when we began working with the Mountain Arapesh it was a subject to which I paid a lot of attention. However, the results seemed to be disappointing.

In Arapesh, both men and women were expected to be succoring and cherishing and equally concerned with the growth of children. Boys helped to feed and grow their small betrothed wives, and husbands and wives together observed the taboos that protected their newborn children. The whole adventure of living centered on making things grow—plants, pigs, and most of all, children. The father's role in conception was essentially a feeding role, for many acts of intercourse were believed to be necessary to build up the baby, which was compounded of father's semen and mother's blood.

Aggressive behavior—behavior that involved disregard for the rights of others and also for the rules forbidding a man to eat his own pigs, the game he killed, or the yams he grew—was heavily disapproved. And it was not the aggressor who was disapproved and punished, but anyone who roused anger and violence in another person.

The Arapesh accepted with wonder and resignation the things that went wrong in the world. Some girls grew up too fast and became women before their betrothed husbands, who were supposed to mature first, did in fact mature. And some people, men and women, did turn out to be violent, uncontrollable people; the best course in such cases was to avoid provoking them. But the expectation was that men and women would be equally cherishing, gentle people who anxiously responded to the needs of others.

Reo and I responded very differently to the Arapesh. I too found this culture, in which there were few ceremonies and little elaboration, very thin, and it taxed all my by now well-developed field skills to make anything of it. On a first field trip it might have been a devastating experience to have to work day after day with a mere handful of people who were in the village to rest after heavy work and spent their time pottering about in a desultory way. However, I found the people pleasantly congenial, although intellectually aggravating. There were individuals who were capable of good, clear thinking and some of the little boys did a fine job on the "ball and field test" of the Stanford-Binet intelligence test. These were, however, deviant individuals who had difficulty in dealing with the soft, uncertain outlines of the culture, in which no one did skilled work, no one could interpret accurately a shouted signal, and everyone called everyone else by a kinship term that fitted the situation in the overall pattern of helpfulness; so a man might call one of two brothers "mother's brother" and

In Alitoa, Arapesh: with Mausi, Kule her father, and Nigimarib

the other "brother-in-law," depending on whom he was currently helping, his mother or his sister.

Reo, struggling to wrest a grammar from grudgingly dictated texts, found the whole thing—the people and the culture—formless, unattractive, and thoroughly uncongenial. When he became furiously aggravated by one of the boys who formed our household he was likely to threaten him physically. I, in turn, would be moved to throw myself quickly between the boy and Reo's lifted hand. Reo came from a culture in which boys were physically disciplined and men beat women, whereas I came from a family tradition within which probably no man had lifted a hand to strike a wife or child for several generations. And so when I seemed to identify with the hapless Arapesh this irritated Reo even more. I began to think of the Arapesh and the Samoans, together, in a category that was opposed in some degree to the Manus and certainly to the Dobuans, those fierce fighters, those dour and dangerous sorcerers.

In Arapesh I had too much time to think. I could not leave the village because the trails were too steep and dangerous for my bad ankle. But often there were no people at all in the village. Even by the most ingenious manipulation of the information I already had—so that anyone I could catch to talk to would provide something useful—there were too many empty spaces. I took single individuals through the whole census. They could respond to a genealogical tree with a systematic kinship statement. But it turned out that this was not the way in which they used the kinship system at all. I also spent many hours replicating in watercolor miniatures the method of painting bark panels. In a busier society I probably would never have had time for activities like these.

And I had two profound experiences. One was a pleasant one, as I came to feel that I had by now, in my field work, repaid all that the world had invested in my training—that I had, in American terms, made good. This gave me the sense that I was from now on free— free of obligation and free to choose what I would to do.

The second experience was of another order. I felt that we were stymied—that we were making no theoretical advances. And our personal relations were not easy. When *Sorcerers of Dobu,* beautifully produced in England, finally reached us, Reo looked at the book sadly and said, "That's the last book I'll ever write alone. You'll be in all the others." I learned Arapesh, but I had lost the thrill of great difficulty that had buoyed me up through the task of spending eight hours a day learning vocabulary in Manus and Samoa. I felt somehow finished.

I had invented a new kind of field work. I knew how to study children and place their rearing within the total culture, in this way giving a dynamic element to what would otherwise be a fairly flat picture of the life of another society. We had invented a method of event analysis and had learned how to place small events within larger contexts. But the problem that I had taken to the field, the question of how culturally attributed contrasts in masculine and feminine behavior differentiated the character structure of men and women, seemed to have yielded very little. Among the Arapesh there was so little difference in the culturally expected character of men and women that I felt nothing new had been discovered. I realized that, just as the Manus emphasized anality, the Arapesh emphasized orality, and that this emphasis on orality and food fitted in with the earlier work of Freud and Abrahams. But this, too, lacked firmness of theoretical reference.

So while Reo made brief trips into neighboring hamlets and longer expeditions toward the sea or toward the interior, I sat in Alitoa and felt that somehow my intellectual life was finished. It seemed to me that I would go on studying more cultures in the same way forever, that there was little new intellectual excitement ahead. Perhaps it was the deadening effect of Reo's continual preoccupation with Malinowski, so different from the stimulation experienced by the students who were actually working with Malinowski. Perhaps it was my response to troubles that had developed at home.

A foundation, as Ruth wrote to me, had offered to give a million dollars for anthropological research. But there was a difficulty: Radcliffe-Brown was to be in charge. When I heard the news I made a beautiful plan. If we really got the money, it seemed to me that the most useful thing we could do would be to offer fellowships to do field work to the most promising students in all the social sciences. This would mean that a large number of living cultures would be studied from the standpoint of economics, political science, and psychology and also that a whole group of specialists in the budding social sciences would each know at first hand what a culture was. It would have been a different world had this been accomplished.

But it soon became clear that intractability on both sides was going to defeat any plan for using the money. Radcliffe-Brown, for all his brilliance, was arrogant, dogmatic, and dictatorial. And Boas and other leading American anthropologists decided that it was better to have no money than to have Radcliffe-Brown in charge of planning and allocating its use. By the time money was again available, in the late 1940's, each of the social sciences had gone its own way and social scientists—

In Alitoa, Arapesh: with Nemausi and her mother Wasimai

cultural and social anthropologists, social psychologists, and sociologists—were working in a kind of crazy tandem in which the traces had been cut. Where they attacked the same problems, each worked with different units and different conceptual schemes.

I think I sensed that the great scheme was going to fail and that this was part of my depression. By the standard of depressions, it was mild enough. It was, I think, somewhat like the depression many men experience in middle life when they realize that they are unlikely to go higher in their profession. I was thirty. Since then I have never felt depressed for more than a few days. But sitting on that mountain, where the mists hid the view and the great leaves of the pawpaw trees were all I could see within the engulfing cloud, I felt that everything ahead looked pallid and uninviting.

When at last we came out of Arapesh in August, 1932, neither of us was very happy with the theoretical implications of what we had found. The language work had inevitably become duller as the main outlines became clear and nothing remained but to fill in detail. Reo had enjoyed his expeditions to the interior, especially as he was able to enlarge the picture of the threatening sorcerers of the plains who blackmailed our mild-mannered mountain people by promising temporarily not to sorcerize their relatives, providing they were given food and an adequate supply of trade goods. But in many ways it was an experience that lacked any high point. We had seen no big ceremony and no initiation; we had not even seen confrontations with any style or drama.

Of course, the very fact that the culture was so thin did make it possible for me, later, to document it very thoroughly. In contrast, Theodore Schwartz—who began his field work in Manus in 1953—and I have calculated that it would take some thirty years of continuous observation to document the whole Manus repertoire, and Manus is not a very complex culture. For the Iatmul, the Sepik people on whom Gregory Bateson did the initial work, I believe that many years of work by different people using all our modern techniques of recording would probably not suffice.

After we came down from the mountains we spent six weeks at Karawop, the hospitable plantation on the coast where I had stayed originally during the period when Reo was in the interior organizing carriers. We rested, kept an eye on the plantation for the absent owners, reorganized and replenished our supplies and then, ready to work again, started up the Sepik River to find another field site.

While we were still in Arapesh we had received the issues of *Oceania* in which Gregory Bateson's short report on the Iatmul was published, and neither of us thought it was very good. Reo still felt, as he had earlier, that Gregory had been overpreferred simply because he came out of the Cambridge tradition. And now he began to ruminate over conversations he had had with Gregory in Sydney at the time when he had returned from Dobu with material for a complete and well-ordered monograph, whereas Gregory had had nothing to report but frustration in his efforts to study the Baining. (Now, some forty-five years later, the Baining are still breaking the hearts of fieldworkers attempting their first field research.) We knew that Gregory was back on the Sepik—and why, Reo demanded, should he, and not we, have that magnicent culture?

In those days the ethics of field work were very strict. Boas had refused to let us work among the Navaho because they "belonged" to Gladys Reichard—and this in spite of the fact that we could have done work that she would never do. I had never met Gregory Bateson and had no reason to be his defender. While we were in Manus I had written asking him to do some collecting for the Museum; he had refused, expressing a complete lack of interest. He had, however, sent us some notes he had taken in Bipi, a distant village in the Admiralties, where he had stopped briefly in 1929 when he was on a New Britain schooner that was taking him on an exploratory trip up the Sepik. But whether or not Gregory had a better right to Iatmul culture in terms of what he would make of it, he had chosen it, he was there, and it was his. In fact, although we did not know this at the time, it was Professor Haddon's suggestion that he could go up the Sepik River to do field work that had tipped the balance in Gregory's decision to leave biology for anthropology. On his first field trip in 1927, E. P. W. Chinnery, the government anthropologist, had refused to let him work on the Sepik and had insisted that he go to the Baining. But now he was on his third trip to the Iatmul.

So when we decided to go to the Sepik, I concentrated on making sure that we would not invade Gregory's territory. I insisted that we, Reo and I, go somewhere where no one else had done any work. This also cut out the Keram River, a lower tributary of the Sepik, where the German ethnographer Richard Thurnwald was working with the Banaro at the beginning of World War I. At that time the Australians received a report of a "German expedition" on the Keram, but when the war party, sent to take over the expedition, arrived on the river, they found only Thurnwald peacefully studying a native village. What we decided, finally, was that we would go up the Sepik as far as the first tributary above the Keram River and study the first people on that river. It was a perfectly arbitrary decision, but one that kept us well below the area of the Middle Sepik.

This brought us to the Yuat River (locally also known as the Biwat) and to the Mundugumor people, who had been under firm government control for about three years. The district government office, with a new patrol officer in charge, knew almost nothing but the names of the villages and approximately where their language began. Recruiters could tell us nothing more except that the Mundugumor liked buttons. But the Mundugumor also proved to be a disappointing choice.

They were a fierce group of cannibals who occupied the best high ground along the riverbank. They preyed on their miserable swamp-dwelling neighbors and carried off their women to swell the households of the leading men. In German times, the Mundugumor told us, the government had sent an occasional punitive expedition to burn down a village and kill anyone they found in the neighborhood. This neither distressed nor deterred them. The Australian administration, when it took over, devised a quite different method of stopping warfare. Instead of destroying villages, the village leaders were put in prison. So the two big men in Kenakatem, the village where we settled, had been imprisoned for a year, during which they sat wondering who had seduced each of their many wives.

When the leaders returned, they announced that warfare was over. This meant that all ceremonial life came to an abrupt end as well. Women had already been admitted to initiation, and so the central point of the ritual —the separation of men from women and children—was lost, and the ceremony would probably be abandoned. Furthermore, all the young men were to leave the village and go to work. This absolute acceptance of a break with the past, which is very characteristic of Sepik cultures, led to a kind of cultural paralysis.

We worked, of course. Reo decided that this time he would do the culture and that I could do the language, the children, and the technology. Since there was only one very good informant, we worked with him alternately. Reo collected endless accounts of battles about women; I worked out the details of the technology. The mosquitoes were frightful, and we found that the people themselves included in their anecdotes allusions to the mosquitoes and whether or not they were biting. It was extraordinarily hard and unrewarding work trying to record everything we could about a culture which the people themselves believed had ceased to exist.

In the middle of our stay I discovered that Reo, who had insisted that he alone would work on the kinship system, had missed a clue. The clue had come from the children's terminology, on which I was working. I felt that if he had not drawn so rigid a dividing line between his work and mine, we would have been able to put the material together much sooner. As it was, we might have missed the clue altogether, and this went against the grain. It was a flat contradiction of good scientific practice. I did not mind a division of labor based on what Reo wanted to do, in which I was left to do whatever he thought was least interesting, as long as the work got done. What worried me was the chance that it might not have got done.

In addition, I felt that I was getting no further in my exploration of sex styles. The Mundugumor contrasted with the Arapesh in every conceivable way. Fierce possessive men and women were the preferred type; warm and cherishing men and women were culturally disallowed. A woman who had the generosity to breast-feed another woman's infant simply did not find another husband when she was widowed. Both men and women were expected to be positively sexed and aggressive. In general, both rejected children and, where the children that were allowed to survive were concerned, adult men and women strongly favored children of the opposite sex. In Arapesh the women were kept away from the gardens for their own protection, because yams disliked anything to do with women. In Mundugumor people copulated in gardens belonging to someone else, just to spoil their yams. Here again, in Mundugumor, I found a very strong cultural styling of personality, but as in Arapesh, both men and women were expected to conform to a single type: the idea of behavioral styles that differentiated men and women was wholly alien. As far as my central problem was concerned, I felt completely stalemated. There would, of course, be plenty of new material, but not on the subject on which I had particularly wanted to work. On my two previous field trips I had had tremendously good luck working in cultures that had been as arbitrarily chosen as the Arapesh and the Mundugumor were. But it seemed that this time my luck was not holding.

Furthermore, I loathed the Mundugumor culture with its endless aggressive rivalries, exploitation, and rejection of children. The Mundugumor had developed a variation on the kinship systems of the area which was neither patrilineal nor matrilineal in its emphasis. People belonged to a "rope"—a woman belonged to her father's rope, to which his mother belonged, and a man belonged to his mother's rope, to which her father belonged. This meant that a man belonged to the same group as his mother's father, but he was not allied either with his father and his father's brothers or with his mother's brothers. And, of course, he belonged to a different "rope" from his sisters. With this system went ruthless intra-sex competition and rivalry and merciless exploitation of the emotions of small children. Little boys of seven or eight were expected to stand up to their fathers who wanted to trade a daughter for an extra wife when, correctly, the boy's sister should have been kept to be given in exchange for the boy's wife. And little boys were sent as hostages to live for months among temporary allies; when they went they were told to learn the bush tracks carefully so that later they could guide a raiding party to the village. Lovemaking was accompanied by scratching and biting, and people committed suicide by getting into a temper tantrum and drifting down the river in a canoe to be captured and eaten by the next tribe.

Most difficult of all for me to bear was the Mundugumor attitude toward children. Women wanted sons and men wanted daughters, and babies of the wrong sex were tossed into the river, still alive, wrapped in a bark sheath. Someone might pull the bark container out of the water, inspect the sex of the baby, and cast it away again. I reacted so strongly against the set of the culture that it was here that I decided that I would have a child no matter how many miscarriages it meant. It seemed clear to me that a culture that so repudiated children could not be a good culture, and the relationship between the harsh culturally prescribed style and the acts of individuals was only too obvious.

Reo was both repelled and fascinated by the Mundugumor. They struck some note in him that was thoroughly alien to me, and working with them emphasized aspects of his personality with which I could not empathize. His way of treating illness in himself was to go out and climb a mountain, however raging his fever, in order to fight the sickness out of his system. When we were first married, he had taken care of me very gently during my first attack of malaria—which is frightening because one gets so cold that it is hard to believe one will ever be warm again and stop shaking. But later, as I became more of a wife—and so a part of him—he turned on me the same fierceness with which he treated his own fevers. When I had an infected finger that required a hot poultice, I was told to make it myself. And once in

New York when I was ill, he refused to go out and get a thermometer; and when I called in a neighbor, I found that my temperature was 105°. So I had ceased to expect any sympathy. In Mundugumor I had a good deal of fever, and this, combined with Reo's unrelenting attitude toward illness, the mosquitoes, and the general sense of frustration over the people, made it a very unpleasant three months.

Just before Christmas we packed up our camp and went down to the mouth of the Yuat where it converged with the brown, swiftly flowing waters of the Sepik. The night we spent there, waiting for the government launch, was the worst in all our months with the Mundugumor. For the people had made a door to the latrine from a kind of palm frond that is edged with tiny thorns, and when I tried to open it, I ran hundreds of thorns into my hands.

Finally, in the morning, the patrol officer and the government launch arrived, and we began the long trip upstream to spend Christmas at Ambunti, the main government station on the river, some 250 winding miles above the river's mouth. This stretch of the Sepik is wide and deep with fens that stretch far back from both banks, and only here and there, on slightly rising land, tall trees make a dark green splash against the sky. We sailed past Tambunam, deep in shade, the most impressive village on the Sepik and one of the most beautiful villages in New Guinea with its great dwelling houses that have rattan faces woven into the gables and its great double-peaked men's house set in a green plaza planted with crotons. Again Reo and I responded with a pang of envy. This was a culture we would like to have studied.

16 Tchambuli: Sex and Temperament

Late in the afternoon the launch pulled in at Kankanamun, the Iatmul village where Gregory Bateson was working. We walked up to his crazy screen room that had a tree growing through the roof so that his cat—and of course the mosquitoes—could come and go at will. The long hours under the brilliant sun on the river had been exhausting. After the first greeting as we came inside, Gregory looked at me and said, "You're tired," and pulled out a chair. I sank into it feeling that these were the first cherishing words I had heard from anyone in all the Mundugumor months.

In an extraordinary way this first encounter redintegrated the state of mind in which I had come out of Samoa. But the situation was much more complicated. This time there were three of us and Gregory was, if anything, even more starved for talk than Reo and I were. He had been working alone and was depressed and discouraged about the way his field work was going. He and Reo sat up all night talking, while I kept a conversation going with the young patrol officer who was accompanying us, so that the others could talk without interruption.

However, less than an hour after our arrival Gregory brought out a copy of *Growing Up in New Guinea* and challenged my statement that Manus men were ignorant of the fact that girls menstruated between menarche and marriage. I explained that it was a secret only because no one knew that the men did not know—just as, in our society, many girls who have been taught "the facts of life" nevertheless grow to womanhood ignorant of the most elementary facts about the human reproductive system. It is taken for granted that they know, but they do not. This was Gregory's opening gambit. He was later to remark that anthropologists who had read my work but did not know me tended to doubt my conclusions because they could not allow for the speed with which I worked.

The next day as the launch chugged slowly upstream on the broad, swiftly flowing river, we went on talking, intoxicated with the excitement of encountering someone so differently trained from ourselves. For whereas all Reo's education and mine had been in the social sciences, Gregory had been trained as a biologist and in his discussions of problems he moved easily from one science to another, choosing analogies now from physics and now from geology.

Boas' intrinsic grasp of scientific method was so sure that he almost never discussed it, as such, with his students. He never loaded us down with talk about the paraphernalia of science; we heard nothing about hypotheses or paradigms and we did not discuss formal epistemology. In his teaching Boas presented material in such a way that his students simply absorbed the correct procedures. As a result, we were quite unaccustomed to the kind of heightened awareness of science that characterized men trained in the English tradition of the period—men like C. H. Waddington, Evelyn Hutchinson, Joseph Needham, "Sage" Burnell, and, of course, Gregory as well.

However, Gregory had had no contact with the kind of anthropology in which we had been trained. Neither the approach of A. C. Haddon and J. H. Hutton at Cambridge nor the somewhat differing functionalist approaches of Bronislaw Malinowski and A. R. Radcliffe-Brown made allowance for the study of individuals or for sustained, systematic observation of the minutiae of behavior.

Gregory was floundering methodologically; we were feeling starved for theoretical relevance. And for a year none of us had met anyone with whom we could talk about what we were doing. In addition, I felt wonderfully released from prison—the prison of that Arapesh mountaintop, where I had not been able to take a step outside the village for seven and a half months, and the nightmare prison of the disintegrating, hostile, and mosquito-ridden Mundugumor village.

We talked all day and most of the time during the days we spent in Ambunti in the midst of that most fantastic New Guinea Christmas celebration. Our party consisted of seventeen men, who came from the most various backgrounds, and one other woman, who had just been released from prison for having killed her baby and had somehow managed to get up the Sepik. Drinking went on all day, and our inexperienced little Arapesh boys, whom we had brought with us upriver, watched with astonishment the events that took place as dishes were smashed and furniture was pitched out of the door of one of the houses down on the flat. At ten o'clock at night our jovial, much-loved, and alcoholic host, "Sepik Robbie," would say, "We have had dinner, haven't we?" I learned to cajole large slices of bread and butter from Robbie's cook to fortify me during the long, dinnerless drinking. There was a labor recruiter in the party, a man who was notorious for his mistreatment of his boys. For Reo he was a kind of red rag to a bull, and he kept threatening to beat him up.

On Christmas Eve the first toast of the already highly inebriated gathering was "To the ladies!" But when someone next proposed "The King, God bless him," Gregory's Cambridge voice cut through the racket with unmistakable English authority, "You can't do that!" Drunk or sober, the toast to the King came first—or not at all. By Christmas morning the beer was exhausted, and the men broke open a case of champagne that had been cached by some prospectors for a celebration when—and if—they found gold. As they began drinking the champagne before breakfast, the Australians muttered that they wished it were beer.

Two days after Christmas, Gregory took us up to look

at the Washkuk, one of the peoples that had been recommended to us for our next field work. His big canoe with an outboard motor—a motor the Sepik peoples still remember with nostalgia—had been towed behind the launch, and now the three of us set off. The first night we slept in the guesthouse of a village that was seething with excitement and tension. The people claimed—and we never knew whether or not it was true—that they were expecting a raid at any moment and feared for their safety and ours. Although they spoke an upper Sepik version of Iatmul, they could understand Gregory, and so he sat outside in the plaza talking with them while Reo covered the scene with a revolver from inside the guesthouse. That night we kept the lamp lit and took turns staying awake as we lay on the floor of our improvised mosquito room. No attack came, but Reo woke once to hear Gregory and me talking. There is much to be said for the suggestion that the true oedipal situation is not the primal scene but parents talking to each other in words the child does not understand. And by then Gregory and I had already established a kind of communication in which Reo did not share.

The situation was made more difficult the next day when we began to climb the Washkuk mountain. I was walking barefoot because that is the only way I can climb a New Guinea mountain. On the way Gregory proposed that we have a swim, assuming, with the Bohemian standards of his university youth, that we would all swim in the nude—a suggestion that horrified Reo. Gregory came out of a world in which multiple and complex love affairs were commonplace; Reo came from a world in which the sternest Victorian values still obtained. It had been hard for him to cope with the fact that I had, after all, been married before and that when he married me, he was, in his own view, taking another man's wife. And it was always hard for him to cope with rivalry at any level. The fact that he himself was enjoying Gregory's company as much as I was did not help at all.

We spent a couple of troubled days in Washkuk while I was making up my mind that this was not the place in which we wanted to work. It was very much like Arapesh, only worse. The houses were scattered far apart along precipitous roads. From one house you might have to walk a mile to find the next house and one man, one woman, one child, and two dogs. We wanted a village with a big population and the kind of rich ceremonial life we had expected to find on the plains beyond Arapesh. So we scrambled down the mountain and returned to Kankanamun.

From there Gregory promised to take us to look at another good possibility, a group of people who lived on Tchambuli (now spelled Chambri) Lake, said to be the most beautiful lake in New Guinea. On its black polished surface thousands of pink and white lotuses and blue water lilies are spread, and in the early morning white osprey and blue herons stand in the shallows. Almost nothing was known about the Tchambuli people except that they had elaborate men's houses and a compact population, but there was a vague idea that they somewhat resembled the Iatmul.

We spent a week in Kankanamun and got a feel for Iatmul culture as Gregory took Reo into the great men's house—the only traditional men's house of its kind still remaining on the Sepik today—and I walked around the village. This visit gave us a sensory base from which to understand Gregory's discussions of the culture later when we were making complicated comparisons between the Tchambuli and the Iatmul. Before we left, I told my little Arapesh boy, Saharu, that I thought the one thing worth copying in Gregory's camp was his very elegant latrine that had a double maze wall leading into it. Saharu replied, "I have taken notice of it." Gregory and I had already begun a playful competition in techniques, for although Reo and I had far more sophisticated verbal field techniques, Gregory had a sure sense for the technology of research that we eventually embodied in the complexities of our work in Bali.

Early in the morning we set off again in the big canoe and wound our way through the narrow man-made canals cut in the high grass that stretches for miles between the main river and Chambri Lake. It was very hot and still; the black water of the channels—black from its deposits of decaying vegetable matter—had a pungent odor that mixed strangely with the taste of the tinned anchovies we had for lunch. The lake, smooth as glass, was as beautiful as it had been pictured, and the Tchambuli villages looked prosperous and full of promise for the work we wanted to do. Gregory, of course, could talk to the people, who used Iatmul as a trade language as their own language was so difficult that surrounding peoples refused to learn it. It was even said that young men, when they returned from several years of work, would claim that they had forgotten their own language and would use Iatmul in talking with their fathers.

At this stage there were complex reversals in our relationships. At times Reo and I felt that Gregory was years younger than we were. Actually, Reo and he were only a year apart in age and they had begun their field work at about the same time. But Gregory, who was very thin, still retained the slight figure of an adolescent, and then there was so much that we could teach him about anthropology. At other times, however, Gregory seemed to be our senior. He had all the assurance of his English background and the intellectual certainty of his Cambridge education in the natural sciences. In addition, Tchambuli seemed to be a rather minor and special version of the great Middle Sepik Iatmul culture. This meant that Gregory already understood a great deal about the content of Tchambuli culture, whereas we had everything to learn both about the culture and the language—a difficult multigender language that was just beginning to break down into a two-gender, animate and inanimate, system.

There were three divisions of the Tchambuli that once had been ceremonially and socially separate. In the past they had exchanged their criminals and delinquents to be executed as first-kills by the boys of the other groups. About twenty years earlier, the Iatmul had chased the Tchambuli away and had appropriated their land; each of the divisions had run away to a different set of trade

friends. They had been able to return, under government protection, only a few years before to reclaim their
land and rebuild their villages. When they came back they
had plenty of steel tools and, exhilarated by their success,
they built a string of beautiful new men's houses all
along the lake shore.

Even now the three divisions were exceedingly rivalrous. We selected a house site next to the guest house
because this was the most convenient location. But as
it turned out, we had to build two houses and promise to
live in the better one, and the building groups sent spies
to watch each other's progress. Inevitably, the one close at
hand, where we could supervise the work, was the one we
chose to live in. However, the second house gave us a
base at the far end of the village. This was convenient,
for although the dwelling houses were built fairly close
together on a steep hillside, with the men's houses down
below at the edge of the lake, the distances were formidable when one was trying to cover two or three events
that were taking place simultaneously. And Tchambuli
buzzed with activity.

We had our wish—a place where things were going
on. But I began to show signs of fatigue from the effort
of learning three new languages in so short a space of
time. I would dream that I was standing outside a house,
asking politely whether I might come in—and no one
would answer me. Then I would wake up and realize
that in my dream-speech only the nouns and verbs were
Tchambuli; I had put in particles in Samoan.

After a short time Gregory decided that he would
do some work in Aibom, the village of another group of
people, specialists in pottery-making, who also lived on
Chambri Lake, and he had a house built for himself
there. He used to come over fairly frequently and we
maintained a messenger service between the two camps,
through which we sometimes exchanged long, theoretical
discussions. Under the stimulus of these exchanges and
our conversations whenever we got together, Gregory's
analysis of Iatmul culture was beginning to take definite
shape, and a pattern was emerging that was in many ways

complementary to the one we were finding in Tchambuli.

And now at last, after working in two cultures in which I had thought I was finding nothing really relevant to the problem with which I had come to the field, Tchambuli was providing a kind of pattern—in fact, the missing piece—that made possible a new interpretation of what we already knew. Very often it is only this kind of comparison of different cultures that reveals what the dimensions of a problem actually are, and so enables one to restate the problem in new terms. Contrast through comparison is necessary to complete a picture.

Among the Tchambuli the expected relations between men and women reversed those that are characteristic of our own culture. For it was Tchambuli women who were brisk and hearty, who managed the business affairs of life, and who worked comfortably in large cooperative groups. Each woman had a clay fireplace, which was shaped like a big pot with a terraced ornament on one side and was set in a woven rattan ring. The women carried these fireplaces around with them to the big ample houses that accommodated several families and set the fireplaces down wherever there was work to be done.

The little girls were as bright and competent as their mothers. Tchambuli is the only culture in which I have worked in which the small boys were not the most upcoming members of the community, with the most curiosity and the freest expression of intelligence. In Tchambuli it was the girls who were bright and free, while the small boys were already caught up in the rivalrous, catty, and individually competitive life of the men.

Warfare had long ago ceased to interest Tchambuli men, and—up to the time when headhunting was abolished by government decree—headhunting honors, necessary for nominal manhood, were achieved through exchanges. The mother's brother held the helpless captive while his nephew thrust the spear. This was the final state in a system of headhunting in which taking a head—any head, even that of an old woman or a child, would do—was much more important than a man's display of bravery. In this the Sepik peoples were in extreme contrast with American Plains Indians, who accorded a warrior greater honor for stealing a horse or touching a living enemy than for taking a scalp. But in Tchambuli even the association of warfare and the taking of heads had broken down.

Formally, the men were in charge of their households, but in fact the women managed all the valuables, dressed up the men and children, and went about their business unadorned, businesslike and competent. Meanwhile, down by the lake shore in the ceremonial houses, the men carved and painted, gossiped and had temper tantrums, and played out their rivalries.

In Tchambuli, while Reo was working out the kinship system, he had one of those flashes of technical insight that make all scientific work worthwhile, as he realized that two types of kinship systems, which hitherto had been described as inherently different, were in actuality mirror images of each other. Gregory came over the afternoon Reo worked this out and marveled at our gaiety. Reo published his finding in *Oceania,* in an article modestly entitled "A Note on Cross-Cousin Marriage." Little notice was taken of his analysis, although, twenty years later, it was the kind of thing on which a man could found his career. But that afternoon in Tchambuli we felt it was a triumph.

As we talked over Tchambuli with Gregory, the central emphasis of Iatmul also began to emerge. Gregory was interested in what he later came to call ethos, the emotional tone of a society, which he had first glimpsed in reading Doughty's *Arabia Deserta,* and he felt that he now had a sense of the ethos of Iatmul culture. In Kankanamun and Palimbai, the villages in which he was working, the women were modest, simply dressed, and unassuming, while the men strutted and performed with great harshness and masculine bravura.

There was one Iatmul ceremony, however, in which men and women reversed their customary roles. This ceremony, *naven,* among other things honored a child's first performance of some act, such as killing an animal or a bird, beating a drum or playing a flute, traveling to another village and returning, or (for a girl) catching a fish or cooking sago pancakes. On such an occasion mother's brothers, dressed in old and filthy worn-out grass skirts, mimed a grotesque femininity, while father's sister, decked out in male finery, strode around proudly and noisily grated their husbands' serrated lime sticks in and out of their lime gourds, a sound that expressed masculine pride and self-assertion. These ceremonial reversals, played out with great verve, had the effect of emphasizing the true contrast between the sexes—a type of masculine-feminine contrast that was quite familiar to the Euro-American world.

As we talked, week after week, about Gregory's material and ours, a new formulation of the relationship between sex and temperament began to emerge. We asked ourselves: What if there were other kinds of innate differences—differences as important as those between the sexes, but that cut across sex lines? What if human beings, innately different at birth, could be shown to fit into systematically defined temperamental types, and what if there were male and female versions of each of these temperamental types? And what if a society—by the way in which children were reared, by the kinds of behavior that were rewarded or punished, and by its traditional depiction of heroes, heroines, and villains, witches, sorcerers, and supernaturals—could place its major emphasis on one type of temperament, as among the Arapesh and the Mundugumor, or could, instead, emphasize a special complementarity between the sexes, as the Iatmul and the Tchambuli did? And what if the expectations about male-female differences, so characteristic of Euro-American cultures, could be reversed, as they seemed to be in Tchambuli, where women were brisk and cooperative, whereas men were responsive, subject to the choices of women, and characterized by the kinds of cattiness, jealousy, and moodiness that feminists had claimed were the outcome of women's subservient and dependent role?

As we discussed the problem, cooped up together in the tiny eight-foot-by-eight-foot mosquito room, we moved back and forth between analyzing ourselves and each other, as individuals, and the cultures that we knew and were studying, as anthropologists must. Working on the assumption that there were different clusters of inborn traits, each characteristic of a particular temperamental type, it became clear that Gregory and I were close together in temperament—represented, in fact, a male and a female version of a temperamental type that was in strong contrast with the one represented by Reo. It also became clear that it would be nonsensical to define the traits that Gregory and I shared as "feminine" and equally nonsensical to define the behavior of the Arapesh man as "maternal," in this culture in which both men and women were predominantly nurturing and parental in their behavior. Equally, Mundugumor men and women, who were strongly sexed, proud, and individualistic, could be said to fit into a single, but very different, temperamental type. In thinking about different societies, what we were working toward was a way of delineating in a systematic way the temperamental types that were standardized by the organization of particular cultures.

The intensity of our discussions was heightened by the triangular situation. Gregory and I were falling in love, but this was kept firmly under control while all three of us tried to translate the intensity of our feelings into better and more perceptive field work. As we dealt with the cultural differences between Arapesh, Mundugumor, Tchambuli, and Iatmul, we talked also about the differences in temperamental emphasis in the three English-speaking cultures—American, New Zealand, and English— that we represented and about the academic ethos that Gregory and I shared. No part of this was irrelevant to our struggle to arrive at a new formulation of the relationships between sex, temperament, and culturally expected behavior.

Our thinking owed a great deal to Ruth Benedict's formulation of the great arc of personality potential from which each culture selected, so to speak, only certain human traits to emphasize. While we were on the Sepik, we had the manuscript of *Patterns of Culture,* a draft of which she had sent us. But Ruth Benedict used the term "arc" as a figure of speech and she did not think of different culturally patterned types of personality as systematically related to one another. In my own thinking I drew on the work of Jung, especially his fourfold scheme for grouping human beings as psychological types, each related to the others in a complementary way. Gregory, who tended to use biological analogues, invoked the formal patterns of Mendelian inheritance.

As we progressed, we tried to work out patterns within a fourfold scheme and to place the cultures we knew best in terms of the temperamental type—or types—emphasized in each culture as a whole. In doing so, we came to the conclusion that there must be one kind of culture of which we had no good example. I made a guess that Bali would exemplify that missing type. When at last we went to Bali, it turned out that my guess had been an accurate one.

Using the fourfold system we developed, we placed the cultures that formed the basis of our discussions as follows, in terms of the culturally defined temperamental expectations for men and women in each one. Those placed at opposite compass points, as it were, were complementary to each other:

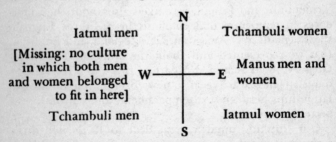

Mundugumor men and women

Iatmul men — N — Tchambuli women

[Missing: no culture in which both men and women belonged to fit in here] — W————E — Manus men and women

Tchambuli men — S — Iatmul women

Arapesh men and women

We also thought over what we knew about Polynesian societies, in which the language was basically the same and the members of which shared a common ancestry.

Here our emphasis was not on sex contrast, but on similarity of temperament in the cultural expectations for both sexes. This is what we suggested might be found:

Maori men and women

	N	
Tahitian men and women	W——┼——E	Hawaiian men and women
	S	

Samoan men and women

From this, we went on to elaborate the possibilities that seemed to be inherent in the formulations we had worked out, namely, that there are a limited number of temperamental types, each of which is characterized by an identifiable cluster of inborn personality traits, and that these several types are systematically related to one another. If this was so, it seemed clear that an individual whose temperament was incompatible with the type (or types) emphasized in the culture in which he was born and reared would be at a disadvantage—a disadvantage that was systematic and predictable for that culture.

Furthermore, it seemed to us that one could make certain predictions about a society in which the behavior of the two sexes—or, for example, of different age groups, status groups, or racial groups within the society—was culturally styled in accordance with contrasting temperamental models. In a society in which boys were expected to be bold, brave, and actively initiating and girls were expected to be modest, responsive, and passive, some men and some women would fail to meet the expected requirements. This would not be because the men who failed were less masculine or the women less feminine, but because the individual's inborn temperament was at variance with that standardized for his or her sex within that society.

We also discussed the implications for personal relationships. For example, what were the implications for a marriage in which the partners had essentially the same temperament? Or in which the temperaments of the marriage partners were strongly contrasting? Or were somewhat different, but less contrasting? At the time it seemed to us that a marriage between two persons of similar temperament, like the relationship of brother and sister, might lack intensity and contrast.

Forty years later it seems to me that *likeness of temperament* can best be appreciated in two individuals who are of the same sex and have been reared within the same culture. And the *contrast between maleness and femaleness* can best be appreciated in a relationship between a man and a woman of essentially the same temperament who have been reared within the same culture.

Our ongoing discussions, of course, threw light upon each of us as a person. Both Gregory and I felt that we were, to some extent, deviants, each within our own culture. Many of the forms of aggressive male behavior that were standardized in English culture did not appeal to him. My own interest in children did not fit the stereotype of the American career woman or, for that matter, the stereotype of the possessive, managing American wife and mother. It was exciting to strip off the layers of culturally attributed expected behavior and to feel that one knew at last who one was. However, Reo did not have as great a sense of revelation about himself. Temperamentally, he fitted the expectations of his culture, even though New Zealand expectations about male behavior were milder and more pastoral and he himself was more concerned with the dangers of unbridled impulse.

At this stage we felt we had made a tremendous discovery. Reo and I cabled Boas that we were coming home with immensely important new theoretical points. But we also recognized that there were dangers in such a formulation because of the very human tendency to associate particular traits with sex or age or race, physique or skin color, or with membership in one or another society, and then to make invidious comparisons based on such arbitrary associations. We knew how politically loaded discussions of inborn differences could become; we knew that the Russians had abandoned their experiment in rearing identical twins when it was found that, even reared under different circumstances, they displayed astonishing likenesses. As yet, however, we were not aware of the full terror of Nazism, with its emphasis on "blood" and "race." The very limited news that reached us gave us no real sense of Hitler's political potential.

At the time we knew very little about attempts that had been made to connect temperament with body type. Although there were some vague notions about physique back of these first formulations, we had little to base them on. One of the first things we did when we got back to libraries was to look up Kretschmer's work, in which he linked types of mental disorder with specific constitutional types. But it was a confused field of inquiry. The theories about such a linkage had been developed among localized populations in Europe and then had been tested and found wanting when they were applied to the immensely diverse population in the United States. Our own formulations were already more sophisticated. For we recognized that persons of the same temperament in different societies would have different body builds and, moreover, that posture and stance were shaped by the culture in which the individual was reared.

When we came out of the field we still saw the world with eyes that seemed freshly opened to every slightest act and gesture; our friends all seemed to have become more intelligible to us. But we were also very clear about the possible dangers of emphasizing any inborn differences between human beings, and this held us back from publishing our hypotheses to the world at that time.

After we returned to Australia from the Sepik River in the spring of 1933, Reo and Gregory and I went separate ways. I returned to America to take up my job at the Museum and reopen the apartment that Reo and I had shared. Reo went to England by way of New Zealand, where he again met Eileen, the girl with whom he had originally been in love. Gregory went home to

Cambridge on a freighter, and it was many weeks before I heard from him.

The developments that followed on our first theoretical formulations about temperament took several forms. Beginning with the contrast between expected male and female behavior and the way in which this contrast was institutionalized and made theatrical in Iatmul, Gregory wrote a first paper on the ethos of the Iatmul *naven* ceremony for an international congress in London.

I spent a summer month at a multi-disciplinary seminar organized by Lawrence K. Frank and held at Dartmouth, in the course of which I learned from John Dollard a much firmer way to describe cultural character. Afterward I began to write *Sex and Temperament,* a book in which I took into account only the different ways in which the behavior of the two sexes was stylized in Arapesh, Mundugumor, and Tchambuli. Although I had in mind the whole problem of temperament as a cross-cutting type of differentiation, I did not discuss it in this book. In the summer of 1934, Gregory, C. H. Waddington, Justin Blanco-White, and I met briefly in Ireland. Here again we discussed the problem of temperamental types and attempted to further clarify the original formulations. That summer I finished *Sex and Temperament,* and the book was published in the spring of 1935.

How very difficult it was for Americans to sort out ideas of innate predispositions and culturally acquired behavior was evident in the contradictory responses to the book. Feminists hailed it as a demonstration that women did not "naturally" like children, and recommended that little girls should not be given dolls to play with. Reviewers accused me of not recognizing the existence of any sex differences. Fourteen years later, when I wrote *Male and Female,* a book in which I dealt carefully with cultural and temperamental differences as these were reflected in the lives of men and women and then discussed characteristics that seemed to be related to primary sex differences between men and women, I was accused of anti-feminism by women, of rampant feminism by men, and of denying the full beauty of the experience of being a woman by individuals of both sexes.

During the following winter, 1934–1935, I began work on a study of cooperation and competition among primitive peoples. This was a pioneering effort in collaborative work—the phrase "interdisciplinary research" had not yet been invented—involving graduate students and younger fieldworkers who worked together with me to produce insights, based on research on thirteen primitive cultures, that might be used in work within our own culture. The central question had to do with the relationship between forms of social organization and types of character structure. Through this study we were able to demonstrate the interdependence of specific styles of living and certain associated character traits.

In the spring of 1935 Gregory came to the United States. Working together with Radcliffe-Brown, we made a further attempt to define what is meant by society, culture, and cultural character. By then it seemed clear to us that the further study of inborn differences would have to wait upon less troubled times. On his return to England, Gregory completed the manuscript of *Naven,* his magnificent study of Iatmul culture.

In London, Reo had repudiated any psychological formulations. We were now divorced, and from England he had gone to China to teach. Gregory was awarded a fellowship at Cambridge, and he and I were at last free to meet in Java and begin field work in Bali.

17 *Bali and Iatmul: A Quantum Leap*

We arrived in Bali in March, 1936, on the Balinese New Year's Day, Njepi, when for a whole day absolute silence is imposed on the island. No one walks the roads, no gong sounds, no voice is raised, no fire is lit, children hush their crying, and no dog barks. By a special dispensation we were allowed to drive across Bali to our destination in Oeboed, alone upon the usually thronged roads and seeing the island as we were never to see it again, a silent setting without a human actor anywhere in all the delicate variety of changing patterns of planting and harvesting, for in each small part of the island there is a different agricultural rhythm. The car climbed the steep road into the cool mountains, where we later elected to live, and swept down again into the lush fields of South Bali, where that day no ducks walked in solemn profile procession amid the rice fields.

Just at noon the car stopped in front of Walter Spies' house. We walked down the winding stone steps set between masses of tropical plants arranged to give a feeling of a pictorial jungle. Walter Spies, fair and full of grace, looked up from his conversation with Beryl de Zoete, with whom he was working on a book on Balinese drama, and said, "We'd given you up." We were in time for lunch, but we were indeed later than we had promised.

We had found it impossible to get married in Java and so we had had to fly to Singapore. From there we decided to go to Bali by boat, a boat that wound its way slowly through the islands and around Macassar. On the boat Gregory read the proofs of *Naven* and made an analytical index for the book. He had made the completion of this book a prerequisite to our getting married—proof that he would be able to accomplish the kind of work he wanted to do if we worked together.

Naven brought together the materials of his three field trips to the Sepik and the crash of illuminations in Tchambuli, when Gregory's long years of patient but unsatisfying field work had combined with Reo's and my years of energetic and fruitful field work to produce both new insights into the way in which cultures evolved and a ground plan for work we could do together. What we now hoped was that we could develop a new methodology out of the combination of Gregory's training in biology and his fascination with the subtleties of cultural ethos

In the American Museum of Natural History with a New
Guinea figure. *Photograph by Irving Browning*

and my years of experience in following the way in which human infants, born, we believed, with the same range of potentialities, developed into adults who differed from one another as conspicuously as the Baining and the Iatmul, whom he had studied, and as the people Reo and I had studied, Samoans, Dobuans, Manus, Omaha, Arapesh, Mundugumor, and Tchambuli.

We had chosen Bali with knowledge and forethought as the culture we wanted to study next in order to obtain material on one temperamental emphasis we had only hypothesized must exist. We had seen just enough material in films and still photographs, had heard just enough of the music studied by Colin McPhee, and had read just enough in Jane Belo's careful records of the ceremonies with which the Balinese greeted the terrible disaster of the birth of twins to assure us that this was the culture we wanted to work on.

I was thirty-four and Gregory was thirty-one. I had what amounted to a lifetime of completed work behind me; Gregory had a lifetime of work he wanted to do, and felt he had not yet done, ahead of him. We looked about the same age—a little younger than we were. But in many ways there was a tremendous age difference between us. I had grown up at eleven and so had been grown up for over twenty years; Gregory kept his slight asthenic figure and adolescent silhouette until the war ended, almost ten years later. Moreover, the kinds of intensity each of us brought to our field work were of a very different order. But Bali was to provide just what both of us needed—for me, the perfect intellectual and emotional working partnership in which there was no pulling and hauling resulting from competing temperamental views of the world; for Gregory, materials that made sense as he worked with them, so that he did not have to wait until his notebooks were filled to know the direction his thinking was taking him.

We both had behind us field work in New Guinea— the dourness of the New Guinea bush, which was relieved only intermittently by a bright bird or a bright flower, and experience with peoples who were divided from one another by fear and hostility, who pursued their own paths and were only slightly willing, when it suited them, to man a canoe or carry something over the mountains for visiting Europeans. The Europeans we had met in New Guinea, for the most part Australian explorers, adventurers, and civil servants, were often kind and sometimes picturesque, but they were not people with whom one could talk about what one was learning and thinking. To most of them, the peoples of New Guinea were very alien and strange—souls to be saved, although lodged in strange bodies; bodies to be worked in utter disregard of mind or soul; intractable and unteachable men and women—as they judged them to be—who had, nevertheless, to be controlled, governed, and slightly civilized. Field work was grueling, especially on the Sepik where we had met, the mosquitoes and the heat providing a constant irritation of bites, cuts, itches, and small vexatious infections that might turn into tropical ulcers. There was no skilled help, no way of getting anything done that one did not initiate and take responsibility for oneself.

And no matter how long one managed to stay in the field, managed to piece together meals of local foods and scarce canned food, and managed to outlast the heat and the fatigue and, on the Sepik, the discomforts of high water, the torrents of the rainy season, and recurrent attacks of malaria, there never was any guarantee that one would in the end see the ceremony that might provide the key to an understanding of the culture. Perhaps in the whole of a field trip one would see no major ceremony, no important man would die, there would be no dramatic clash that would suddenly illuminate the plot of a people's lives. Fieldworkers have waited for months for a feast that was postponed from week to week, only to hear that it was finally celebrated two weeks after they had to leave.

In New Guinea fieldworkers were, in a real sense, at the mercy of the situation in the village in which they were finally able to settle and of the available talent and ability at that time in that village—perhaps there would

With Gregory Bateson. *Photograph by C. H. Waddington*

be only one capable and interested informant, perhaps none at all. In addition they had to face the uncertainties of the weather, the caprices of shipowners and district officers, and the almost certain exhaustion brought about by malaria, for which there was then no real remedy.

On his first field trip to the Baining, Gregory had sat patiently with an old man who was making masks and, with a sharp thorn under his tongue, spitting blood on the white bark cloth. He was preparing, Gregory thought, for a ceremony of some sort. And then one morning Gregory woke up to find the camp empty; all the people had moved away. In Arapesh the carriers had dumped Reo and me on a mountaintop in a village in which we had not planned to work, a village I never left for seven and a half months. The only ceremony we saw in Alitoa took place when we had been there only a few weeks. For the rest I had to extract the culture laboriously from men and women, most of whom got headaches when they were asked to think for more than ten minutes at a stretch. I had to base much of what I learned on lists of names and samples of leaves. And sometimes nothing at all happened for days.

Gregory had been reared as a biologist. When he was born, his geneticist father, William Bateson, was opening eggs to measure sex distribution; the house in which he lived was surrounded by fields that were planted to yield Mendelian types of information. He had a naturalist's training in attending to ongoing reality, instead of forcing nature in the laboratory to give limited answers to limited questions. His first publication had been a report on a creature not previously recorded in England. As an anthropologist he wanted to be able to systematize his observations—to have enough of them so they could be treated in an orderly fashion. *Naven* literally had been put together from bits and pieces, fragments of myth and ceremony, recorded in the field as they happened or as an informant thought to mention them, some of the most illuminating so slight that one could easily have missed them altogether.

To all these vicissitudes, Bali presented an extraordinary

contrast. Bali was beautiful with its carefully terraced and planted hills and its roads that were always crowded with people carrying on their heads or shoulders loads under which they trotted lightly and tirelessly. Villages were compactly built and were close together. There were over a million people who spoke the same language, as compared with the few hundreds—or at most a few thousands—in any one of our New Guinea cultures. The Balinese had been partly literate for centuries, and the Dutch had taught some of them modern writing so that from the very start we had a Balinese secretary who could write, as well as speak, the language we were learning and record the most tiresome, time-consuming, and repetitive parts of ceremonies. Bali teemed with expressive ritual. We were never again, after the silence of our first day, out of the sound of music, if it was only the tinkle of the bells that women fastened to their knives or the flute played by some lonely peasant watching over his crops in a far field. As one drove along the well-kept roads—for the Dutch administrators believed in good roads—one passed from a feast in one temple to a feast in another and met people dressed in glowing colors and carrying offerings, or a whole orchestra on its way to a performance in another village, or dancers in trance, or a bride borne in a palanquin.

The Europeans we met were, many of them, artists and dancers and musicians—people who had come to Bali for months, sometimes for years, to paint or write or simply to delight in the painting and dancing of the Balinese. Instead of feeling helpless, as we so often did in New Guinea, to communicate to Europeans the simple fact that the native people among whom one had come to work were as real as their colonial administrators and had minds as able and affections as passionate as theirs, we encountered, in Bali, continuing active interest and enjoyment. It made little difference whether we talked with a visitor like Beryl de Zoete, or with those who, like Walter Spies or Jane Belo and Colin McPhee, had built themselves homes in Bali. In their houses they brought together carvings from one village, wall paintings from another, and musicians from still another. And as Bali changed, as new materials were used and new themes appeared in paintings and dances, artist residents both enjoyed and guided, criticized and facilitated, so that the standards of new forms were high.

Walter Spies found a house for us within easy distance of his own, a little house built in modern style, and provided us with servants. The food, cooked in the traditional fashion that had been modified over several centuries by Dutch taste, was delicious. It consisted of rice and garnish, accompanied by spicy, pungent condiments, each meal different, and each diminutive chicken or duck cut up and prepared in three or four different ways. In New Guinea I routinely lost between twenty-five and fourty pounds on each field trip; in Bali I never lost any weight at all. A medium, to whom a friend had taken me in New York, said of Gregory, "Feed that man, feed him chicken, for he's good clean through." In Bali this was easy to do.

In due course we would choose a village and build a house; it was only a matter of deciding where and then of finding the appropriate craftsmen. Only those who have worked in societies where money has no power to persuade people who do not, at the moment, feel like doing something can realize what a paradise Bali was for us. Ceremonies every day—if not in this village, then in another only a short distance away. Informants, scribes, secretaries were ready to be trained for the asking. Household help, too, and when we came home at midnight, dinner would be waiting, hot and delicious, when we were ready. And every group—the people walking on the roads, or sitting behind the little roadside stalls in which refreshments were sold, or standing, close packed, listening to music—all of them were rewarding for the photographer, their whole stance explicit and revealing to the eye.

And we had two years in which to do our work.

So for two months we worked on the language with Made Kaler, our incredible Balinese secretary who knew five languages and had a vocabulary of some 18,000 words in English, although he had never before met a native speaker of English. We decided to learn Balinese rather than Malay, although it was more difficult, and Gregory always regretted the choice. Malay, used as a lingua franca, was much simpler and avoided all the restrictions and endless small conventions that governed the speech of people of different rank and caste in Balinese. We had to learn to deal with seventeen levels of vocabulary; we were never answered in the vocabulary we used in addressing another person. And words were extraordinarily specific. If you showed a Balinese a loaf of bread and asked him to slice it, but used another verb instead of the one that meant to cut in even slices the thickness of which was less than their length and breadth, he would look at you with an absolutely blank expression. Gregory felt that this kind of precision reminded him too vividly of the exactions of English culture. But having enjoyed my earlier experience with formal courtesies in Samoan, I also enjoyed the intricacies of Balinese. And I took advantage of my sex. Balinese women did not learn the ancient Sanskrit-derived script. and so I, too, remained illiterate in ancient ecclesiastical Balinese.

During the two months we lived in Oeboed, Beryl was working on her book, and this meant excursions almost every day to watch calendrical ceremonies or ones that had been specially ordered. For in Bali, where every theatrical performance is also an offering to the gods, those who wish to make a thanks offering or a propitiatory offering can order the performance of a shadow play or a trance dance—sheer heaven for the anthropologist. One of our most successful films was made when we ordered a group to play in the daytime that ordinarily performed only late at night. We had no movie lights and we wanted to film the different ways in which men and women handled their razor-sharp krises in the trance dances when they turned the kris, in mock self-destruction, against their own bodies. The man who made the arrangements decided to substitute young beautiful women for the withered old women who performed at night, and we could record how women who had never before been in trance flawlessly replicated the customary behavior they had watched all their lives.

Gradually we developed a style of recording in which I kept track of the main events while Gregory took both moving pictures and stills—we had no means of recording sound and had to rely on musical recordings made by others—and our youthful Balinese secretary Made Kaler kept a record in Balinese, which provided us with vocabulary and a cross-check on my observations. We soon realized that notes made against time provided the only means by which the work of three people could be fitted together and which would enable us, later, to match the photographic records of a scene with the notes. For special events, such as trance, we used stopwatches.

This brought us into some conflict with our artist-hosts, a conflict that was intensified when Jane Belo first arrived and rebelled against what she called "cold and analytical" procedures. Beryl, who had an acid tongue and a gift for destructive criticism, effectively satirized this conflict between science and art, and I identified her with the witch, a prevailing Balinese figure. And so, periodically, I would note moments of special felicity in my diary with the initials *r. p.*, which stood for *ranga padem*—the witch is dead—and conveyed my feeling that the influence of Beryl and the malign influences of Balinese culture, which emphasized nameless fear as a sanction, were temporarily in abeyance.

While we feasted on riches, day after day, and found each temple, each theatrical performance, and each shadow play more delightful and more intelligible than the last, we searched for a village. We had made a decision that contravened the usual approach of Europeans to the high cultures of the East. Bali was a high culture, Hindu in religion, and the Sanskrit texts, art, music, and ritual were derived from India by way of Java. Except for Dutch jurists and an occasional antiquarian who ventured into the remote mountain villages, those who studied Bali concentrated on the high culture of the courts of the rajahs and the ceremonies presided over by Brahmin priests—the great cremations or the deification of the father of a rajah. We decided that we would not do this. We would approach Balinese culture as we were accustomed to approaching a primitive culture, by using our eyes and ears. We would not pore over ancient texts or dictionaries in which the roots of words had been laboriously traced by Dutch scholars or rely on erudite comparisons which were alien to the villagers themselves.

We decided that we would start our work in as simple a village as we could find and learn Balinese culture as it was expressed in the life of villagers and record the prayers of the village priest, not the mangled versions of Buddhist or Hindu rituals that were performed by priests in the lowlands. Several things followed from this choice: living in the mountains meant rough roads and some walking and carrying. The mountain people muffled themselves in drab imported cloth and only rarely wore the expensive handwoven and beautifully dyed Balinese materials, and they often stuffed their mouths unaesthetically with lumps of shredded tobacco. They were a dour people and suspicious of strangers; they lacked the easy openness to any patron that characterized the people of the lowlands, who were warmer, more sophisticated, and accustomed to the life of the courts and priestly palaces, to gold and silver betel boxes, to wet rice fields and abundant food.

Our choice of the village of Bajoeng Gede, which was to be our headquarters for two years, was one of those lucky accidents that have accompanied me all my life. It was a village in which most courtyard walls consisted of bamboo fencing, instead of the clay walls which, in other villages, shut each courtyard off from sight. I had already learned how much time was consumed in courtesies and gifts of refreshment on every occasion when one entered a courtyard, and I realized that in Bajoeng Gede one could catch a glimpse of what was going on in a courtyard as one walked along a street without actually entering the house. But I did not yet know about the contaminations that had to be avoided; for example, no one who had entered a house in which there was a new-born infant could, on that same day, enter a house where

In Balinese festival dress, with children,
in Bajoeng Gede, Bali, 1938

a god was kept. Later, we tried to be sure that one of us,
Gregory or Made Kaler or I, would remain "pure" until
sundown, so that at least one of us could enter the holier
houses. Having chosen Bajoeng Gede, we also found that
everything there went on in a kind of simplified slow
motion. An offering that elsewhere would have a hundred
items might have only ten in Bajoeng Gede. The entire
population suffered from hypothyroidism, and about 15
percent of the people had a conspicuous goiter. This deficiency of thyroid had the effect of slowing things down
so that there was a simplification of action, but without
a loss of pattern.

Had we attempted to learn Balinese culture in the
complex and highly elaborated lowlands—or even in a
mountain village in which there was no hypothyroidism—
I do not believe we could have accomplished what we did
in the time we had. As it was, after a year during which
we paid the most intense attention to the relatively simplified forms in Bajoeng Gede, we were able to follow
the complex ceremony in which the rajah of Karangaam

deified his father, in preparation for which hundreds of women worked for months making the offerings that were built up into towers that reached the sky.

So we had our house built in Bajoeng Gede—a set of pavilions roofed with bamboo shingles, with polished cement floors and covered walks leading from one to another. We had our furniture made by Chinese carpenters and Balinese craftsmen—in the end we had seventeen tables—and we lighted the pavilions at night with a multitude of tiny glass lamps with tall slender chimneys.

When we planned our field work, we decided that we would make extensive use of movie film and stills. Gregory had bought seventy-five rolls of Leica film to carry us through the two years. Then one afternoon when we had observed parents and children for an ordinary forty-five minute period, we found that Gregory had taken three whole rolls. We looked at each other, we looked at the notes, and we looked at the pictures that Gregory had taken so far and that had been developed and printed by a Chinese in the town and were carefully mounted and catalogued on large pieces of cardboard. Clearly we had come to a threshold—to cross it would be a momentous commitment in money, of which we did not have much, and in work as well. But we made the decision. Gregory wrote home for the newly invented rapid winder, which made it possible to take pictures in very rapid succession. He also ordered bulk film, which he would have to cut and put in cassettes himself as we could not possibly afford to buy commercially the amount of film we now proposed to use. As a further economizing measure we bought a developing tank that would hold ten rolls at once and, in the end, we were able to develop some 1600 exposures in an evening.

The decision we made does not sound very momentous today. Daylight loaders have been available for years, amateur photographers have long since adopted sequence photography, and field budgets for work with film have enormously increased. But it was momentous then. Whereas we had planned to take 2,000 photographs, we took 25,000. It meant that the notes I took were similarly multiplied by a factor of ten, and when Made's notes also were added in, the volume of our work was changed in tremendously significant ways.

It also meant that we had to wait almost twenty-five years before our work had much impact on anthropological field work. And there are still no records of human interaction that compare with those that Gregory made in Bali and then in Iatmul. In 1971, when the American Anthropological Association held a symposium on the newest methods of using and analyzing film and tape, Gregory's films of Balinese and Iatmul parents and children still were shown as models of what can be done with photography.

When we returned to the United States, we decided to prepare one publication, even though we were already becoming involved in wartime work, that would demonstrate the new techniques of photography and recording notes that we had developed. *Balinese Character,* our only joint book on Bali, involved looking sequentially at a large proportion of the 25,000 frames and selecting from these the key pictures, which Gregory enlarged and from which we chose some 759 for publication. In this book we developed a method of presenting details from different scenes—a man asleep, a mother carrying a sleeping child, and thieves falling asleep during their trial—that were thematically related, without violating the context and the integrity of any one event. It was a challenge that no one took up.

It was not only in photography that our field work took on new dimensions. Gregory also invented new methods of verbal recording that made it possible to follow a whole sequence of both major events and minor incidents, to know just when a new insight occurred, and later to include in the record cross-references and further theoretical ideas. The places where there were still photographs and stretches of film also were indicated. With this kind of record, thirty years later, I can place each moment or write captions that include the identification of a child's foot in the corner of a picture.

Then, because of the density of the population and the

richness of the ceremonial life, we were able to put together many new kinds of samples. We had not one birth feast but twenty; fifteen occasions, all carefully recorded, when the same little girls went into trance; six hundred small carved kitchen gods from one village to compare with five hundred from another village; and one man's paintings of forty of his dreams to place in the context of paintings by a hundred other artists.

The opportunity to get this kind of material was dazzling. We responded to it by working at fever pitch, as each continually stimulated the other to investigate some new dimension of the culture or to develop some new refinement of method. When Gregory was working in Iatmul, he invented the term schizmogenesis, a concept that was later identified as positive feedback, that is, a vicious circle in which the opposition between two persons—or two groups—accelerates to a breaking point. In Bali, he added the concept of zygogenesis, in which acceleration leads not to a breaking point but to a harmonious equilibrium. Most of the time as we worked together far into the night—went to bed after washing our faces in the remaining pint of water when the last films had been developed, or after we had labeled the last film or had worked out a new theoretical point—we felt that we were working in harmony. Our working pace slackened only during fits of weariness and was interrupted only when we visited our friends' luxurious lowland houses, where, however, we also worked hard.

For we had expanded our working team to include Jane Belo and a secretary whom Made Kaler trained for her and also Katharane Mershon, a former dancer, who lived with her husband in the beach village of Sanoer, a village where even small children went into trance, where witches abounded, and where there was one wise old priest who was willing to think independently and whom we could consult. We also trained an intelligent boy, who had formally adopted the Mershons as his parents, to be Katharane Mershon's secretary. When we visited the Mershons we worked together on large ceremonies, and when we visited Jane Belo and Colin McPhee

we worked on the village of Sajan or on the trance behavior Jane Belo was studying. It did not seem to be
very hard work. The material was so rich and the sense
we had of making progress in method and theory was so
exhilarating.

At the end of two years, when we had planned to
finish our work and go home, we again looked at each
other. We had, it was true, an unprecedented amount of
material. But the essence of anthropological work is comparison. There was nothing anywhere to compare with
what we had. The war was approaching. Even with newspapers two months late, it was clear that the outbreak
of war would not be long delayed. But even as war became more imminent we had planned for a great interdisciplinary expedition, complete with endocrinologists
and psychiatrists, which was to come to Bali and have a
headquarters in the Bangli Palace—where we went to
study the ruling caste and worked intensively, protected
by royal prerogatives. Each visiting scientist was first to
be taught about Bali from texts and film and then was
to be presented with a trained secretary-interpreter and
with a village all his own. We even took a three-year lease
on the palace, although we knew that the plan probably
represented no more than a dream. We had taken seriously Nolan Lewis' request that I plan an expedition to
study schizophrenia in some other culture and, when
there were no immediate funds to carry out the plan, we
had done much of the work ourselves by enlisting Jane
Belo and Katharane Mershon and getting the cooperation of Dutch specialists. And the larger plan might still
be feasible.

Meanwhile, what were we to do with our incomparable
material? We had daydreamed of going home by way of
Angkor Wat, the place in the world I wanted most to
see—and which has now been badly damaged by a by-
product of the war in Vietnam. But our intensified
anthropological consciences won out. We decided, instead, to go back to the Sepik and work with the Iatmul.
Gregory knew the culture well, and it was an area where
I had high familiarity and a mastery of the lingua franca.

In the mosquito room, Tambunam, New Guinea, 1938

There we hoped within a much shorter time to make films and still sequences and do the kind of detailed recording we had developed in Bali.

We took a Dutch ship to Port Moresby. Hitler took over Austria while we were on the voyage, and the Austrian ambassador bound for New Zealand was suddenly a man without a country. We set up our camp in Tambunan, a large and complex Iatmul village in which Gregory had not worked before, and tried to replicate the kind of work we had done in Bali. But there was no Made Kaler to do part of the recording, Sepik names were four and five syllables long and could not be abbreviated, and Gregory was ill almost a third of the time. In addition, it was an unusually dry season and the people gave up almost all their ceremonial life in order to devote themselves enthusiastically to crocodile hunting, and they often returned to the village only to quarrel over the disposition of the smoked crocodile meat. What had seemed to be a possibly slightly feverish dream in Bali came closer to being a nightmare on the Sepik River.

But in six months we got the necessary materials. We could contrast the way the Balinese mother and the Iatmul mother handled a whole range of behavior—the way, for instance, the Balinese mother borrowed another baby in order to send her own child into a frenzy of jealousy in contrast to the way the Iatmul mother protected her child from jealousy, even as she kept her breast steady for a newborn infant which she was nursing for the first time. We could contrast the way the Balinese confined drama and action to the theater and maintained their everyday relationships placidly and evenly, never allowing children to contend even for a toy, whereas the Iatmul, who struggled and screamed and quarreled in real life, used their artistic performances to introduce moments of static beauty into their more violent lives.

We got the contrasts we were looking for and were ready to work on new theoretical advances at home—to take part in the development of cybernetics and group decision theory and, with the illumination provided by Erik Erikson's modal-zonal theories, to incorporate a new and more sophisticated handling of ideas about temperament.

But our days of working together in the field were over. For the next two years, including a brief six weeks' return to Bali to fill in small bits and to make a record of another year's growth of the children we had been following in Bajoeng Gede, we worked just as hard. We analyzed and catalogued our materials, worked with people in other disciplines on the theoretical implications of what we had accomplished, cut a few films, and prepared *Balinese Character*. But then, as the war engulfed us, Gregory turned to other interests and never came back to this kind of field work. Instead, he has preferred to generate small stretches of data, based on tape recordings and films of interviews with schizophrenics and observations of octopuses in tanks, otters at the zoo, or dolphins in captivity, making records that are not in themselves priceless or timelessly valuable and that can be discarded when the thinking they were meant to underpin is done.

I have tried to replicate the Balinese experience in many different and, on the whole, unsatisfactory ways. I have worked on the analysis of photographs, including many of our Balinese sequences. I have gone with photographers to cultures I knew and other cultures I did not know. I have tried twice to work with a husband-and-wife team in Manus.

And the work on Bali and Iatmul has gone on. In 1957, I took Ken Heyman to Bali, where he photographed still sequences of things I had seen that had never been photographed in this way before, and in 1968, he returned alone to make a photographic study of a single Balinese family in the village of Bajoeng Gede, where all the schoolteachers and the schoolchildren in the last grade of school had been killed in the political massacres. Rhoda Métraux has gone back to Iatmul to add music and sound and her own complex perceptions to the work that Gregory and I did. Colleagues and students have used small pieces of the Balinese material for very fine theoretical analysis. After years, Colin McPhee completed his massive work on Balinese music. Jane Belo's books and monographs also have been finished, and just before she died she edited a collection of the papers we all wrote while we were working together. Last year Katharane Mershon finally published an account of her work in Sanoer. Recently, working from a quite different base, Clifford and Hilred Geertz have done beautiful work on Bali, elaborating that middle distance that was lacking in our own work, for Gregory was so intent on the faces and the hands of cockfighters that sometimes we had no pictures of the cockfight at all.

In the new Hall of the Peoples of the Pacific at the American Museum of Natural History, there is an exhibit based on the collection of 1,300 Balinese carvings analyzed by Claire Holt on cards, using a method that predated computer analysis. But the material remains unworked up, as she left it to write her great work on Indonesian art.

We have made other attempts to reproduce some of the conditions of the Balinese research. The big research project, Columbia University Research in Contemporary Cultures, which was started almost immediately after the war under Ruth Benedict's direction, was one of these. In this project we worked in small overlapping groups, whose members differed widely in background and experience and who were trained in a variety of disciplines —scientists, artists, and students of the arts. In each of the nine cultures we studied at a distance, we worked with informants and used films, novels, autobiographies, artistic production, records of congresses, manuals of child care and other didactic literature, and many other kinds of materials available in complex modern societies. Geoffrey Gorer did some of the principal work. He himself had been in Bali, and his letters to us from Sikkim where he was studying the Lepchas, while we were in Bali and I was writing him accounts of our work there, were part of the whole Balinese experience. Jane Belo also worked with us in Research in Contemporary Cultures. But interviews about childhood in a distant country, films made far away in the Soviet Union or France, minutes of meetings, paintings and sculpture by artists one has never seen at work—all these are pallid compared with working in the midst of a culture, watching people day by day, and testing out theory against the next gesture or the next trance performance.

When I returned to Bali in 1957, the Balinese knew that none of our marriages, then such vivid partnerships in delight in Bali, had survived. They knew that Jane Belo had been very ill, and when I told them that her memory of Bali was unimpaired, they said seriously: "She left her soul in Bali, you know, for she failed to ask permission of the gods to depart." Walter Spies died on a ship in which prisoners were being evacuated just before the Japanese occupation. My daughter has one of his rare and beautiful paintings on her wall. Colin McPhee died two weeks after the page proofs of his book had been corrected, Jane Belo before *Traditional Balinese Culture* was published, and Claire Holt in the midst of directing a new project on Indonesia.

As I write, Gregory is teaching, traveling with a selected

group of students who are planning to spend six weeks in Bali, which he will see again after an absence of thirty-three years.

I think it is a good thing to have had such a model, once, of what anthropological field work can be like, even if the model includes the kind of extra intensity in which a lifetime is condensed into a few short years.

PART THREE

18 On Having a Baby

I was always glad that I was a girl. I cannot remember ever wanting to be a boy. It seems to me this was because of the way I was treated by my parents. I was a wanted child, and when I was born I was the kind of child my parents wanted. This sense of satisfying one's parents probably has a great deal to do with one's capacity to accept oneself as a kind of person. As a girl, I knew that someday I would have children. My closest models, my mother and my grandmother, had both had children and also had used their minds and had careers in the public world. So I had no doubt that, whatever career I might choose, I would have children, too.

All through my childhood I enjoyed taking care of younger children. At family parties I would collect the smaller children and play games with them or tell them stories, and I enjoyed holding a baby in my arms until it fell asleep. I had dolls, but I never cared very much for them; I preferred real babies. And I never cared very much for pets, cats or dogs, because babies were more interesting. And there always were babies, our own or other people's babies, to hold, watch over, play with, and observe. I remember Ruth Benedict commenting that the baby of one of her acquaintances was "horrid." This surprised me. I had known horrid children and horrid adults, but in my mind babies, before they could walk and talk, were exempt. It was only later, when I watched births in the field, that I learned how the newborn baby does somehow embody the personality it will have and, if it dies soon after birth, epitomizes the person it would have become. But when Ruth made that remark I had seen only one newborn baby, my sister Priscilla, who was beautiful from her birth.

When I became engaged to Luther, I felt that this pledged us to have a child, and as he planned to enter the ministry I built up a picture of a rectory—modeled on Charlotte M. Yonge's stories of English rectories—with six children. Charlotte M. Yonge also wrote stirring stories of high adventure. These provided me with themes for adventurous daydreams, but in the end it was her domestic tales, in which she pictured children in the world of their day and night nurseries, that caught my imagination. When I was seventeen I gave a big Shrove Tuesday party for my sisters and made pancakes for some fifteen children. Grandma said, "Well, if you can keep as steady as you are now, with one in your arms and one pulling at your skirt, you'll do all right." And I never doubted that one day there would be one in my arms and one pulling at my skirt.

In the 1920's, we believed that children should be wanted and planned for. We were all very conscious of the new possibilities of birth control and safer childbirth, which meant that one could have a child even late in life. Luther and I wanted to finish our graduate work before we had a child, and then my field trip and Luther's traveling fellowship in Europe meant another postponement. But I was so sure that we would have children that Edward Sapir's advice that I would do better to stay at home and have a child than to go off to Samoa to study adolescent girls seemed peculiar to me. After all, men were not told to give up field work to have children! And I felt, rather than knew, that postponement—even postponement for a whole lifetime—need do no harm. A nun who loves children, but who devotes her life to the care of many of God's children, comes out unharmed, even though she may sometimes be wistful.

And then, in 1926, when I was told that I could never have children, I took this as a kind of omen about my future life. I had married Luther with the hope of rearing a houseful of children in a country parish. But now he was giving up the ministry and I was told that I could not have a child. I believed he would make a wonderful father, but this was no longer a possibility— for us.

On the other hand, I did not think that Reo, who wanted to marry me, would make an ideal father. He was too demanding and jealous of my attention; he begrudged even the attention I gave to a piece of mending. I had always felt that my father demanded too much of my mother and took her away from us to satisfy his own immediate and capricious requests to do something or find something for him. I did not want a marriage that repeated this pattern. But without children, the future looked quite different, and I decided to choose a life of shared field work and intellectual endeavor. I do not remember being terribly disappointed. There had always been the alternative of another kind of life. But Ruth was not pleased. Even though neither she nor anyone else questioned the doctor's verdict, she felt that I was somehow making an ascetic choice, a choice against the fullness of life.

So I married Reo. And, having made a commitment to work, I wrote to Professor Boas that he could send us anywhere he would send a man, since I would no longer need any special protection. I had accepted the need to give potentially childbearing women greater protection in the field than men. I still accept it, for the illness or death of a woman in the field makes for far more trouble for everyone—the people one is working with and the officials who have to deal with the situation. But this stricture no longer applied to me.

However, when we went to Mundugumor, I saw for the first time what the active refusal of children could do to a society. I had known many childless couples—some who did not want children and others, like the kings and queens in fairy tales, who had everything they wanted except a child. Mother had often spoken about the "selfishness" of childless couples who "preferred to go to Europe every summer," and she would say, self-righteously, "*Our* extravagances are our children." But as an anthropologist I learn best when I see what happens when a whole society embodies some particular trait—and among the Mundugumor both men and women actively disliked children. They are the only primitive people I have ever known who did not give an infant the breast when it cried. Instead, the child was hoisted up on the mother's shoulder. Sleeping babies were hung in rough-textured baskets in a dark place against the wall, and when a baby cried, someone would scratch gratingly on the outside of the basket.

The Mundugumor presented a harsh contrast to the Arapesh, whose whole meager and hardworking lives were devoted to growing their children. They had a strange kind of fascination for Reo, but I simply felt repelled. Added to this, we lived under constant tension. The Mundugumor had so recently been brought under control that it was not safe to let more than two or three people up into our house at a time, lest a head so easily taken might prove too tempting. In the village I walked about them quite freely, but I always kept the initiative. Probably this reinforced my distaste. But it was the Mundugumor attitude toward children that was decisive. I felt strongly that a culture that rejected children was a bad culture. And so I began to hope—not very logically, but with a kind of emotional congruence—that perhaps after all I could have a child, perhaps I could manage it.

I pointed out to Reo that one child would not interfere very much with our work. One child could always be put to bed in a bureau drawer. It was having two children that really changed life. Reo in no sense had made having no children a condition of our marriage, but I myself felt that our marriage had been a pact that committed us to field work as a way of life—and by this time we were very heavily committed to field work. And in spite of the difficulties, it was a more peaceful existence than our life in an academic setting, where Reo was almost unendurably harassed by his constant feelings of rivalry. A little later, while we were in Tchambuli, I had a miscarriage, but this did not weaken my renewed belief that somehow I was going to have a child.

Later, when Gregory and I were married and working in Bali, I continued to hope for a child, but once again I had several early miscarriages. Then, in 1938, when we went to the Sepik, it appeared that I might be having a premature menopause—again a doctor's theory. I was sad, but it was the kind of sadness that accompanies a hope that has been sustained. I wanted a child, but I did not feel, as Ruth had felt, that there was no possible compensation for not having a child. If I was now reaching a stage in my life in which it was certain that I could never have a child, I could face that, not with remorse or guilt, but only with regret.

Something very special sometimes happens to women when they know that they will not have a child—or any more children. It can happen to women who have never married, when they reach the menopause. It can happen to widows with children who feel that no new person can ever take the place of a loved husband. It can happen to young wives who discover that they never can bear a child. Suddenly, their whole creativity is released—they paint or write as never before or they throw themselves into academic work with enthusiasm, where before they had only half a mind to spare for it. I think that if I had had six children, I would have had energy to spare for other things, especially when the children were older, but they would have come first. And six children who come first take up most of one's time and energy, and, if they are deeply wanted, in a very satisfying way.

I remember the flash of insight I had in 1940 as I sat talking to a small delegation that had come to ask me to address a women's congress. I had my baby on my lap, and as we talked I recalled my psychology professor's explanation of why women are less productive than men. He had referred to a letter written by Harriet Beecher Stowe in which she said that she had in mind to write a novel about slavery, but the baby cried so much. It suddenly occurred to me that it would have been much more plausible if she had said "but the baby smiles so much." It is not that women have less impulse than men to be creative and productive. But through the ages having children, for women who wanted children, has been so satisfying that it has taken some special circumstance—spinsterhood, barrenness, or widowhood—to let women give their whole minds to other work.

When we returned to Bali for a brief stay in 1939, it appeared that I was, after all, pregnant. And so I was carried up and down the muddy, steep mile from the main road to Bajoeng Gede. The villagers had rigged up a kind of sedan from one of our old bamboo chairs. But the bamboo had dried out, and in the middle of the trip the chair suddenly collapsed on itself and held me as in a vise. That night, in the guesthouse in which we were staying in Kintamani, I had a rather bad miscarriage and the Dutch doctor was summoned. In those days Dutch doctors—indeed all the Dutch—strongly believed in having children. Every hotel room in the Indies had at least one crib, sometimes more. Instead of advising me not to try again for a while, the Dutch doctor said, "You want a child, yes?" and continued with homely advice.

By the time we reached Chicago, on our way back to New York, I thought I was pregnant again. One of the complications in the field is the difficulty of knowing whether you are, or are not, pregnant. But now it was possible to find out and to take precautions. However, we were visiting friends at the University of Chicago and had little time to ourselves; and so, instead of consulting a physician, I asked the secretary of the Anthropology Department to arrange for a test. The result was negative. I was heartbroken. Hope deferred was quite a different thing from resignation to what could not be changed.

Nevertheless, the first few weeks in New York were inexplicably peculiar. Without any good explanation for my mood, I was fretful, irritable, and cantankerous. I even had a sudden attack—the only one I ever had—of morning sickness. But I knew I was not pregnant. Finally, because I felt so strange, we went to a doctor, who said that either I was very pregnant or else I had a tumor and would have to be operated on immediately. The danger of a little knowledge! No one had warned me not to touch alcohol before taking a pregnancy test—and in Chicago, on the night before, we had gone to a big, gay party given by the Ogburns.

From the moment it was certain that I was pregnant, I took extreme precautions. I took a leave of absence from the Museum and gave up riding on streetcars, trains, and buses. I was given vitamin E as an aid to nidification, and I kept the baby.

We had planned to stay in the United States only briefly and then to go to England. There we intended to live in Cambridge, where Gregory held a fellowship in Trinity College. Now it appeared that I might have to have the baby in America and cope with all the tiresome regulations of hospitals and doctors that made breast feeding difficult and prevented a mother from keeping the baby in the room with her.

But perhaps there was a way around the problem. I decided to start with the coming baby and work backward. I looked for a pediatrician first, and talked with Ben Spock, a young pediatrician who had been psychoanalyzed and who was recommended to me by my child development friends. I explained to Ben that I wanted him to be present at the birth, so that he could take over the baby's care immediately, that I wanted to have a film made of the baby's birth, so that afterward it could be referred to with some degree of accuracy; that I wanted a wet nurse if my milk was slow in coming in, and that I wanted permission to adjust the feeding schedule to the baby instead of the clock.

Ben replied genially—for after all he was dealing with someone more or less of his own age with a reputation in his field—that he would come to the delivery and that I could feed the baby as often as I pleased. He also knew of a good obstetrician, Claude Heaton, who had some odd ideas and might be willing to listen to me.

It turned out that Dr. Heaton was deeply interested in American Indian medicine and that he was delighted to consider my ideas—including the fact that I wanted no anesthesia unless it was absolutely necessary. He happily entered into plans to persuade the nursing sisters at the French Hospital to cooperate with my wish to breast-feed the baby in response to the baby's own needs. As part of his efforts in this direction he showed them one of our New Guinea films depicting a scene just after childbirth.

While all these arrangements were being made, we still hoped that it might be possible for me to travel to England before the baby was born. In August I was once more allowed to travel. As a first trial, we made the long, slow train journey to New Hampshire to visit Larry and Mary Frank, who were to provide a second home for all of us in the years to come. While we still were at Cloverly, the Franks' summer home, after several days' fascinating discussion with J. H. Woodger, the philosopher-biologist, the stunning news came of the Soviet-German neutrality pact. Then, when we were back in New York, the German armies invaded Poland.

It was clear that unless the British government could find some use for Gregory in the United States, he would have to leave for England immediately. He went to see the British consul, who told him, "If you were forty-nine and had a bad heart, I'd say stay. As it is, I'd advise you to go back." Four days later, when Geoffrey Gorer came to New York from a vacation in Yucatán, the orders had changed and he was advised to remain in America. Gregory, however, had to sail. He cabled his mother the date on which the ship was expected to arrive and added, "Inform National Register." He assumed that he would at once be used as a social scientist. Actually, although highly trained scientists were reserved from active military service, it was some time before the British were ready to put their intellectuals to work at specialized tasks.

And so it came about that at thirty-eight, after many years of experience as a student of child development and of childbirth in remote villages—watching children born on a steep wet hillside, in the "evil place" reserved for pigs and defecation, or while old women threw stones at the inquisitive children who came to stare at the parturient woman—I was to share in the wartime experience of young wives all around the world. My husband had gone away to take his wartime place, and there was no way of knowing whether I would ever see him again. We had a little money, a recent bequest from Gregory's aunt Margaret, so I would not have to work until after the baby was born. But that was all. Initially, we had thought that I might join Gregory in England, but my mother-in-law wrote that they were sending away busloads of pregnant women. Obviously it was better to stay in America than to become a burden in Britain as the country girded itself for war.

As a temporary measure, my friend Marie Eichelberger organized her ground-floor apartment so that I could live with her for the three months before the baby was expected. She even brought in a large armchair, strong enough for Gregory to sit in, if he should be able to return to New York. She carefully fed me low-calorie vegetables and rationed me on high-calorie foods. I also was given calcium and a little thyroid. This was about all that was known about feeding a pregnant woman.

At that time physicians were obsessed with the idea that pregnant women should not gain weight—in almost total disregard for the well-being of their unborn babies. Today, extravagant disregard for the safety of the baby has taken another form, as pregnant women, determined not to give in to coddling, engage in hazardous sports, work full time, take no precautions to have a responsible person nearby in the last weeks of pregnancy, and cheerfully risk having their babies born in taxis or police cars or at the office. Mothers even risk being alone when the new baby is born with all the difficulty of having to cope with the frightened older children. And wholly inexperienced young fathers aspire to act as midwives. These extreme rejections of our contemporary social regime are contrapuntal to "natural childbirth"—the elaborate and beneficent preparation for child bearing invented and elaborated by men to indoctrinate women (the phrase is a masculine one) with the idea that childbirth is natural!

I was rosily healthy and happy and had on my cheeks the rare "mask of pregnancy." I did not experience the extreme dimming of mental activity that affects some women—I suspect particularly women who very much enjoy carrying a child. During the whole summer Gregory and I had worked very hard cataloguing our Balinese films and 25,000 stills. The stills were on long rolls of film that Gregory would hold up to the light, while I followed my notes, to identify the scenes and the actors. Periodically we invited colleagues to come to see the films and help us to develop hypotheses from these first comparative films of human behavior. I also did some writing and in the autumn I taught at Vassar in the Child Development Department. While I lectured, Mary Fisher (Mary Fisher Langmuir Essex) sat on the steps of the little podium to be sure I would not fall off.

During these months I had all the familiar apprehensions about what the baby would be like. There was some deafness in my family, and there had been a child who suffered from Mongolism and a child with some severe form of cerebral palsy. There also were members of my family whom I did not find attractive or endearing, and I knew that my child might take after them. Distinguished forebears were no guarantee of normality. But what I dreaded most, I think, was dullness. However, I could do something about anxieties of this kind by disciplining myself not to expect the child to be any special kind of person—of my own devising. I felt deeply—as I still feel—that this is the most important point about bringing into the world a child that will have its own unique and clear identity.

So I schooled myself not to hope for a boy or a girl, but to keep an open mind. I schooled myself to have no image of what the child would look like and no expectations about the gifts he or she might, or might not, have. This was congenial to me, for I had already learned to watch carefully the power that my imagination could have over the thoughts and dreams of other people. People would come to me with some vague stirring of ambition, some vague glimpse of a possible future, and unless I was careful, I would find myself imagining a whole future and the course of action necessary to grasp it. As students or friends talked about what they wanted to be or do, a panorama would unfold before my eyes in which I could see how some special combination of talent and experience might make possible a unique contribution to the world. It was better, I had learned, to listen and occasionally suggest some alternatives or some of the complications of the course chosen by the other person. In the same way, I determined not to limit the child that was to be born—not to hope for it to be beautiful or intellectually gifted or temperamentally happy.

There was another problem, too, of which I was quite aware. I had been a "baby carriage peeker," as Dr. David Levy described the child with an absorbing interest in babies, and he identified this as one of the traits that predisposed one to become an overprotective mother. When I told him, in a telephone conversation, that I was expecting a baby, he asked, in that marvelous therapeutic voice which he could project even over the telephone, "Are you going to be an overprotective mother?" I answered, "I'm going to try not to be." But I realized that whatever predisposition in this direction I might have must have been reinforced by hope that was so often disappointed, and I knew that I would have to work hard not to overprotect my child, but to ensure my child's freedom to find its own way of taking hold of life and becoming a person.

I did not, of course, have to contend with the kinds of ambivalence that bedevil the newly married, who are afraid of sharing their so recently established intimacy with a newcomer. Nor did I worry about what having a child might do to my career. I already had a reputation on which I could rest for several years, and our Balinese and Iatmul field trip had provided materials on which I could work for the rest of my life. Before the war disrupted plans to live in England, I had intended to stay at home in Cambridge in order to look after the baby and work up our field notes. I had never cared about having any particular professional status; in the Cambridge of

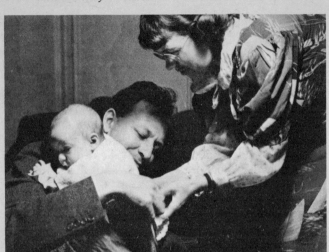

Catherine with her parents, 1940.
Photograph by Jane Belo

those days, in any case, feminine aspirations were meaningless. Men dined in hall several times a week and left their wives at home. I expected to have the baby to care for, and there was plenty of work to do.

The day before the baby was born, while I was working on Balinese films with Colin McPhee, a cable came from Gregory telling me that he had applied for a permit to come to America. There seemed to be nothing to be gained by staying in England. In fact, he had finally been rebuked for not getting on with the analysis of his field materials, the purpose for which he had been given the fellowship at Trinity.

The following night my father came over from Philadelphia and took me out to dinner. Soon after he brought me home, the water broke. It is astonishing how seldom things of this kind, which are apparently innerly determined, happen in the wrong place and at the wrong time. Six weeks earlier, I had spoken at Barnard's seventy-fifth anniversary celebration. When my former professor, Miss Howard, telephoned to ask whether I would do this, I had said, "But I'm expecting a baby at about that time." Her response came crisply, "Well, you won't have it at the dinner, will you?" And as I was getting ready to go to the hospital, Dr. Beatrice Hinkle telephoned to ask me about accepting an award and did not see any reason why the imminent birth of the baby should interfere with my speaking to her.

At the hospital I was made to time my own pains with an ordinary watch, and I remember my annoyance at not having a stopwatch. They were convinced that as a primipara I could not be so ready for birth and I was given medication to slow things down. In the end, the baby's birth had to be slowed down for another ten minutes while Myrtle McGraw, who was making the film of the birth, sent for a flashbulb that had been left in her car. All night I felt as if I were getting an attack of malaria, but I did not know—one of those things one does not know—whether the sensation of having a baby might not feel like malaria. And I was fascinated to discover that far from being "ten times worse than the worst pain you have ever had" (as our childless woman doctor had told us in college) or "worse than the worst cramps you ever had, but at least you get something out of it" (as my mother had said), the pains of childbirth were altogether different from the enveloping effects of other kinds of pain. These were pains one could follow with one's mind; they were like a fine electric needle outlining one's pelvis.

Today, preparation for natural childbirth gives women a chance to learn and to think about the task of labor, instead of simply fearing how they will endure the pains. In fact, the male invention of natural childbirth has had a magnificent emancipating effect on women, who for generations had been muffled in male myths instead of learning about a carefully observed actuality. I have never heard primitive women describe the pains of childbirth. But in societies in which men were forbidden to see birth, I have seen men writhing on the floor, acting

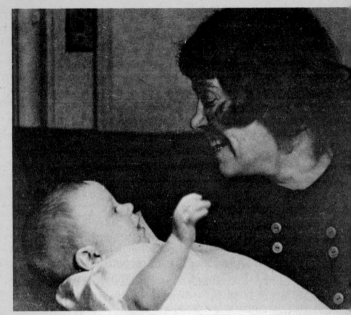

With Catherine, 1940

out their conception of what birth pangs were like. In one such society, the wife herself had squatted quietly on a steep hillside in the dark and had cut the cord herself, following the instructions not of a trained midwife but of the woman who had most recently borne a child.

Mary Catherine Bateson was born on December 8, 1939, and looked very much herself.

But I did have malaria, and the day after the baby's birth my fever shot up. Now my original choice of an obstetrician, as someone who would support what I wanted for the baby, paid off in the mysterious way that a correct choice so often determines that the outcome will be felicitous. For Dr. Heaton, who was open-minded beyond most men of his day, believed me when I said that this was an ordinary attack of tertian malaria, with familiar timing. He said reasonably, "She's had it, and none of us knows anything about it." And he found an ancient book in which quinine was prescribed as a post-partum drug and let me have the thirty grains a day I was accustomed to taking. Someone else might well have diagnosed the malaria as puerperal fever. I would then have been banished from the birth pavilion and my baby would have been put into a nursery to learn the lazy habits of bottle-fed babies and perhaps would never have learned to feed from the breast.

For with all the positive forces at one's disposal—I had enough money, I had knowledge, I had reputation and prestige, I even had a film of a newborn baby in New Guinea to show to the nurses—there are limits to what one can do within a culture. The pressures of an economy building up for wartime were already felt in the hospital. Nurses were in short supply. Keeping one's baby in the same hospital room was forbidden by state law. Four-hour feeding intervals were enjoined for babies weighing more than seven pounds, and my baby was several ounces over that.

The best that could be done—the closest approximation to rooming-in and self-demand feeding, as these practices later came to be called—was to give me the baby to be fed every three hours, as if she weighed less than seven pounds, and to allow me to feed her at night. According to hospital practice, then and now, a baby should go home from the hospital ready to sleep the night through —already, at a few days old, resigned to a world whose imposed rhythms are strange and uncongenial. Although Dr. Heaton's wooing of the nurses' interest had been successful, they were too busy to manage any further alterations of the customary routine. The night I arrived the nursing sister in charge had said to me, "I understand we are to let you do just what you want." An astonishing statement, but however willing she was, there were limits beyond which she could not move.

Before Gregory left for England, we had discussed the question of the baby's name. We had already decided that if the baby were a boy, we would make our home in England, because the English did a better job of bringing up a boy; but if it were a girl, we would live in the

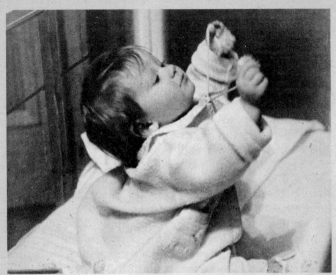

ABOVE Catherine, 1940

RIGHT Catherine with
Nanny Burrows, 1940

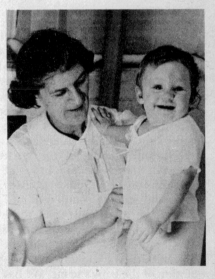

United States, where girls are better off. But in any event, the child's surname would be Bateson, and so we considered Bateson names. We decided that we would name a girl Mary, after the most distinguished of Gregory's paternal aunts, a pioneer historian, who had died young, much loved and deeply regretted. Naming a child after someone who has died young is in some sense, I think, a promise that an interrupted pattern will, after all, be completed.

But when I suggested that a boy should be named William, Gregory dissented. "Too hard on librarians," he commented. His geneticist father was William Bateson and his theologian grandfather, Master of St. John's College, had been William H. Bateson. Evidently Gregory already expected that the child would one day write books. And in this case, another William would simply add confusion.

After a time I found that I did not really feel at home with the name Mary. I wanted to name our child Katherine after my lost little sister, whom I had named. I proposed that we spell the name Catherine, to match her Bateson grandmother's initials, C. B. I had written about this to Gregory, and he had agreed. We had also discussed circumcision, which Gregory disapproved of, but the question was left unresolved. When the cable was sent, "Mary Catherine Bateson, born December 8th," Gregory started to cable, in a return message, "Don't circumcise," and then, remembering he had a daughter, cabled instead, "Don't christen."

Three days after her birth, a package arrived in the mail addressed to Miss Mary Catherine Bateson. Reading this, I started the process of learning to treat my daughter as a separate person with an identity completely her own.

In my family I was treated as a person, never as a child who could not understand. My grandmother shared her worries about my parents with me as she combed my hair. My mother took me with her when she did field work among recently arrived immigrants. My father taught me to look him in the eye when I recited a poem to an audience. To them I was an individual. It might be necessary to keep me—as a child—from reading too much or sitting up too late. But it was never suggested that because I was a child I could not understand the world around me and respond to it responsibly and meaningfully.

Now there was Catherine, a new person.

19 *Catherine, Born in Wartime*

We called her Cathy. She was fair-haired, her head was unmarred by a hard birth or the use of instruments, and her expression was already her own. I was completely happy.

As she was born on the Feast of the Immaculate Conception, it pleased the sisters at French Hospital that she was also named Mary. But she has never been called by this name. More recently as she has grown older, she has wanted to be called Catherine. Try as I do to call people by whatever name they wish, I find this difficult. Perhaps it is because I have lived so long among peoples for whom names were too vital a part of the personality to be treated lightly, among whom true names were not pronounced. For me the name Catherine carries a heavy weight, compounded as it is not only of all the Katherines who preceded my daughter but of her complete self as well. Here we have compromised. I speak of her as Cathy when I refer to her as a child, but when I talk about her older years, she is Catherine.

My friend Margaret Fries, who did pioneering work on the propensities of the newborn, came to the hospital to give Cathy her tests and found her to be well on the quiet side. Although she did not fall asleep, as some new-

born babies do when they are frustrated, she did not
fight for the nipple when it was taken away from her.
Margaret Fries' counsel was that she was just quiet
enough so that it would be unwise to subject her to
much frustration. Some babies can adapt to life only by
occasional hard crying, but we saw to it that Cathy had
as little occasion as possible to cry.

Inevitably her arrival was accompanied by a good deal
of excitement. I had so many friends, and so many of
them came from circles in which children were a major
preoccupation—educators, child analysts, and child psychologists. They all shared my delight in having a child.
And so did my childless friends—Jane Belo, who had been
so close to us in Bali and who had been with us in Kintamani when I lost a baby there, and Marie Eichelberger,
who took Cathy as her special charge and became "Aunt
Marie" forever. In England, Nora Barlow began to plan
all over again for a Darwin-Bateson marriage as she
visualized Cathy as a prospective bride for her grandson
Jeremy, who was born four months earlier.

Cathy's paternal grandmother wrote that the baby's
hands were like her own father's hands. He had been a
surgeon at Guy's Hospital in London and it was fabled
that when his students watched him operate they were
hypnotized by the beauty of his hands. My mother-in-law
added that "Margaret has nice hands, too, though small."
This gave me a twinge of surprise, for I had always
thought that small hands were embellishment in a
woman, not to be dismissed with a "though." All the
Batesons and Durhams were tall, and I had a momentary
worry—that did recur from time to time—that Cathy
might have my features, which are better in a small
face, but that she might grow like a bean pole to match
her paternal inheritance.

One of the most fascinating preoccupations when one
has a child of one's own is watching for the appearance of
hereditary traits and predispositions that can be attributed to—or blamed upon—one side of the family or the
other. Like everything else about biological parenthood,
it is a mixed blessing. The traits in which one takes pride

and the traits of the other parents whom one loves are doubly endearing in the shared child. The child who is born with such a combination, as I was, starts off in life with a special blessing. But the child who displays repudiated parental traits starts life with a handicap. The parents have to make an extra effort not to respond negatively to those traits in their child which they dislike or fear in themselves.

Cathy inherited a felicitous combination of family traits. Her eyes were blue, bluer than her father's or mine, and her hair, blond that changed to light brown, was indistinguishable from ours. Her long fingers are her father's. When she is still, she uses her hands as her father does, with the fingers arranged asymmetrically; when she moves and talks, she uses her hands symmetrically, as I do. There is one photographic sequence, made when she was about three, in which she shifts back and forth in just this way, a dozen times on one reel of film.

Bringing up Cathy was an intellectual as well as an emotionally exciting adventure. I believed that the early days of infancy were very important—that it made a difference how a child was born, whether it was kept close to its mother, whether it was breast-fed, and how the breast feeding was carried out. I also realized that when we began to regulate child feeding by the clock and a measured formula in a bottle, this was done with the best intentions. For if babies were to be fed cow's milk, milk that came in unlimited quantities from a dairy— and bottle feeding was initially an urban phenomenon— then a system had to be devised that somehow approximated the delicate self-regulating system that develops between a breast-feeding mother and her breast-fed baby. And if more babies were to be protected from weakening and dying because their mothers' milk was not adequate or because a particular child could not be well nourished by its own mother, then some babies—perhaps a majority —might have to be bottle-fed. But in 1939 I only vaguely understood these things.

At that time it was believed that the crucial thing for a child's survival and well-being was the mother's acceptance of her baby and her acceptance of breast feeding. Only later we heard about the rejecting baby—the baby that could not adapt to its mother. Still later we heard about the failed nursing couple—the mother and infant who, although they did not reject each other, were physiologically unadapted to each other.

I was trying to invent something new—to adapt breast feeding to modern living conditions and to use a clock in a situation in which the mother who constantly carried her baby under her breast or in a net bag on her back had no need of a clock. And I introduced the idea of taking notes on the progress of the breast feeding, so that I would know—and not retrospectively falsify, as it is so easy to do—what actually happened. My mother had expressed her love for me by taking voluminous notes on my development. And I myself had been watching and recording the behavior of children for many years. For me note-taking was, and it is, part of life.

From the moment we left the hospital and escaped from the hospital rhythm, I struggled to establish breast feeding in response to Cathy's expressed need. Until then I could not have distinguished her spontaneous cry from the crying of all the babies segregated in the hospital nursery, where they suffered all the disadvantages—and lacked the advantage of having a mother nearby—of creatures born in a litter, kittens or puppies.

As so many war wives were to do, I took my newborn baby home to my father's house in Philadelphia. As there had been no baby there for thirty years, Mother had forgotten almost all the lore she had ever known. But she did remember that little babies cried because they were bored, and she recommended that we prop Cathy up on pillows so she could see the world. I had a young nurse from Appalachia, who had been trained to concentrate on keeping the baby warm. It was a very cold winter, and the old house was drafty. When the nurse was away, there was our large, warm, black housekeeper on whose lap the baby immediately became placid.

I used to sit up in the low armless rocking chair in which my grandmother had rocked my father and listen to the strange nighttime radio programs as Susie or Lucy, at two o'clock in the morning, asked for a special piece to be played for Johnny or Bill traveling east or west on some numbered road. I had nothing to do except keep my milk up and feed and hold the baby. I did not have to go anywhere, I had no housework to do, no uneasy husband to placate, no worries about money—in fact, I faced none of the problems that can make the first baby so difficult for an inexperienced young mother. But I was trying to do something, consciously and in a new way, that combined our best knowledge and my own observations of mothers and babies in many cultures.

I drank three quarts of milk a day to be sure there was enough milk for Cathy. But then Dr. Joseph Stokes, the pediatrician who was the friendly surrogate for Ben Spock while I was in Philadelphia, said that my milk was too rich and advised feeding the baby water first. This infuriated her. And once when she raged, I found myself stamping my foot in the kind of blind responsive rage a mother can feel when her child screams unappeased. I caught it, realized what it was. Experienced only once, it was enough to make me recognize what lies back of the desperation of a young mother, innocent of all knowledge of babies, who feels that she will never be able to cope with her baby and goes into a postpartum depression.

But this, too, is something I understand better in retrospect. In 1939, we did not know how intimately a postpartum depression is related to helpless isolation. What the young mother needs most is affectionate counsel and helping hands—and especially someone she trusts who can say, "In a few days or at most a few weeks you won't feel that you can't manage it all. Suddenly, one day, your step will lighten and you will feel like yourself again and know you are a mother with a baby you can enjoy —just as you wanted to."

So Cathy cried and I fed her when she cried and kept careful notes. She was an early-responsive child who responded with real tears when I shifted her to a room where I thought I could hear her immediately but came late in answer to her cry. Gregory came home from England when she was six weeks old. We let the nurse go and took care of her ourselves for a whole weekend during which she had a bad episode of colic. This was the only time he took much physical care of her. But it was enough to establish a very close relationship between Gregory and Cathy.

Until the early 1950's, when so many young student fathers lived in cramped quarters with their tiny infants and shared in their care, we did not know how much depended on such an intimate relationship between father and child. There is something in the kind of response a very young baby evokes, perhaps with its hand that still retains the infantile grasping reflex and curls so firmly and trustfully around an adult finger, that brings the father in and wins his enthusiasm. If this close contact is postponed—if the father believes that a baby must be approached gingerly or must be kept at arm's length—his relationship to his child will be drastically different from the mother's, and the experience of children of the two sexes also will be forever different.

Almost immediately, Gregory worried about the effect of my young Appalachian nurse's grammar on the baby. It seemed clear that I must try to find a trained English nanny, who would fit her father's picture of how a child should be brought up. It would also prepare her to live in England, if this was what we would do at some time in the future.

As soon as we could, we went back to New York. With a safe base in Marie Eichelberger's apartment, where the baby slept in a padded bureau drawer, we set out to find an apartment and a nurse-housekeeper. As before, when I searched for an obstetrician, I began with the baby. We would find the nurse first and then get an apartment that would fit the new household. My mother, with her imaginative humanism, had employed servants with children, so that their domestic work was a way of keeping with them, instead of separating them from, their children. I decided that we, too, should look for a mother-child pair.

Catherine and her father

Once again I was extraordinarily fortunate. Helen Burrows, who became Cathy's nurse for two and one-half years, had begun her working life as the third nursemaid in a great house in the English countryside, and eventually, having crossed the Atlantic during the submarine peril of World War I, she became the nanny of a child of the Governor-General of Canada. She married a butler, who disappeared after a stormy marriage and left her with a daughter to support. Audrey was now fourteen, a big strong girl, able and ready to engage in jolly physical play with a baby. Helen was very intelligent and a great reader. She said she took the job with us because she liked the look of the baby—for babies do play a part in their own fate from the very first days of their lives—and because she was intrigued by the things I told her. For example, we planned to have photo floodlights in every room so that we could catch important moments in Cathy's life.

Helen was devoted and endlessly patient. She knew just how to bring up a baby and still focus its affection on its mother, away from herself. She would have Cathy on the floor learning to "love that teddy," and then, when I would enter the room, she would say, without changing the tone of her voice, "There's your mummy. Love your mummy."

The years that Helen and Audrey stayed with us were grueling ones as far as work was concerned. The first semester I taught at New York University at noon and after class was rushed home in a car provided by a devoted student. By that time Cathy had established her own comfortable schedule of feeding. Very considerately, she had dropped the early nighttime feeding that had made any kind of evening life impossible, but I continued to feed her at one or two in the morning until she was six months old. I went back to work at the Museum parttime also, and with the deepening war crisis we both became heavily involved in the kind of contributions that social scientists could make. Gregory could get only small sums of money from England, and I had to supplement this with whatever lecturing and teaching I could do.

This meant that I had less time with Cathy than I had hoped for. But I continued to breast-feed her and taught her to feed herself with a spoon when Ben Spock insisted, "All the brightest babies I know feed themselves at this age." Nanny demurred. Watching the way Cathy handled her sand shovel, she insisted that she was not yet ready to use a spoon, but she could not stand the imputation that her baby was not as bright as the brightest child. In the the afternoon, when we came home, we spent a couple of hours with the baby. In the morning, too, she was brought to us, ready to play with the motes in the shafts of sunlight or to marvel at the "light birds" on the ceiling, made by stirring a sunlit cup of tea.

Nanny was so intelligent and embodied such a long, wise tradition of child care that I felt Cathy was physically and mentally completely safe with her. Once in the middle of the night I stopped outside the nursery door to listen to a spirited argument about how many elephants they had seen at the zoo, an argument that was conducted on a perfectly equal basis with no holds barred. Like every good nurse, Nanny put the child before all other tasks. Consequently she had the patience, which few harried mothers can afford, to let a child dawdle—put on one shoe and then play with the kitty before she put on the other shoe. And when Nanny was busy, Audrey would "go and talk to the baby, she's lonely." At night she was rocked to sleep, actually shaken in a portable baby carriage that could be folded up and taken wherever I went on lecture and conference trips. For then Gregory and I took care of Cathy, as Nanny had to stay at home with Audrey.

By the time she could talk, she would waken beside me in a strange room and say, "Mummy," even though she had slept with Nanny every night in the whole previous month. I saw to it that she was never left in a strange place with a strange person. First a familiar person introduced her to the new place, or the stranger who was to care for her was introduced to her in a familiar place. She went easily and happily to strangers and showed discomfort only in the presence of visitors who, like her grandfather, were themselves a little too anxious.

She learned to talk very early and began to use the intensive mode, which makes it very easy to transpose sentences. For example, when someone would ask her, "Did you sit on a rock in Central Park?" she would answer, "Yes, I did sit on a rock in Central Park." This gave an impression of enormous comprehension, and as a result, people talked with her using more and more difficult constructions. Her warm responsiveness, her trustingness, and her outgoing interest in people and things all evoked lively responses from others and set the stage for her expectation that the world was a friendly place.

When she was eighteen months old, we were asked to plan a film that dealt with the problem of childhood trust. This brought us up against the problem that bedevils all the news media—how to represent adequately

LEFT Catherine

BELOW Catherine
and her mother

something that is good. Fear and rage are easy to photograph, but trust is not. Finally we settled for pictures of Cathy, wearing a baby harness, hurling herself over the edge of a steep decline, completely secure in the knowledge that her father was firmly holding on to the leash. This film was never made.

Later, when she was almost three, a plan was made for a film of a child being given a routine physical examination. This was to be shown to working mothers who were shy of letting their children go to day-care centers. Cathy was chosen to portray the child because she was so unfrightened and so accustomed to photography. But no one considered the response of the pediatrician. The film turned into a sequence in which Cathy, smiling and nude, put the pediatrician, who was shaking with stage fright, at his ease. But the film was never used.

How much was temperament? How much was felicitous accident? How much could be attributed to upbringing? We may never know. Certainly all a mother and father can claim credit for is that they have not marred a child in any recognizable way. For the total adult-child situation could be fully understood only if one also had the child's own interpretation of the parts that adults played in its life.

In the winter our household consisted of Nanny, her daughter Audrey, Cathy, Gregory, and myself. But in summer we went to Holderness, New Hampshire, and lived near the Franks. There we were joined by two English children, Philomena and Claudia Guillebaud, whom we had brought over at the time of Dunkirk and who lived with my parents during the winter.

These summer households were filled with continuous hard work. It was there we viewed the whole set of Balinese stills in the evenings, with Audrey counting frames because the old film had no frame numbers. And during the day Gregory worked in an improvised darkroom, printing the pictures we had chosen for *Balinese Character*.

But in New Hampshire there was time, too, for long, restful hours with the Franks at Cloverly, for picnics and play, for taking photographic sequences, for hilarious rescue scenes as Cathy raced in her walker toward the shining strips of film that were hanging ready for work, for battles between the big children and the rampaging baby, and for the adventure of swimming in White Oak Pond.

In the summer months I had an opportunity to realize what it had been like to bring up a child in a household in which there were many willing hands ready to hold the baby and someone to do the endless chores and to sleep with the baby at night, so that the mother's contacts with her child were both intense and relaxed. In a sense it was all anachronistic and war-determined. Without the war we would have had only one adolescent, Audrey, instead of three. And, of course, having a nanny was a survival from an earlier day. Even before the war, nannies were disappearing in England; often the older ones stayed on to be the only servants in great houses that had been built to be cared for by a large staff of men and maid servants.

In those first two summers the two households—ours and the Franks—were drawn close together by mutual interests and warm concern into a happy friendship. I had first visited Cloverly in the summer of 1934, when Larry recruited me for the interdisciplinary seminar at Dartmouth at which I began my interdisciplinary work. At that time he was a widower who had lost two wives by death, and he had five children, two of them very small. When we came back from Bali, we found a beautiful young third wife, Mary, who with astonishing courage had taken on the household of five children, the eldest her own age, and a husband whose warmth made him ready to include a great number of colleagues and friends as part of his world.

Cloverly in the summertime became the center of the intellectual and human lives of a large group of friends, some of whom built homes nearby while others came up to take part in the conferences that Larry planned. At Cloverly there was a big sloping flower and vegetable garden where Larry and his visitors talked in the sunny

Catherine, Mary Frank, and her son Colin

afternoons while they weeded the beans or helped to pick peas for dinner at the long, hospitably crowded table. There were tennis courts and several little houses, one of them built for the boys and others intended to shelter those who needed quiet for work on a paper or a book. There were corn roasts down by the side of the lake and evenings of singing by a great blazing fire in the high-roofed living room.

But Cloverly was only the beginning. On Pearl Harbor Day, while we were taking part in a conference, Ruth Benedict asked whether I would go to Washington to take a job working on cultural change; Larry Frank, who was also at the conference, proposed that we spend the next summer not near but at Cloverly and then come to share the Franks' big house on Perry Street in New York City. Gregory was already working on a wartime project at the Museum of Modern Art, and I began to commute

ABOVE Larry and Mary
Frank at Cloverly

RIGHT Larry Frank
and his son Colin

to Washington, coming home for weekends. In the spring everything changed. We gave up our apartment and became part of a large joint household organized for wartime. Nanny began gently to prepare Cathy for her leaving at the end of the summer, during which I wrote *And Keep Your Powder Dry* and Gregory worked on the proofs of *Balinese Character*.

Cloverly and Perry Street gave us a way of life that sustained us all through the war. I formed with Larry the same kind of working alliance that I had formed long ago with Julian Gardy in Holicong. We worked and planned together, and he included me in one interdisciplinary enterprise after another. Meanwhile Mary included Cathy in the nursery which Mary's son Colin, a year younger, shared with her. When Cathy moved to Perry Street, she expressed both sides of her feeling. "This is a very big house, Aunt Mary," she said. "Can't we move into a little tiny house with Mummy and Daddy and Philomena and Claudia and Nanny and Audrey and you and Uncle Larry and Ladd and Allen and Margie and Harley and Barbie and Colin . . . ?"

Living in Perry Street, Cathy had all the benefits of a large household and at the same time had periods when she had her mother and father to herself. Larry and I worked in Washington and spent weekends in New York. In the summer of 1943, when I went to England to lecture, Gregory went to Washington for war work and then, in February, 1944, he went overseas for the duration of the war. But the joint life we had organized continued for Cathy and me until Larry retired in 1955 and sold the Perry Street house.

The atomic bomb exploded over Hiroshima in the summer of 1945. At that point I tore up every page of a book I had nearly finished. Every sentence was out of date. We had entered a new age. My years as a collaborating wife, trying to combine intensive field work and an intense personal life, also came to an end. From that time on I worked not with one other person but with many others, as my child grew up secure within the generosities of the Frank household.

From Cathy's birth I had tried to let her to be free to choose her own path, and in January, 1947, I wrote—for her—the last poem I have ever written:

> That I be not a restless ghost
> Who haunts your footsteps as they pass
> Beyond the point where you have left
> Me standing in the newsprung grass,
>
> You must be free to take a path
> Whose end I feel no need to know,
> No irking fever to be sure
> You went where I would have you go.
>
> Those who would fence the future in
> Between two walls of well-laid stones
> But lay a ghost walk for themselves,
> A dreary walk for dusty bones.
>
> So you can go without regret
> Away from this familiar land,
> Leaving your kiss upon my hair
> And all the future in your hands.

20 On Being a Grandmother

As the years went by, I had carefully not let myself hope that I would have grandchildren, as I knew before Catherine had children I would be old enough to be a great-grandmother. Great-grandmotherhood is something we do not think of as a likely possibility of the human condition, even now when it is becoming more common.

But I did think how delightful it would be, if it happened, to see my daughter with a child. And I wondered what kind of child Catherine and Barkev Kassarjian would have—she with her long ancestry from the British Isles and he with his long Armenian heritage in the Middle East, she with her English fairness and he with his dark eyes and black hair. Thinking back to my grandmother and my mother and the kind of mother I had tried to be and remembering all the different kinds of mothering people who had cared for my daughter in her childhood—her English nanny, her lovely young aunt Mary, and her devoted godmother, Aunt Marie, who brought in the generation of my grandmother's day when people respected heirlooms and passed their dolls on from generation to generation—I wondered what kind of child my daughter would have and what kind of mother she would be.

Rather carefully I also did not think too much about the kind of father my son-in-law would be, just as, earlier, I had not permitted myself to daydream about a son-in-law. When Biddy Barlow asked me, just before Catherine was married, "Whose side are you going to take?" I realized with a jolt that such a contingency had not occurred to me. So carefully had I restricted my daydreaming to what Barkev meant to Catherine that I had left myself out. It was an added delight, then, to discover that I enjoyed him very much. I appreciated and took great pleasure in his analytical mind, his keen enjoyment of all the concrete details of life, his sensitive regard for persons and lively respect for the nature of things.

When Catherine and Barkev lost their first baby in the Philippines—Martin, who was born too soon and lived only long enough to be christened and registered as a citizen—I knew that they both wanted a child very much. I knew also that bereavement had catapulted Catherine into the same position in which I had been placed by a long series of disappointed hopes; just as I had been, she was potentially an overprotective mother. And as I had done, she would have to school herself to give her child the freedom to take risks. I could feel again the terrible tingle in the calves of my legs that I had felt when Cathy became an intrepid climber of tall pine trees.

The baby they now expected was to be born in one of the best hospitals in the country, a hospital that had respect for fathers and one in which a mother had some hope of establishing breast feeding. Catherine had already selected as her pediatrician T. Berry Brazelton, who is playing an avant-garde role in his concern for child development. She had decided to combine motherhood with her work. During the summer before the baby was born she went to Austria to take part in a seminar organized by her father, and she planned to teach in the fall. The baby was due in September. Like so many other young people in the United States, Catherine and Barkev planned to move just before the baby was born, and so added to other complications all the confusion of making a new home.

When they moved in, the newly remodeled house—in which there was a small apartment for a baby-sitting young professional couple—was not finished. Teaching began, and the baby was not yet born. In the end, in spite of careful planning, something went wrong with the telephone connection to Barkev, a few blocks away, and Catherine was taken to the hospital in the fire chief's car summoned from the concerned fire department across the street. It was a modern version of having the baby born while the mother is out fishing in a canoe, far from the village and the waiting midwife.

When the news came that Sevanne Margaret was born, I suddenly realized that through no act of my own I had become biologically related to a new human being. This was one thing that had never come up in discussions of grandparenthood and had never before occurred to me. In many primitive societies grandparents and grandchildren are aligned together. A child who has to treat his father with extreme respect may joke with his grandfather and playfully call his grandmother "wife." The tag that grandparents and grandchildren get along so well because they have a common enemy is explicitly faced in many societies. In our own society the point

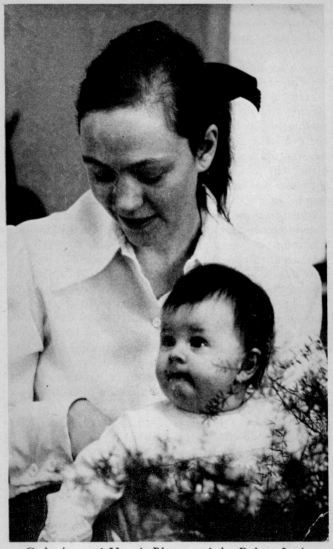

Catherine and Vanni. *Photograph by Robert Levin*

With my granddaughter. *Photograph by Robert Levin*

most often made is that grandparents can enjoy their grandchildren because they have no responsibility for them, they do not have to discipline them, and they lack the guilt and anxiety of parenthood. All these things were familiar. But I had never thought how strange it was to be involved at a distance in the birth of a biological descendant.

I always have been acutely aware of the way one life touches another—of the ties between myself and those whom I have never met, but who read *Coming of Age in Samoa* and decided to become anthropologists. From the time of my childhood I was able to conceive of my relationship to all my forebears, some of whose genes I carry, both those I did not know even by name and those who helped to bring me up, particularly my paternal grandmother. But the idea that as a grandparent one was dealing with action at a distance—that somewhere, miles away, a series of events occurred that changed one's own status forever—I had not thought of that and I found it very odd.

I felt something like the shock that must be felt by those who have lived all their lives secure in their citizenship in the nation of their birth and who then, suddenly, by the arbitrary act of some tyrannical government, find that they are disenfranchised—as happened to the old aristocracy in Russia after the revolution, to the Jews in Germany in the 1930's, and to the Turkish Armenians in Turkey. But of course what happened to me was not an arbitrary denial of something I had regarded as irreversibly given, but rather an arbitrary confirmation of a state which I felt that I myself had done nothing to bring about. Scientists and philosophers have speculated at length about the sources of man's belief that he is a creature with a future life or, somewhat less commonly, with a life that preceded his life on earth. Speculation may be the only kind of answer that is possible, but I would now add to the speculations that are more familiar another of my own: the extraordinary sense of having been transformed not by any act of one's own but by the act of one's child.

Then, as a new grandmother, I began both to relive my own daughter's infancy and to observe the manifestations of temperament in the tiny creature who was called Vanni—to note how she learned to ignore the noisy carpentry as the house was finished around her but was so sensitive to changes in the human voice that her mother had to keep low background music playing to mask the change in tone of voice that took place when someone who had been speaking then answered the telephone. I remarked how she responded to pattern in the brightly colored chintzes and the mobiles that had been prepared for her. I showed the movies of Cathy's birth and early childhood, to which my daughter commented, "I think my baby is brighter"—or prettier, or livelier—"than your baby!"

However, I felt none of the much trumpeted freedom from responsibility that grandparents are supposed to feel. Actually, it seems to me that the obligation to be a resource but not an interference is just as preoccupying as the attention one gives to one's own children. I think we do not allow sufficiently for the obligation we lay on grandparents to keep themselves out of the picture—not to interfere, not to spoil, not to insist, not to intrude—and, if they are old and frail, to go and live apart in an old people's home (by whatever name it may be called) and to say that they are happy when, once in a great while, their children bring their grandchildren to visit them.

Most American grandparents are supported in their laborious insistence on not being a nuisance by the way they felt toward their own parents and by the fierceness with which, as young adults, they resented interference by their parents and grandparents. But I had none of this. I had loved my grandmother and I had valued the way my mother nursed and loved her children. My only complaint when I took Cathy home as a baby was that Mother could not remember as much as I would have liked about the things it was useful to know. And I had quite gladly shared my baby with her nurse and with my closest friends.

I had hoped that Helen Burrows could come back to Catherine to take care of the new baby. But she was ill. Instead, Tulia Sampeur, my godson's Haitian nurse, went up to Cambridge to look after the new baby with her sure and practiced hands. Watching her, Catherine was able to explore the tremendous suggestibility of a new mother, who initially learns to follow the procedures in the care of her baby to which she is exposed immediately after delivery with a rigidity that is strangely reminiscent of the way in which young ducklings are imprinted to follow whatever moving figure they see. Catherine learned, as I had learned, that having a baby teaches you a great deal about mothers, however much you already may know about babies.

Sevanne Margaret, called Vanni, is the child her parents wanted. At birth she was petite and she has remained petite, so that people still respond to her as if she were almost weightless. She has a beautiful head of dark curling hair, her eyes dance with responsiveness, her laughter echoes her mother's laughter, and her confidence matches her father's as he tosses her, easily and surely, up in the air.

Last week I took her, now a little more than two years old, to the aquarium in Boston. It is a place that may well be a nightmare to many small children, for it is dark and crowded with shouting, rushing older children, and intermittently lights flash and loudspeakers boom. But Vanni, dressed in bright green, her astonishing hair blowing out behind her, fearlessly darted here and there, her progress interrupted only by a guard who picked her up to show her fish swimming too high for her eyes to see. She is already making a place for herself and in her minuteness and responsiveness evokes delight and response from others.

And I wonder again about special privilege. I think we shall continue to value diversity and to believe that the family—perhaps more widely assisted by grandparents, aunts and uncles, neighbors and friends, and supplemented by more varied experience in other settings— provides the context in which children are best reared to become full human beings. But how then are we to deal with the special privilege that is conferred on a child simply by being the child its parents wanted, which in turn sets the stage for becoming a person other people, too, will think they want?

There are some changes that can be made. In a very few years parents will be able to decide, in advance, the sex of the child they want, so that every child will be the desired son or daughter. Then, for the first time, every girl will know that she was chosen by her parents and is not, as so often has happened, the by-product of a search for boys. The kings and queens in the fairy tales that Catherine wrote as a child had daughters, and within the complexities of the Armenian tradition about the role of the firstborn, Barkev's elder brother already had a son. Among Armenians, "The Princess and the Pea" is a favorite fairy tale—a story about a princess who is so light and delicate that she feels the pea through a pile of mattresses, but a princess who is also ready to ride her own horse through the steepest and most dangerous mountain passes.

Perhaps we shall also be able to develop a climate of opinion in which a mother waits with suspended imagination for her unknown child, ready to greet a stranger. And adoption may become so common that the drama of waiting for the unknown child with all the weight of longing that is part of having a child by a deeply loved person will be balanced by the drama of going with a loved person to choose a child already born and ready to curl its hand around its adopting father's finger. Children may face gladly the knowledge that they were chosen for what they could be seen to be, a boy or a girl with white or black or brown or saffron skin and with eyes bright as stars or tranquil as dreams. Or they may know, happily, that they came as strangers and that they were welcomed by their parents who had not chosen them but in whose being they had a creative part.

The whole dilemma of humanity—to yield to and glory in the characteristics we share with other living creatures or, alternatively, to work at and glory in our capacity to

ABOVE Vanni with her parents Catherine and Barkev Kassarjian. *Photograph by Paul Byers*

LEFT Vanni. *Photograph by Ken Heyman*

transcend our creatureliness—is summed up in the acceptance of the biological child, however different it may be from the parents' dream of a child, and in the dignity and responsibility of those who, forgoing personal creativity, make a full and conscious choice of a child to bring up as their own.

But when all this comes about and the beliefs about such choices are expressed in ritual and art, people still will be faced—parents, real and adoptive, still will be faced—with the extraordinary unevenness, the uncontrollable inequalities of the kind of child that any baby, adopted or biologically one's own, turns out to be. It is true that parents play a considerable role in this. Catherine is a laughing, delighted, imaginative mother, and she gives her child, as she was given, the gift of complete attention. It is true that identical twins, one adopted by a smiling and open mother and the other by a mother who is dour and sour, will respond to the very different behavior of those two mothers. But there is still the possibility that a more smiling baby would have made the dour mother smile and that a fretful, unresponsive baby might have made the smiling mother fretful and anxious.

Not long before Christmas a television program showed a group of miserable children who were screaming and fearful of the department store Santa Claus onto whose lap they were reluctantly pulled. For any child who saw this televised scene, it was a prescription for fear and dread. However, Catherine and I took Vanni downtown to see Santa Claus. On the lower floors of the department store she rollicked through the aisles, got lost under stacks of bargain dresses, and emerged laughing to mock at any effort to dampen her delight. Upstairs, we stood in the long, roped-off line of waiting parents and children, the children becoming more anxious by the minute as they were constrained by their parents to stand still, while Vanni raced up and down the line swinging on the ropes that bound us in. As they approached Santa many of the children squirmed and fretted and some of them screamed, as they had been instructed by television to do. But Vanni, sitting contentedly on Santa's lap, "niced" his beard, his truly magnificent beard, as she had learned to do by stroking the fur of cats, the coats of dogs, and the smooth hair of other children.

Watching Vanni, I can see her mother's childhood reflected and intensified in many ways. She is very daring, but also very cautious. Just as her mother used to test every branch when she climbed a tall tree, so Vanni, learning to walk, measured the distance between table and chair. If the distance was too great, she dropped down to creep, but if she could just make it, she walked. She has her mother's reasonableness. If you can explain why you are asking something, she will accede—especially if you give her a part in the action. "Help" and "self"— meaning "I will do it myself"—are important words in her vocabulary. She also has her mother's tendency to dream out something without telling anyone what it is, and when the unwitting adult turns down a different path or enters a door first instead of last, she will burst into tears. Her dark eyes, inherited from her father, flash with some of the intensity that made my grandmother look so much fiercer than I ever did. My responses to her are compounded of my responses to the particularities of my own younger brother and sisters, of my own daughter, of all the babies I have held and cared for, and of all the babies I have observed and studied.

I discovered when I had a child of my own that I had become a biased observer of small children. Instead of looking at them with affectionate but nonpartisan eyes, I saw each of them as older or younger, bigger or smaller, more or less graceful, intelligent, or skilled than my own child. This troubled me. I felt that I learned a great deal about mothers by being one, but that I had become in some way a less objective observer of children. If I think of myself as a scientific observer of children, I would still say that this is true, that being a mother or a grandmother introduces a definite observational bias into descriptions of children of the same age as the child one sees most of from day to day.

But if I think of myself not as a professional student of childhood but simply as a human being, then it seems

Sevanne Margaret Kassarjian, photographed by her father

to me that the effect of my daughter and granddaughter on my view of children—and the world—has to be described quite differently. Instead of a bias that must be compensated for, I have acquired a special and perhaps transient sensitivity. It is as if the child to whom one is bound by greater knowledge and the particularity of love were illuminated and carried a halo of light into any group of children. When Vanni is present, I see the children around her with greater clarity; when she is not there, I visualize two-year-olds—all the two-year-olds I have ever known—with new comprehension. I see their faces more clearly. I understand again, or anew, how they formed their first words. I grasp the meaning of puckered eyebrows, a tensed hand, or a light flick of the tongue. The known and loved particular child makes it possible for one to understand better and care more about all children.

It is far more clear to me now than when I came out of Mundugumor that a society that has ceased to care about children, a society that cuts off older people from meaningful contact with children, a society that segregates any group of men and women in such a way that they are prevented from having or caring for children, is greatly endangered. It seems to me that this is one reason why, today, in the Catholic missions in New Guinea, the faith of the priests and the lay brothers may falter, while the sisters, who care for little children and are close to them, can work on. It is extraordinarily difficult to love children in the abstract, to devote oneself exclusively to the next generation, or in speaking to actual children to tell them with conviction, "Boys and girls of America, you are the hope of the world"—as we were told by a speaker whose eyes ranged unseeing over the heads of my high-school class in 1917. It is only through precise, attentive knowledge of particular children that we can become—as we must—informed advocates for the needs of all children and passionate defenders of the right of the unconceived to be well born.

Early this year I spent a month living in my sister's hospitable home so that I could be a resource, but not a burden, in the nearby Kassarjian household while Catherine and Barkev were preparing for a two-year work period in Iran. This crowded month, during which I could be a full-time grandmother to Vanni, has rounded out my understanding of something for which I have pleaded all my life—that everyone needs to have access both to grandparents and grandchildren in order to be a full human being.

In the presence of grandparent and grandchild, past and future merge in the present. Looking at a loved child, one cannot say, "We must sacrifice this generation for the next. Many must die now so that later others may live." This is the argument that generations of old men, cut off from children, have used in sending young men out to die in war. Nor can one say, "I want this child to live well no matter how we despoil the earth for later generations." For seeing a child as one's grandchild, one can visualize that same child as a grandparent, and with the eyes of another generation one can see other children, just as light-footed and vivid, as eager to learn and know and embrace the world, who must be taken into account—now. My friend Ralph Blum has defined the human unit of time as the space between a grandfather's memory of his own childhood and a grandson's knowledge of those memories as he heard about them. We speak a great deal about a human scale; we need also a human unit in which to think about time.

21 *Epilogue: Gathered Threads*

Where life and work are so closely interwoven, writing an autobiography raises a great many different kinds of questions. Some are very old questions that came to my

mind when I first wrote letters home from the field in
Samoa. Others were an accompanying refrain during the
many months while I was writing, months in which I
was also going back over my own footsteps, retracing the
seaways and airways I had traveled and spending time
once more among peoples I had studied and restudied to
see how their lives today fitted my memories and the
written records of earlier visits. Many questions came up
as I talked about the past I was writing about with some
of those who have been very close to my life and who are,
inevitably, part of this book. And then, as a recurrent
motif, there is the question of next steps in anthropology.
These questions, it seems to me, are also part of the
record.

Would I be able to say the things that would make
what I wrote intelligible to those who had lived in a very
different world, either because they did not do the kind
of work in which personal relations and working relations are inseparable or because they had never been in
any situation remotely resembling field work, in which one
lives isolated for many months, alone or with one companion, among a strange and initially incomprehensible
people? And would the life I had lived be intelligible to
young people born since World War II, reared in the
shadow of the bomb, alienated from the life of their
parents, and nurtured on television, which has made so
much that was high adventure for me into the trivia of
a morning newscast?

And then, a question that concerned all those whose
lives touched mine: Would I be able to write in a way
that would not hurt or offend those about whom I wrote
or those who read what I wrote about others? This is
one of the difficult things I have learned, as an anthropologist writing about the culture of another people and
the individuals who embody that culture. What one says
must be intelligible and bearable for those about whom
one writes and, at the same time, for the members of
one's own culture and for the people of all the other
cultures in the world who may read what one has written.
Sometimes anthropologists write about the peoples they

have studied in ways that deeply offend members of their own culture, who sense a rejection of themselves lying back of what the anthropologists themselves thought were sympathetic presentations of the other cultures. Sometimes, too, those who cannot bear any discussion of their own feelings also find unbearable any discussion of the feelings of others.

When I wrote a biography of Ruth Benedict, *An Anthropologist at Work,* I tried to meet these different and sometimes conflicting demands. But of course there was no way of being certain that I had done so. There was the problem, for example, of letters. Although the actual letters belong to the recipients, the original writer —or his family or literary executor—has a continuing right to release or withhold the use of the content of the letters. I had the rights to Ruth Benedict's own letters. Franz Boas' letters, which were deposited in the archives of the American Philosophical Society in Philadelphia, had become the property of the scholarly world. But the content of Edward Sapir's voluminous letters to Ruth Benedict—her letters to him had not survived—remained the property of his family. I submitted to them the excerpts from this correspondence that I planned to reproduce, and I omitted anything which they felt would violate his expressed dislikes. There were also those whom Ruth had known well who did not wish even their names to be mentioned in a book about her, and I honored their wishes. There were, in addition, a few friends who objected to any discussion of the way Ruth had felt about her childlessness. But this she had written about at length and over many years' time in her diaries and journals.

There was also, always to be considered and never to be known with certainty, how Ruth herself would have felt about this book about her life. All I had to go on was my own sense of how she had felt and the knowledge of her own feelings that she had entrusted to me, knowing who I was as well as she did.

When I wrote *An Anthropologist at Work,* Franz Boas and Edward Sapir and Ruth Benedict were dead. I could not ask them how they felt. Had they been alive, had it been necessary for me to consult them, much of what I wanted to say could not have been written, either because of their own sense of modesty or because of the difficulty of seeing themselves in the mirror of my writing. Ruth could never accept any direct comment on her beauty. Edward Sapir continually berated himself for idleness, when, in fact, he was turning out whole grammars of complex and difficult languages. Franz Boas found it impossible to believe that his behavior, in planning for those for whom he had responsibility, ever embodied the kind of dictatorialness that he so thoroughly repudiated.

For better or worse, the biography of Ruth Benedict was one expression of my responses to those who had already died and who, in their lifetime, had left their mark forever on my life and on the lives and work of American anthropologists. Necessarily, what they meant to me is also an integral part of this account of my own life.

But in this book there are others.

Larry Frank stands midway between the living and those who died long enough ago so that, in writing about them, I can feel that I am writing about a past that now belongs to the next generation—Franz Boas and William Ogburn, Ruth Benedict, Edward Sapir, and A. R. Radcliffe-Brown, my grandmother and my mother and father, Eleanor Steele and Howard Scott, Jane Belo, Colin McPhee, and Walter Spies, and my youngest sister, Priscilla, who died in 1959. But Larry Frank died in 1968. His papers are not yet entirely sorted, and some of his manuscripts have not yet been published. We can just speak about him without a break in our voices. And in this book I have tried to convey something of what working with him meant to me.

There are those, also, who are very much alive. My own contemporaries, my brother Richard and my sister Elizabeth, will remember our parents and each of them quite differently from the way I remember them. There are also my mother's sisters and my father's cousins, all of whom have their own memories of those they loved.

And there are my youngest sister's husband and many of those with whom I went to school and college or with whom I worked in the field and elsewhere. There are my former husbands, all anthropologists and all as deeply involved as I am in the ways in which their lives and work are interrelated. And there are their present wives, all three of whom I know and like. Their several versions of the events that linked together our lives, as well as of the events that followed our separations and that have brought us together again for occasional meetings—all these will be different from mine.

There are the children—my daughter and her husband, Elizabeth's two artist children, Priscilla's son and two daughters, Luther's daughter, and Gregory's son and little daughter, Nora, who is only a year older than Vanni. The children of the next, the grandchild generation—Vanni and Melinda, Joshua, Benjamin, and Pamela—may not read this book in the lifetime of their grandparents; I am in effect presenting them with ancestors about whom they may know very little. But the generation of our children is already an adult generation, and whatver I write is, in a sense, an intrusion into their lives and their own memories. Yet to ask each one of them to pass judgment on what I am writing would involve all of us in the curious unrealities of a committee approach to work without any of its rewards.

The alternative has been to resolve the difficulties in my own mind as best I could. As I also have resolved the way in which I have been publicly discussed, lambasted and lampooned, lionized and mythologized, called an institution and a stormy petrel, and cartooned as a candidate for the Presidency, wearing a human skull around my neck as an ornament. I have taken the stand, in my own mind and replying to others, that I have no right to resent the public expression of attitudes that I arouse in those whom I do not know and who know me only through what I have written or said and through the words that the mass media, correctly or incorrectly, have attributed to me.

Those whose lives I have touched—and still touch—

have to deal with all this also. It is not as if I were a quiet and private person who has suddenly stepped into public view. All those about whom I write here, as well as many people who are closely connected with those about whom I am writing, have already had to put up with me in one way or another. I come into their living rooms, unannounced, on television. Léonie Adams, living in the country, hears my televised voice through an open door as she walks home from church along the quiet Sunday streets of a small town. The mothers of my students send them clippings, often accompanied by the most uncomplimentary remarks, or they write critical letters to the deans under whom their sons and daughters are studying. When my daughter was ten, she commented, "It's hard to have a mother who is half-famous." I asked her why, and she replied, "Because when I assume that people know who you are, so often they don't." And when I asked her what being famous meant, she laughed and said, "Being in crossword puzzles."

For better or worse, none of those whose lives have touched mine closely have been spared the consequences of being known to have known me. Nuisance or point of pride, reason for asking outrageous favors or a sufficient reason for failing to claim a relationship openly, there it is. I do not think the truth as I have tried to set it down can make it worse.

When I began this book I wrote to Luther to tell him about it. He and I had agreed that as ours was a student marriage, out of which neither a book nor a child had come—either of which must, of course, have been acknowledged—it was not necessary to introduce our marriage into later public records. Occasionally, an industrious journalist, going through newspaper files, has come across the columns of comment, all around the nation, that greeted my decision to keep my own name when Luther and I married in 1923. Otherwise, by and large, our marriage has remained part of our young and private past.

Just as I was writing to him, he sent me one of his recent papers in which he expressed, in the setting of the discipline we have long shared, many of the things I have always valued in his approach to the world. Feeling that he should be heard, speaking in his own person, I have set down here a paragraph from this paper:

Perhaps I can best illustrate the meaning of my thoughts by going back to Oppenheimer's felicitous metaphor of the house called "science." I would like to see us build a NEW room in that vast and rambling structure. This room, like the others, would have no door and over the entrance would be the words, THOUGHT, REFLEC-TION, CONTEMPLATION. It would have no tables with instruments, no whirring machinery. There would be no sound except the soft murmur of words carrying the thoughts of the men in the room. It would be a Commons Room to which men would drift in from those rooms marked geology, anthropology, taxonomy, technology, biology, paleontology, logic, mathematics, psychology, linguistics, and many others. Indeed, from without the walls of the House would come poets and artists. All these would drop in and linger. This room would have great windows: the vistas our studies have opened. Men, singly or together, would from time to time walk to those windows to gaze out on the landscape beyond. This landscape in all its beauty, sometimes gentle, sometimes terrible, cannot be seen fully by any one of the occupants of the room. Indeed, it cannot be known fully by a whole generation of men. Explorers of each generation travel into its unknown recesses and, with luck, return to share their discoveries with us. So the life of the NEW room would go on—thought, reflection, contemplation—as the explorers bring back their discoveries to share with the room's occupants. This landscape that we gaze on and try to understand is an epic portion of the human experience.

Having brought in Luther, I also thought what single paragraph from their work, early or late, recalled something that was deeply significant to me in my relationships to Reo and Gregory.

For Reo I have chosen one of his recurrent statements

of his differences with Malinowski, this one from a revised edition of *Sorcerers of Dobu:*

> In this edition . . . Malinowski's introduction to the first edition is retained but is not all endorsed. Malinowski has written that his purpose was to state natural universal laws of behaviour, i.e., laws of culture independent of period, place, and circumstance, and to reduce the social sciences to terms of behaviouristic psychology. Radcliffe-Brown, who supervised the work on which this book is based, wrote that the social sciences are natural sciences, which stem from Aristotle, ethics, and politics, do not, like medicine, rest upon a knowledge of the biological sciences, or upon any known natural laws. They are not any of the natural sciences. There is no doubt that, in so far as Malinowski and Radcliffe-Brown predicted the discovery of natural universal laws of behaviour and society, they were, of course, wrong. It is therefore wrong to discuss mistaken detail in their work as if there were a correct solution within the terms of their presuppositions. Outside such terms there may be something said introductory to a discussion of late Oceanic neolithic society. A knowledge of the politics or of the ethics of a particular society is not necessary to an understanding of general works on such subjects, such as those written by Aristotle, John Locke, David Hume, John Dewey, and Bertrand Russell.

From Gregory's work, I have chosen a paragraph from the comment he made on a paper, "The Comparative Study of Culture and the Purposive Cultivation of Democratic Values," which I presented in a symposium in 1941:

> As to the reward component, this, too, should not be beyond our reach. If the Balinese is kept busy and happy by a nameless, shapeless fear, not located in space or time, we might be kept on our toes by a nameless, shapeless, unlocated hope of enormous achievement. For such a hope to be effective, the achievement need scarcely be defined.

All we need to be sure of is that, at any moment achieve-
ment may be just around the corner, and, true or false,
this can never be tested. We have got to be like those few
artists and scientists who work with this urgent sort of
inspiration, the urgency that comes from feeling that great
discovery, the answer to all our problems, or great creation,
the perfect sonnet, is always only just beyond our reach,
or like the mother of a child who feels that, provided she
pay constant enough attention, there is a real hope that
her child may be that infinitely rare phenomenon, a great
and happy person.

Each of them would perhaps have chosen some other
passage, for, just as I do, each of them has his own sense
of what was significant to us and of the way in which his
work fits into the anthropology of our generation. And
the story is by no means finished. All of us are actively
working and writing.

But more often now than in the past I am asked what
I would choose to do if I had my life to live over again.
About this there is no doubt in my mind. I would elect
to be an anthropologist. However, there are also those
who ask me a different question: If I were twenty-one
today, would I now elect to become an anthropologist?

The real question that is being asked, it seems to me,
has to do with the future of anthropology. Won't all the
primitive peoples of the world soon be extinct? Or won't
the cultures of the surviving peoples be so changed, so
transformed by contact into various versions of the emerging worldwide culture, that they no longer will be of interest? There is even a group of young anthropologists—
and of others who have abandoned their original interest
in anthropology—who have become so involved in immediate change in our own society that they deny the
value of working with primitive peoples and believe that
any further recording of primitive life-styles will yield
only bits and pieces, curiosities not worth the thought
and effort involved in recording them.

In a strange way, I feel that this is where I came in.
For even now, when for fifty years intensive field work

on living primitive societies has been carried out with sophisticated methods, relatively few human scientists understand what our aims have been—and still are—or the nature of the materials that are available to them. Instead of making use of these beautiful materials, materials incorporating the fine details made possible by modern techniques of filming and taping, some of the most brilliant synthesizers still write about a kind of mythical primitive man, much as nineteenth-century armchair philosophers did, as Freud did. When I am given manuscripts to read, brilliant discussions organized with the intention of breaking through the limits of current social science theory, I find, for example, first-class biology but only rags and tatters of what is known and has been well recorded about primitive cultures and the people who embody them.

Fifty years ago, very few people knew the meaning of the word anthropology, and a liberal reviewer could protest Goldenweiser's choice of a title, *Early Civilization*, for his book about the cultures human beings had so laboriously built up. But even then it was clear that anthropologists must work on contemporary problems using contemporary tools while there still were primitive peoples, relatively untouched primitive peoples, among whom we could work.

When I was a graduate student I used to wake up saying to myself, "The last man on Raratonga who knows anything about the past will probably die today. I must hurry." That was when I still dimly understood anthropology as a salvage operation, and knew that we must go to the old men and old women who alone knew about the old ways which, once destroyed, could never be reconstructed.

But I did not go to Samoa in 1925 to record the memories of old people about the way titles had once been distributed or how hieroglyphic taboos had been put on trees or to collect still other versions of the tales of Polynesian gods. I did not go as an antiquarian or as a representative of a discipline whose members were chiefly preoccupied with the peculiarities of kinship systems or with constructions based on primitive myths in which primitive peoples, treated as fossilized ancestors, served to prop up contemporary beliefs about the superiority or degeneration of Western society.

I went to Samoa—as, later, I went to the other societies on which I have worked—to find out more about human beings, human beings like ourselves in everything except their culture. Through the accidents of history, these cultures had developed so differently from ours that knowledge of them could shed a kind of light upon us, upon our potentialities and our limitations, that was unique. No amount of experimental apparatus, however complex, can simulate what it is to be reared as a Samoan, an Arapesh, a Manus, or a Balinese. We can carry out innumerable carefully controlled experiments with university students and still know nothing about the kind of thing that studying peoples in different living cultures can teach us. But most people prefer to carry out the kinds of experiments that allow the scientist to feel that he is in full control of the situation rather than surrendering himself to the situation, as one must in studying human beings as they actually live.

For the most part, contemporary Euro-Americans are as ethnocentric, as concerned with their own problems and limited world view, as unwilling to think beyond themselves and their own time as they were in the early twentieth century, when the insights of Freud and Durkheim and a little later Piaget were obscured by the lack of careful attention to the real behavior of primitive peoples and by ignorance of the possibilities of making exacting comparative studies of human behavior in cultures based on a different historical tradition from our own. Today, there are those who are willing to search the literature, like medieval scholastics, and then to submit their fragmented findings to all the modern complexities of computer analysis. There are those rebels in search of a "natural" life, who would like to try the experiment of living in the midst of some primitive group. There are the sentimentalists who would like to put fences around the remaining groups of primitive peoples and treat them like wild creatures in a game preserve. And, increasingly, there are those who are attempting to turn primitive peoples, living on the edge of modern civilization, into tourist attractions—as if they were exotic animals set out for public view in a zoo. But how many social scientists are there, today, who are trying to think out ways in which primitive peoples, where they still exist, can become our partners and co-workers in the search for knowledge that may, in the end, save their children and ours?

In certain respects we might still be living in the 1920's, even to the images that came into our minds then when we read Edna St. Vincent Millay's poem, "The Blue Flag in the Bog," in which she wrote, "All the things I ever knew/Are this blaze in back of me." The difference is that things we dreamed of and feared in those days are realities today. The fire Edna Millay imagined is the bomb, the effects of which we have, on a very small scale, experienced. The end of the world—the hellfire about which Billy Sunday preached —is a real possibility. The brotherhood of man and man's common humanity, a religious belief and a scientific hypothesis in the 1920's, are urgent truths today.

In the 1920's we knew that primitive societies were vanishing. Today we know that those still remaining are being destroyed even more rapidly by the over-powering impact of our technological society—in the far reaches of Latin America by the unchecked ruthless operations of commercial greed; New Guinea by exploitation and by ideological pressures for a form of independence that will make exploitation even more devastating in its effects; in Africa and elsewhere by the acts of young bureaucrats who are determined to make over their new countries in the Euro-American, democratic or communist, image.

Nevertheless, there are still, in remote parts of the world, living primitive societies. Not just a handful of old men who remember fragments of initiation rites or who can, slowly and painfully, call back into mind methods of divining or of working black magic, buried deep under two generations of mission teaching, but whole functioning societies. Studying these peoples, who are living now as they have lived for centuries and who embody ways of thinking and feeling we do not know about, we could add immeasurably to our knowledge of who we ourselves are. Using modern techniques for making sound films, for example, anthropologists could provide the materials for far more detailed analyses, far more securely based, than ever could be made as long as we were dependent on what a single observer could see only once, an observer who had only a running pencil to record what he could catch in passing. Unlike the piles of notes in some personal shorthand that do not survive the original observer, such records as now can be made would form a reservoir beyond price for generations of newly trained observers.

It is true that beautiful work has been done in the years since Gregory Bateson and I realized what could be done by studying primitive behavior photographically and made a quantum leap from the two to three hundred still photographs usually taken merely to illustrate a study to twenty-five thousand still photographs that incorporated our observations. But if anthropologists today made full use of the magnificent new technology and went to the field prepared to build into their research the new conceptions about evolution, about man's instinctual equipment, and about the functioning of the brain, as well as all we have learned about the embodiment of patterning and the development of the individual personality, they could come back with materials that would immensely expand what we could do.

But only a handful of people are at work. What meager funds there are for research go more often to support laboratory experiments or fashionable dead ends than to further significant field research. Yet human scientists must have new and appropriate materials to think with. And we must have the best materials we can assemble to educate young human scientists of another generation who will be thinking about the nature of man when, in truth, there will be no more primitive societies and, indeed, no society whose members do not embody some version of a worldwide culture.

For anthropologists there are, however, other possibilities as well. During the war we learned how to take our knowledge and experience, gained from field work among primitive peoples, and use it in studies of cultures in the modern world that were complementary to studies made by those disciplines that work only within modern societies and lack the illumination of comparison and the practice of learning from the observed behavior of living beings. Then what we knew was put to wartime use; now these anthropological skills are sorely needed to work on problems that are worldwide in their dimensions—that no nation, no society, can solve independently of all others. Research among isolated primitive peoples is still the most rewarding for the individual anthropologist and for the sciences of human behavior. But we must also understand the societies within which our growing knowledge is put to work.

Experience of another culture can be gained by work in any other society, not necessarily an isolated and technologically simple one, and, in a modern society, can complement the work of other disciplines. Well equipped with anthropological concepts, the student who learns the language and lives wholly within the society he is systematically studying may acquire sufficient cross-cultural insight to make important contributions to theory and practice. But nowhere are we preparing students for work of this kind by training them to work as anthropologists together with members of other disciplines or by training a new generation of students to use the methods developed for anthropological research in modern societies a whole generation ago. Much of the exploratory work was done on cultures studied at a distance. Studies made at first hand would be an adventure of another kind.

What is there for young anthropologists to do? In one sense, everything. The best possible work has not yet been done. If I were twenty-one today, I would elect to join the communicating network of those young people, the world over, who recognize the urgency of life-supporting change—as an anthropologist.

But even so, I speak out of the experience of my own lifetime of seeing past and future as aspects of the present. Knowledge joined to action—knowledge about what man has been and is—can protect the future. There is hope, I believe, in seeing the human adventure as a whole and in the shared trust that knowledge about mankind, sought in reverence for life, can bring life.

Appendix:
Family Tree

This book has been written in the family unit of grandparent to grandchild's grandchild. The speaker, standing in the middle, gives reality to the generations on either side.

Four generations in the United States usually means that one loses touch with relatives in the old countries. I know that seven of the lines that can be traced from my great-grandparents go back well before the American Revolution; the eighth ancestor was a Tory. Here I do not go back beyond my grandparents' parents.

Each of the vertical columns represents a generation:

In the first I give only the names of my eight great-grandparents.

In the second I give the names of my four grandparents and their brothers and sisters, but not the names of their husbands and wives.

In the third I give my parents' names and the names of my mother's sisters and brothers and their husbands and wives. My father was an only child.

The fourth is my own generation; here I give my own marriages and the marriages of my brother and sisters.

The fifth is the generation of my daughter and her first cousins, the children of my sisters with their husbands and wives.

The sixth is the new generation of my granddaughter and her cousins, the children of my nephew and nieces who have been born in the last six years.

Family Tree

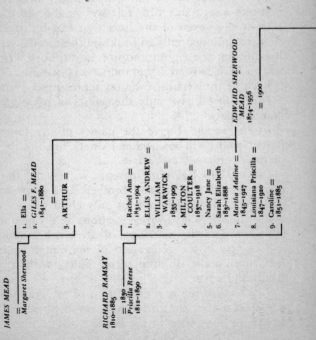

GREAT-GRANDPARENTS	GRANDPARENTS	PARENTS

JAMES MEAD
=
Margaret Sherwood

1. Ella =
2. **GILES F. MEAD**
   1841–1880
3. **ARTHUR** =

RICHARD RAMSAY
1810–1885
= 1890
Priscilla Reese
1812–1890

1. Rachel Ann =
   1831–1904
2. **ELLIS ANDREW** =
3. **WILLIAM WARWICK** =
   1835–1909
4. **MILTON COULTER** =
   1837–1918
5. Nancy Jane =
6. Sarah Elizabeth
   1837–1888
7. *Martha Adaline* =
   1845–1937
8. Louisiana Priscilla =
   1847–1920
9. Caroline =
   1851–1885

EDWARD SHERWOOD MEAD
1874–1956
= 1900

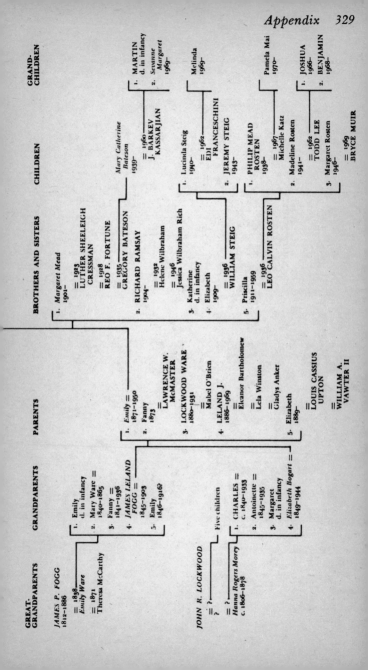

GREAT-GRANDPARENTS	GRANDPARENTS	PARENTS	BROTHERS AND SISTERS	CHILDREN	GRAND-CHILDREN
JAMES P. FOGG 1812–1886	1. Emily d. in infancy				
= 1886 *Emily Ware*	2. Mary Ware = 1840–1865		*Margaret Mead* 1901–		
= 1871 Theresa McCarthy	3. Fanny = 1841–1936	*Emily* = 1871–1950	= 1923 LUTHER SHEELEIGH CRESSMAN		1. MARTIN d. in infancy
			= 1928 REO F. FORTUNE		= 2. *Sevanne* *Margaret* 1969–
	4. *JAMES LELAND* *FOGG* 1845–1903		= 1935 GREGORY BATESON	*Mary Catherine* *Bateson* 1939–	= 1960 J. BARKEV KASSARJIAN
	5. Emily = 1846–1962	Fanny 1873			
		LOCKWOOD WARE 1880–1931	2. RICHARD RAMSAY 1904–	1. Lucinda Steig 1940–	Melinda 1969–
		LAWRENCE W. McMASTER	= 1932 Helene Wilbraham	= 1962 EDI FRANCESCHINI	
			= 1946 Jessica Wilbraham Rich		
JOHN R. LOCKWOOD	= ? ?	LELAND J. 1886–1969	3. Katherine d. in infancy	2. JEREMY STEIG 1943–	
= ? ?	Five children	= Mabel O'Brien	4. Elizabeth 1909–		
		= Eleanor Bartholomew	= 1936 WILLIAM STEIG		
	Hanna Rogers Morey c. 1866–1878	= Lela Winston	5. Priscilla 1911–1959	1. PHILIP MEAD ROSTEN 1938–	Pamela Mai 1970–
	1. CHARLES = c. 1840–1933	= Gladys Anker	= 1936 LEO CALVIN ROSTEN	= 1967 Michelle Katz	
	2. Antoinette = 1845–1935	Elizabeth 1889–		2. Madeline Rosten 1941–	1. JOSHUA 1966–
	3. Margaret d. in infancy	= LOUIS CASSIUS UPTON		= 1962 TODD LEE	2. BENJAMIN 1968–
	4. *Elizabeth Bogart* = 1849–1944	= WILLIAM A. VAWTER II		3. Margaret Rosten 1946–	
				= 1969 BRYCE MUIR	

Index of
Personal Names